The Pocket Handbook

Second Edition

LAURIE G. KIRSZNER
University of the Sciences in Philadelphia

STEPHEN R. MANDELL
Drexel University

THOMSON
✳
HEINLE™

Australia   Canada   Mexico   Singapore   Spain   United Kingdom   United States

THOMSON

HEINLE

The Pocket Handbook, Second Edition
Laurie G. Kirszner, Stephen R. Mandell

Publisher: *Michael Rosenberg*
Acquisitions Editor: *Dickson Musselwhite*
Development Editor: *Camille Adkins*
Production Editor: *Lianne Ames*
Director of HED Marketing: *Lisa Kimball*
Executive Marketing Manager: *Ken Kasee*
Marketing Manager: *Katrina Byrd*
Manufacturing Coordinator: *Marcia Locke*
Text Designer, Compositor: *Thompson Steele, Inc.*
Project Manager: *Nancy Friehofer*
Cover Designer: *Diane Levy*
Printer: *RR Donnelley and Sons*

Printed in the United States of America.
1 2 3 4 5 6 7 8 9 10   07 06 05 04 03 02

For more information contact Heinle, 25 Thomson Place, Boston, Massachusetts 02210 USA, or you can visit our Internet site at http://www.heinle.com

For permission to use material from this text or product contact us:
Tel   1-800-730-2214
Fax   1-800-730-2215
Web   www.thomsonrights.com

ISBN: 0-15-505121-0 (Standard Edition)
ISBN: 0-8384-5250-7 (InfoTrac® Edition)

Library of Congress Cataloging-in-Publication Data
Kirszner, Laurie G.
   The pocket handbook / Laurie G. Kirszner, Stephen R. Mandell, -- 2nd ed.
      p. cm.
   Inclues bibliographical references and index.
   ISBN 0-15-505121-0
   1. English language --Rhetoric--Handbooks, manuals, etc. 2. English language--Grammar--Handbooks manuals, etc. 3. Report writing--Handbooks, manuals, etc. I. Mandell, Stephen R. II. Title.

PE1408 .K6755 2002
808'.O42--dc21   2002027637

PREFACE

We would like to introduce you to *The Pocket Handbook*, a quick reference guide for college students. This book was designed to be a truly portable handbook that will easily fit in a backpack or pocket yet can serve as a valuable resource. Despite its compact size, however, *The Pocket Handbook* offers coverage of all the topics that you would expect to find in a much longer book: the writing process (including a model student paper); sentence grammar and style; punctuation and mechanics; the research process (including two complete model student research papers); and MLA, APA, Chicago, CBE, and Columbia Online documentation styles. In addition, the book devotes a full section to practical assignments (including document and web-page design, writing for the workplace, and making oral presentations) as well as an appendix that addresses concerns facing ESL students. Thus, *The Pocket Handbook*'s explanations and examples of writing can guide college students not just in first-year courses, but throughout their college careers and beyond.

In preparing *The Pocket Handbook*, we focused on making the book inviting, useful, clear, and—most of all—easy to navigate. To achieve these goals, we incorporated distinctive design features throughout that make information easy to find and easy to use.

- A color-coded guide to the nine parts of the book appears on the back cover. Inside the book, the pages of each part are marked by a distinctive color bar that corresponds to a color on this guide.
- A brief table of contents is provided inside the front cover. Here too, the parts are color-coded to link them with the corresponding sections of the text.
- Close-up boxes that focus on special problems are identified by a magnifying glass icon.
- Checklists for quick reference are distinguished by a check mark icon.
- A computer icon identifies information that students will need as they write and revise.
- Boxed lists and charts set off other information that students are likely to refer to on a regular basis.
- Marginal cross-references (keyed to blue, underlined terms in the text) direct students to related discussions in other parts of the book.

Preface

As we revised the text for this second edition, we worked hard to make the book even more useful to students. The book now includes the following new features:

- An expanded and updated four-chapter research section, including complete coverage of the research process, using and evaluating library sources, using and evaluating Internet sources, and integrating sources and avoiding plagiarism
- A revised and updated MLA paper, "The Great Digital Divide"
- A new APA paper, "Sleep Deprivation in College Students"
- Three full chapters on documentation styles, including greatly expanded coverage of MLA style, updated APA coverage consistent with the revised APA publication manual, and new coverage of Columbia Online Style. All three chapters pay special attention to documenting electronic sources.
- A new chapter on Writing for the Workplace (including discussion of résumés, letters of application, memos, and e-mail)
- Coverage of web-page design along with document design
- A new chapter on making oral presentations

With the publication of *The Pocket Handbook,* the *Holt Handbook* series consists of three distinct texts: *The Holt Handbook,* for those who want a full-size, comprehensive reference book with exercises; *The Brief Holt Handbook,* for those who want a compact, tabbed reference guide; and *The Pocket Handbook,* for those who want a concise, portable reference. To give users even more options, *The Pocket Handbook* is also available in several custom versions, which include discussions of research, documentation, and unique assignments that reflect the needs of particular academic disciplines, such as business, sociology, communications, and biology.

In all the different versions of the *Holt Handbook* series, our goal has remained the same: to give students the guidance they need to become self-reliant writers and to succeed in college and beyond. Helping us to achieve these goals has been an extraordinary team at Heinle: Camille Adkins, Julie McBurney, Michael Rosenberg, Dickson Musselwhite, and Lianne Ames. We are very grateful for their help and support, and grateful as well to our families for their continued patience and enthusiasm.

Laurie G. Kirszner
Stephen R. Mandell

CONTENTS

Contents

Contents

Contents

Contents

INFOTRAC®
COLLEGE EDITION
The Online Library

A FREE 4-month Access Card for *InfoTrac® College Edition* comes with every new copy of Kirszner and Mandell: *The Pocket Handbook 2/e.* Indispensable when writing research papers, *InfoTrac® College Edition* offers students 24-hour-a-day access to a database of over 10 million full-length articles from hundreds of scholarly and popular periodicals.

PART 1

WRITING ESSAYS
AND PARAGRAPHS

CHAPTER 1

WRITING ESSAYS

Writing is a constant process of decision making—of selecting, deleting, and rearranging material.

THE WRITING PROCESS

Planning: Consider your purpose, audience, and assignment; choose a topic; discover ideas to write about.
Shaping: Decide how to organize your material.
Drafting: Write your first draft.
Revising: "Re-see" what you have written; write additional drafts.
Editing: Check grammar, spelling, punctuation, and mechanics.
Proofreading: Check for typographical errors.

1a Understanding Essay Structure

The essays you write for your college courses will have a thesis-and-support structure. A **thesis-and-support essay** includes a **thesis statement** (which expresses the **thesis,** or main idea, of the essay) and the specific information that explains and develops that thesis. Your essay will consist of several paragraphs: See an **introductory paragraph**, which introduces your thesis; a 2d1-2 **concluding paragraph**, which gives your essay a sense of completion, perhaps restating your thesis; and a number of **body paragraphs,** which provide the support for your essay's thesis.

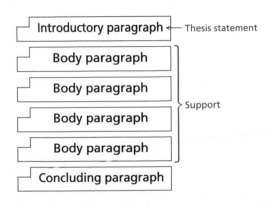

1b Writing Effective Thesis Statements

An effective thesis statement has four characteristics.

1. ***An effective thesis statement should clearly communicate your essay's main idea.*** It tells your readers not only what your essay's topic is, but also how you will approach that topic and what you will say about it. Thus, your thesis statement reflects your essay's purpose.

2. ***An effective thesis statement should be more than a general subject, a statement of fact, or an announcement of your intent.***

   SUBJECT: Intelligence tests

   STATEMENT OF FACT: Intelligence tests are used for placement in many elementary schools.

   ANNOUNCEMENT: The essay that follows will show that intelligence tests may be inaccurate.

   THESIS STATEMENT: Although intelligence tests are widely used for placement in many elementary schools, they are not the best measure of a student's academic performance.

3. ***An effective thesis statement should be carefully worded.*** Your thesis statement—usually expressed in a single, concise sentence—should be direct and straightforward. Avoid vague phrases, such as *centers on, deals with, involves, revolves around,* or *is concerned with.* Do not include phrases like *As I will show, I plan to demonstrate,* and *It seems to me,* which weaken your credibility by suggesting that your conclusions are based on opinion rather than on reading, observation, and experience.

4. ***Finally, an effective thesis statement should suggest your essay's direction, emphasis, and scope.*** Your thesis statement should not make promises that your essay will not fulfill. It should suggest the major points you will cover, the order in which you will introduce them, and where you will place your emphasis, as the following thesis statement does.

   EFFECTIVE THESIS STATEMENT: Widely ridiculed as escape reading, romance novels are becoming increasingly important as a proving ground for many first-time writers and, more significantly, as a showcase for strong heroines.

NOTE: As you write and rewrite, you may modify your essay's direction, emphasis, and scope; if you do so, you must reword your thesis statement.

1c Drafting and Revising

(1) Writing a Rough Draft

When you write a rough draft, you get ideas down on paper so you can react to them. You will generally write several drafts of your essay, and you should expect to add or delete words, to reword sentences, to rethink ideas, to reorder paragraphs—even to take an unexpected detour that may lead you to a new perspective on your topic. To make revision easier, leave room on the page so that you can add material or rewrite. If you type, triple-space; if you write by hand, skip lines. To streamline your revision process, use symbols (arrows, circles, boxes, numbers, and so on) that signal various operations to you.

(2) Revising Your Drafts

Everyone's revision process is different, but the following specific strategies can be helpful at this stage of the process.

- **Outline your draft.** An outline can help you check the logic of your paper's structure.
- **Do collaborative revision.** Ask a friend to give you feedback on your draft.
- **Use instructors' comments.** Study written comments on your draft, and arrange a conference if necessary.
- **Use revision checklists.** Revise in stages, first looking at the whole essay and then considering the paragraphs, sentences, and words. Use the revision checklists that follow to guide you through the process.

✔ CHECKLIST: REVISING THE WHOLE ESSAY

- ✔ Are thesis and support logically related, with each body paragraph supporting one aspect of your thesis statement? **(See 1b)**
- ✔ Is your thesis statement clearly and specifically worded? **(See 1c)**
- ✔ Have you discussed everything promised in your thesis statement? **(See 1c)**

✔ CHECKLIST: REVISING PARAGRAPHS

- ✔ Does each body paragraph focus on one main idea, expressed in a clearly worded topic sentence? **(See 2a)**
- ✔ Are the relationships of sentences within paragraphs clear? **(See 2b)**
- ✔ Are your body paragraphs fully developed? **(See 2c)**
- ✔ Does your introductory paragraph arouse interest and prepare readers for what is to come? **(See 2d1)**
- ✔ Does your concluding paragraph review your main points? **(See 2d2)**

✔ CHECKLIST: REVISING SENTENCES

- ✔ Have you used correct sentence structure? **(See Chapters 3 and 4)**
- ✔ Are your sentences varied? **(See Chapter 9)**
- ✔ Have you eliminated nonessential words and unnecessary repetition? **(See 10a–b)**
- ✔ Have you avoided overloading your sentences with too many clauses? **(See 10c)**
- ✔ Have you avoided potentially confusing shifts in tense, voice, mood, person, or number? **(See 11a)**
- ✔ Are your sentences constructed logically? **(See 11b–c)**
- ✔ Have you strengthened sentences with repetition, balance, and parallelism? **(See 12a)**
- ✔ Have you placed modifiers clearly and logically? **(See Chapter 13)**

✔ CHECKLIST: REVISING WORDS

- ✔ Have you eliminated jargon, pretentious diction, clichés, and biased language from your writing? **(See 14a–d)**

CHOOSING A TITLE

- A title should convey your essay's focus, perhaps using key words and phrases from your essay or echoing the wording of your assignment.
- A title should arouse interest, perhaps with a provocative question, a quotation, or a controversial position.

ASSIGNMENT: Write about a problem faced on college campuses today.

TOPIC: Free speech on campus

POSSIBLE TITLES:

Free Speech: A Problem for Today's Colleges (echoes wording of assignment and uses key words of essay)

How Free Should Free Speech on Campus Be? (provocative question)

The Right to "Shout 'Fire' in a Crowded Theater" (quotation)

Hate Speech: A Dangerous Abuse of Free Speech on Campus (controversial position)

1d Editing and Proofreading

When you **edit,** you concentrate on grammar, spelling, punctuation, and mechanics. When you **proofread,** you reread every word carefully to make sure you did not make any errors as you typed.

EDITING AND PROOFREADING

- As you edit, look at only a small portion of text at a time. If your software allows you to split the screen, create another window so small that you can see only one or two lines of text at a time.
- Use the *search* or *find* command to look for words or phrases in usage errors that you commonly make—for instance, confusing *it's* with *its*. You can also uncover **sexist language** by searching for words such as *he, his, him,* or *man.*

See
14d2

continued on the following page

continued from the previous page

- Remember that a spell checker will not catch a typo that creates a correctly spelled word—for example, *there* for *their* or *form* for *from*. Even after you run a spell check, you still must proofread your papers carefully.

1e Model Student Paper

Masterton 1

Samantha Masterton

Professor Wade

English 101

15 November 2002

Title

The Returning Student:

Older Is Definitely Better

After graduating from high school, young people must decide what they want to do with the rest of their lives. Many graduates (often without much thought) decide to continue their education in college. This group of teenagers makes up what many see as the typical first-year college student. Recently, however, this stereotype has been challenged by an influx of older students into

Thesis statement

American colleges and universities. My experience as one of these older students has convinced me that many students would benefit from taking a few years off between high school and college.

First point in support of thesis

The college experience of an eighteen-year-old is quite different from that of an older student. Teenagers are often concerned with things other than cracking books—

Masterton 2

going to parties, dating, and testing personal limits, for example. I almost never see older students cutting lectures or wasting time as younger students do. Most older students have saved for tuition and want to get their money's worth. Many are also balancing the demands of home and work to attend classes, so they know how important it is to do well.

Generally, young people just out of high school have not learned how to set priorities or meet deadlines. Younger college students often find themselves hopelessly behind or scrambling at the last minute simply because they have not learned how to budget their time. Although success in college depends on the ability to set realistic goals and organize time and materials, college itself does little to help students develop these skills. On the contrary, the workplace—where reward and punishment are usually immediate and tangible—is the best place to learn such lessons. Working teaches the basics that college takes for granted: the value of

Second point in support of thesis

Masterton 3

punctuality and attendance, the importance of respect for superiors and colleagues, and the need for establishing priorities and meeting deadlines.

The adult student who has gained experience in the workplace has advantages over the younger student. In general, the older student enrolls in college with a definite course of study in mind. For the adult student, college is an extension of work rather than a place to discover what

Third point in support of thesis

work will be. This greater sense of purpose makes older students more focused and more highly motivated.

Fourth point in support of thesis

Because of their age and greater experience, older students bring more into the classroom than younger students do. Eighteen-year-olds have been driving for only a year or two; they have just gotten the right to vote; and they usually have not lived on their own. In contrast, older students have generally had a good deal of life experience. This experience enables them to make significant contributions to class discussions and group projects, and it enriches their written work as well. Moreover, their

Masterton 4

years in the real world have helped them to become more focused and more responsible than they were when they graduated from high school. As a result, they are better prepared for college. Thus, they not only bring more into the classroom but also take more out of it.

Conclusion

All things considered, higher education is often wasted on the young, who are either too immature or too unfocused to take advantage of it. Many older students have taken time off to serve in the military, to get a job, or to raise a family. Many have traveled, read widely, engaged in informal study, and taken the time to grow up. By the time they get to college, they have defined their goals and made a commitment to achieve them. Taking a few years off between high school and college would give younger students the breathing room they need to make the most of college. It would also give them the life experience they need to appreciate the value of their education.

CHAPTER 2

WRITING PARAGRAPHS

A **paragraph** is a group of related sentences. It may be complete in itself or part of a longer piece of writing.

✔ CHECKLIST: WHEN TO PARAGRAPH

- ✔ Begin a new paragraph whenever you move from one major point to another.
- ✔ Begin a new paragraph whenever you move your readers from one time period or location to another.
- ✔ Begin a new paragraph whenever you introduce a new step in a process or sequence.
- ✔ Begin a new paragraph when you want to emphasize an important idea.
- ✔ Begin a new paragraph every time a new person speaks.
- ✔ Begin a new paragraph to signal the end of your introduction and the beginning of your conclusion.

2a Writing Unified Paragraphs

A paragraph is **unified** when it develops a single idea. Each paragraph should have a **topic sentence** that states the main idea of the paragraph; the other sentences in the paragraph support that idea.

I was a listening child, careful to hear the very different sounds of Spanish and English. Wide-eyed with hearing, I'd listen to sounds more than words. First, there were English (*gringo*) sounds. So many words were still unknown that when the butcher or the lady at the drugstore said something to me, exotic polysyllabic sounds would bloom in the midst of their sentences. Often the speech of people in public seemed to me very loud, booming with confidence. The man behind the counter would literally ask, "What can I do for you?" But by being so firm and so clear, the sound of his voice said that he was a *gringo;* he belonged in public society. (Richard Rodriguez, *Aria: A Memoir of a Bilingual Childhood*)

[margin note: Topic sentence]

[margin note: Support]

2b Writing Coherent Paragraphs

A paragraph is **coherent** when all its sentences are logically related to one another. **Transitional words and phrases** clarify the relationships among sentences by establishing the spatial, chronological, and logical connections within a paragraph.

Topic sentence

Transitional words and phrases *(after, finally, and so on)* establish chronology of events.

Napoleon certainly made a change for the worse by leaving his small kingdom of Elba. <u>After Waterloo</u>, he went back to Paris, and he abdicated for a second time. <u>A hundred days after</u> his return from Elba, he fled to Rochefort in hope of escaping to America. <u>Finally</u>, he gave himself up to the English captain of the ship *Bellerophon*. <u>Once again</u>, he suggested that the Prince Regent grant him asylum, and <u>once again</u>, he was refused. <u>In the end</u>, all he saw of England was the Devon coast and Plymouth Sound as he passed on to the remote island of St. Helena. <u>After six years of exile</u>, he died on May 5, 1821, at the age of fifty-two. (Norman Mackenzie, *The Escape from Elba*)

USING TRANSITIONAL WORDS AND PHRASES

To Signal Sequence or Addition
again, also, besides, furthermore, moreover, in addition, first . . . second . . . third, one . . . another, too

To Signal Time
afterward, as soon as, at first, at the same time, before, earlier, finally, in the meantime, later, meanwhile, next, now, since, soon, subsequently, then, until

To Signal Comparison
also, by the same token, likewise, in comparison, similarly

To Signal Contrast
although, but, despite, even though, however, in contrast, instead, meanwhile, nevertheless, nonetheless, on the contrary, on the one hand . . . on the other hand, still, whereas, yet

To Introduce Examples
for example, for instance, namely, specifically, thus

continued on the following page

continued from the previous page

To Signal Narrowing of Focus
after all, indeed, in fact, in other words, in particular, specifically, that is

To Introduce Conclusions or Summaries
as a result, consequently, in summary, therefore, in conclusion, in other words, thus, to conclude

To Signal Concession
admittedly, certainly, granted, naturally, of course

To Introduce Causes or Effects
accordingly, as a result, because, consequently, hence, since, so, then, therefore

---

NOTE: <u>Parallel</u> constructions ("He was a patriot. . . . He was a reformer. . . . He was an innovator. . . .") and repeated key words and phrases ("He invented a new type of printing press. . . . This printing press. . . .") also help writers achieve coherence.

See 12a

Writing Well-Developed Paragraphs

A paragraph is **well developed** when it contains all the support—examples, statistics, expert opinion, and so on—that readers need to understand the main idea.

From Thanksgiving until Christmas, children are bombarded with ads for violent toys and games. Toy manufacturers persist in thinking that only toys that appeal to children's aggressiveness will sell. <u>One television commercial praises the merits of a commando team that attacks and captures a miniature enemy base. Toy soldiers wear realistic uniforms and carry automatic rifles, pistols, knives, grenades, and ammunition. Another commercial shows laughing children shooting one another with plastic rocket fighters and tank-like vehicles.</u> Despite claims that they (unlike action toys) have educational value, video games have increased the level of violence. <u>The most popular video games involve children in strikingly realistic combat situations. One game lets children search out and destroy enemy fighters in outer space. Other bestselling games graphically simulate hand-to-hand combat on city streets.</u> The real question is why parents buy these violent toys and games for their children. (Student Writer)

Topic sentence

Specific examples

Specific examples

2d Writing Introductory and Concluding Paragraphs

(1) Introductory Paragraphs

An **introductory paragraph** introduces the subject, narrows it, and then states the essay's thesis.

Thesis statement

> Although it has now faded from view, the telegraph lives on within the communications technologies that have subsequently built upon its foundations: the telephone, the fax machine, and, more recently, the Internet. <u>And, ironically, it is the Internet—despite being regarded as a quintessentially modern means of communication—that has the most in common with its telegraphic ancestor.</u> (Tom Standage, *The Victorian Internet*)

An introductory paragraph may arouse readers' interest with an interesting quotation, a compelling question, an unusual comparison, or a controversial statement.

NOTE: Avoid introductions that simply announce your subject ("In my paper I will talk about Lady Macbeth") or that undercut your credibility ("I don't know much about alternative energy sources, but I would like to present my opinion").

✔ CHECKLIST: REVISING INTRODUCTIONS

- ✔ Does your introduction include your essay's thesis statement?
- ✔ Does it lead naturally into the body of your essay?
- ✔ Does it arouse your readers' interest?
- ✔ Does it avoid statements that simply announce your subject or that undercut your credibility?

---

(2) Concluding Paragraphs

A **concluding paragraph** typically begins with specifics—for example, a review of the essay's main points—and then moves to more general statements.

> As an Arab-American, I feel I have the best of two worlds. I'm proud to be part of the melting pot, proud to contribute to the tremendous diversity of cultures, customs and traditions that make this country unique. But Arab-bashing—public acceptance of hatred and bigotry—is something no American can be proud of. (Ellen Mansoor Collier, "I Am Not a Terrorist")

A concluding paragraph may also offer a prediction, a recommendation, a forceful opinion, or a pertinent quotation.

NOTE: Avoid conclusions that just repeat your introduction in different words or that cast doubt on your concluding points ("I may not be an expert" or "At least this is my opinion"). If possible, end with a statement that readers will remember.

✔ CHECKLIST: REVISING CONCLUSIONS

✔ Does your conclusion sum up your essay, perhaps by reviewing the essay's main points?
✔ Does it do more than just repeat the introduction?
✔ Does it avoid apologies?
✔ Does it end memorably?

PART 2

WRITING GRAMMATICAL SENTENCES

CHAPTER 3

REVISING COMMA SPLICES AND FUSED SENTENCES

A **run-on sentence** is created when two <u>independent</u> <u>clauses</u> are joined incorrectly. See A2.3

A **comma splice** is a run-on that occurs when two independent clauses are joined by just a comma. A **fused sentence** is a run-on that occurs when two independent clauses are joined with no punctuation.

COMMA SPLICE: Charles Dickens created the character of Mr. Micawber, he also created Uriah Heep.

FUSED SENTENCE: Charles Dickens created the character of Mr. Micawber he also created Uriah Heep.

✔ CHECKLIST: REVISING COMMA SPLICES AND FUSED SENTENCES

To revise a comma splice or fused sentence, use one of the following strategies.

✔ Add a period between the clauses.
✔ Add a semicolon between the clauses.
✔ Add an appropriate coordinating conjunction.
✔ Subordinate one clause to the other, creating a complex sentence.

3a Revising with Periods

You can add a period between the independent clauses, creating two separate sentences. This is a good strategy to use when the clauses are long or when they are not closely related.

In 1894 Frenchman Alfred Dreyfus was falsely convicted of treason, ~~his~~ His struggle for justice pitted the army against the civil libertarians.

3b Revising with Semicolons

See
17a

You can add a **semicolon** between two closely related clauses that convey parallel or constrasting information.

Chippendale chairs have straight legs;however,Queen Anne chairs have curved legs.

NOTE: When you use a **transitional word or phrase** (such as *however, therefore,* or *for example*) to connect two indepen-

See
2b

dent clauses, the transitional element must be preceded by a semicolon and followed by a comma. If you use a comma alone, you create a comma splice. If you omit punctuation entirely, you create a fused sentence.

3c Revising with Coordinating Conjunctions

You can use a coordinating conjunction (*and, or, but, nor,*

See
9a1

for, so, yet) to join two closely related clauses of equal importance into one **compound sentence**. The coordinating conjunction you choose indicates the relationship between the clauses: addition (*and*), contrast (*but, yet*), causality (*for, so*), or a choice of alternatives (*or, nor*). Be sure to add a comma before the coordinating conjunction.

Elias Howe invented the sewing machine, and Julia Ward Howe was a poet and social reformer.

3d Revising with Subordinating Conjunctions or Relative Pronouns

When the ideas in two independent clauses are not of equal importance, you can use an appropriate subordinating con-

See
9a2

junction or a relative pronoun to join the clauses into one **complex sentence**, placing the less important idea in the dependent clause.

Stravinsky's ballet *The Rite of Spring* shocked Parisians in 1913, because its rhythms seemed erotic.

Lady Mary Wortley Montagu, who had suffered from smallpox herself, she helped spread the practice of inoculation.

CHAPTER 4

REVISING SENTENCE FRAGMENTS

A **sentence fragment** is an incomplete sentence—a clause or a phrase—that is punctuated as though it were a sentence. A sentence may be incomplete for any of the following reasons.

- It lacks a subject.

    Many astrophysicists now believe that galaxies are distributed in clusters. <u>And even form supercluster complexes.</u>

- It lacks a verb.

    Every generation has its defining moments. <u>Usually the events with the most news coverage.</u>

- It lacks both a subject and a verb.

    Researchers are engaged in a variety of studies. <u>Suggesting a link between alcoholism and heredity.</u> (*Suggesting* is a **verbal**, which cannot serve as a sentence's main verb.) See A1.3

- It is a **dependent clause**, a clause that begins with a subordinating conjunction or relative pronoun. See A2.3

    Bishop Desmond Tutu was awarded the 1984 Nobel Peace Prize. <u>Because he struggled to end apartheid.</u>

    The pH meter and the spectrophotometer are two scientific instruments. <u>That changed the chemistry laboratory dramatically.</u>

MAINTAINING SENTENCE BOUNDARIES

When readers cannot see where sentences begin and end, they have difficulty understanding what you have written. For instance, it is impossible to tell to which independent clause the fragment in each of the following sequences belongs.

The course requirements were changed last year. <u>Because a new professor was hired at the very end of the spring semester.</u> I was unable to find out about this change until after preregistration.

✔ CHECKLIST: REVISING SENTENCE FRAGMENTS

To revise a sentence fragment, use one or more of the following strategies.

✔ Attach the fragment to an adjacent independent clause that contains the missing words.
✔ Delete the subordinating conjunction or relative pronoun.
✔ Supply the missing subject or verb (or both).

4a Attaching the Fragment to an Independent Clause

In most cases, the simplest way to correct a fragment is by attaching it to an adjacent independent clause that contains the missing words.

See A2.3

President Johnson did not seek reelection, ~~For~~ *for* a number of reasons. (**prepositional phrase** fragment)

See A2.3

Students sometimes take a leave of absence, ~~To~~ *to* decide on definite career goals. (**verbal phrase** fragment)

The pilot changed course, ~~Realizing~~ *, realizing* that the weather was worsening. (verbal phrase fragment)

See 7b3

Brian was the star forward of the Blue Devils, ~~The~~ *,the* team with the most wins. (**appositive** fragment)

Fairy tales are full of damsels in distress, ~~Such~~ *, such* as Rapunzel. (appositive fragment)

People with dyslexia have trouble reading, ~~And~~ *and* may also find it difficult to write. (part of compound predicate)

They took only a compass and a canteen, ~~And~~ *and* some trail mix. (part of compound object)

See A2.3

Property taxes rose sharply, ~~Although~~ *although* city services declined. (**dependent clause** fragment)

Subordinating Conjunction

The battery is dead, ~~Which~~ **which** means the car won't start.

(dependent clause fragment)

REVISING SENTENCE FRAGMENTS: LISTS

When a fragment takes the form of a **list**, add a colon to connect the list to the independent clause that introduces it.

See 25a1

Tourists often outnumber residents in four European cities: Venice, Florence, Canterbury, and Bath.

4b Deleting the Subordinating Conjunction or Relative Pronoun

When a fragment consists of a dependent clause that is punctuated as though it were a complete sentence, you can correct it by attaching it to an adjacent independent clause, as illustrated in **4a.** Alternatively, you can simply delete the subordinating conjunction or relative pronoun.

Property taxes rose sharply. ~~Although city~~ **City** services declined. (subordinating conjunction *although* deleted)

The battery is dead. ~~Which~~ **This** means the car won't start. (relative pronoun *which* replaced by *this*, a word that can serve as the sentence's subject)

NOTE: Simply deleting the subordinating conjunction or relative pronoun is usually the least desirable way to revise a sentence fragment. It is likely to create two choppy sentences and obscure the connection between them.

REVISING SENTENCE FRAGMENTS

Sentence fragments are often used in speech and in e-mail as well as in journalism, advertising, and creative writing. In most college writing situations, however, sentence fragments are not acceptable. Do not use them without carefully considering their suitability for your audience and purpose.

4c Supplying the Missing Subject or Verb

Another way to correct a fragment is to add the missing words (a subject or a verb or both) that are needed to make the fragment a sentence.

In 1948, India became independent. ~~Divided~~ It was divided into the nations of India and Pakistan. (verbal phrase fragment)

A familiar trademark can increase a product's sales. ~~Reminding~~ It reminds shoppers that the product has a longstanding reputation. (verbal phrase fragment)

CHAPTER 5

UNDERSTANDING AGREEMENT

Agreement is the correspondence between words in number, gender, or person. Subjects and verbs agree in **number** (singular or plural) and **person** (first, second, or third); pronouns and their antecedents agree in number, person, and **gender**. See 11a4

5a Making Subjects and Verbs Agree

Singular subjects take singular verbs, and plural subjects take plural verbs. **Present tense** verbs, except *be* and *have,* add *-s* or *-es* when the subject is third-person singular. (Third-person singular subjects include nouns; the personal pronouns *he, she, it,* and *one;* and many **indefinite pronouns** .) See 6b1 See 5a4

The <u>President</u> <u>has</u> the power to veto congressional legislation.

<u>She</u> frequently <u>cites</u> statistics to support her points.

In every group <u>somebody</u> <u>emerges</u> as a natural leader.

Present tense verbs do not add *-s* or *-es* when the subject is a plural noun, a first-person or second-person pronoun (*I, we, you*), or a third-person plural pronoun (*they*).

<u>Experts</u> <u>recommend</u> that dieters avoid processed meat.

At this stratum, <u>we</u> <u>see</u> rocks dating back ten million years.

<u>They</u> <u>say</u> that some wealthy people default on their student loans.

In some situations, making subjects and verbs agree can be troublesome.

(1) Words between Subject and Verb

If a modifying phrase comes between the subject and the verb, the verb should agree with the subject, not with a word in the modifying phrase.

The <u>sound</u> of the drumbeats <u>builds</u> in intensity in *The Emperor Jones.*

The <u>games</u> won by the intramural team <u>are</u> few and far between.

This rule also applies to phrases introduced by *along with, as well as, in addition to, including,* and *together with.*

Heavy <u>rain</u>, along with high winds, <u>causes</u> hazardous driving conditions.

(2) Compound Subjects Joined by *and*

Compound subjects joined by *and* usually take plural verbs.

<u>Air bags and antilock brakes</u> <u>are</u> standard on all new models.

There are, however, two exceptions to this rule. First, compound subjects joined by *and* that stand for a single idea or person are treated as a unit and used with singular verbs: <u>Rhythm and blues</u> <u>is</u> a forerunner of rock and roll.

Second, when *each* or *every* precedes a compound subject joined by *and,* the subject takes a singular verb: <u>Every desk and file cabinet</u> <u>was</u> searched before the letter was found.

(3) Compound Subjects Joined by *or*

Compound subjects joined by *or* may take singular or plural verbs. If both subjects are singular, use a singular verb; if both are plural, use a plural verb. If a singular and a plural subject are linked by *or* (or by *either . . . or, neither . . . nor,* or *not only . . . but also*), the verb agrees with the subject that is nearer to it.

<u>Either radiation treatments or chemotherapy</u> <u>is</u> combined with surgery for effective results.

<u>Either chemotherapy or radiation treatments</u> <u>are</u> combined with surgery for effective results.

(4) Indefinite Pronouns

Some **indefinite pronouns**—*both, many, few, several, others*—are always plural and take plural verbs. Most others—*another, anyone, everyone, one, each, either, neither, anything, everything, something, nothing, nobody,* and *somebody*—are singular and take singular verbs.

<u>Anyone</u> <u>is</u> welcome to apply for the scholarship.

<u>Each</u> of the chapters <u>includes</u> a review exercise.

A few indefinite pronouns—*some, all, any, more, most,* and *none*—can be singular or plural, depending on the noun they refer to.

<u>Some</u> of this trouble <u>is</u> to be expected. (*Some* refers to *trouble.*)

<u>Some</u> of the spectators <u>are</u> restless. (*Some* refers to *spectators.*)

(5) Collective Nouns

A **collective noun** names a group of persons or things—for instance, *navy, union, association, band.* When it refers to the group as a unit (as it usually does), a collective noun takes a singular verb; when it refers to the individuals or items that make up the group, it takes a plural verb.

> To many people, the <u>royal family symbolizes</u> Great Britain. (The family, as a unit, is the symbol.)

> The <u>family</u> all <u>eat</u> at different times. (Each member eats separately.)

Phrases that name fixed amounts—*three-quarters, twenty dollars, the majority*—are treated like collective nouns. When the amount denotes a unit, it takes a singular verb; when it denotes parts of the whole, it takes a plural verb.

> <u>Three-quarters</u> of his usual salary <u>is</u> not enough to live on.

> <u>Three-quarters</u> of the patients <u>improve</u> dramatically after treatment.

(6) Singular Subjects with Plural Forms
A singular subject takes a singular verb, even if the form of the subject is plural.

> <u>Statistics deals</u> with the collection and analysis of data.

When such a word has a plural meaning, however, use a plural verb.

> The <u>statistics prove</u> him wrong.

(7) Inverted Subject-Verb Order
Even when the verb comes before the subject (as it does in questions and in sentences beginning with *there is* or *there are*), the subject and verb must agree.

> <u>Is either</u> answer correct?

> There <u>are</u> currently thirteen circuit <u>courts</u> of appeals in the federal system.

(8) Linking Verbs
A **linking verb** should agree with its subject, not with the subject complement.

> The <u>problem was</u> termites.

> <u>Termites were</u> the problem.

See 8a

(9) Relative Pronouns
When you use a **relative pronoun** (*who, which, that,* and so on) to introduce a dependent clause, the verb in the dependent clause should agree in number with the pronoun's **antecedent,** the word to which the pronoun refers.

See A1.2

27

The farmer is among the <u>ones</u> who <u>suffer</u> during a grain embargo.

The farmer is the only <u>one</u> who <u>suffers</u> during a grain embargo.

5b Making Pronouns and Antecedents Agree

Singular pronouns—such as *he, him, she, her, it, me, myself,* and *oneself*—should refer to singular antecedents. Plural pronouns—such as *we, us, they, them,* and *their*—should refer to plural antecedents.

(1) Compound Antecedents

In most cases, use a plural pronoun to refer to a **compound antecedent** (two or more antecedents connected by *and*).

<u>Mormonism and Christian Science</u> were similar in <u>their</u> beginnings.

Use a singular pronoun when a compound antecedent is preceded by *each* or *every*.

<u>Every programming language and software package</u> has <u>its</u> limitations.

Use a singular pronoun to refer to two or more singular antecedents linked by *or* or *nor*.

<u>Neither Thoreau nor Whitman</u> lived to see <u>his</u> work read widely.

When one part of a compound antecedent is singular and one part is plural, the pronoun agrees in person and number with the antecedent that is nearer to it.

<u>Neither the boy nor his parents</u> had <u>their</u> seatbelts fastened.

(2) Collective Noun Antecedents

If the meaning of a collective noun antecedent is singular (as it will be in most cases), use a singular pronoun. If the meaning is plural, use a plural pronoun.

The teachers' <u>union</u> announced <u>its</u> plan to strike. (The members act as a unit.)

The <u>team</u> moved to <u>their</u> positions. (Each member acts individually.)

(3) Indefinite Pronoun Antecedents

See 5a4

Most **<u>indefinite pronouns</u>**—*each, either, neither, one, anyone,* and the like—are singular and are used with singular pronouns.

<u>Neither</u> of the men had <u>his</u> proposal ready by the deadline.

<u>Each</u> of these neighborhoods has <u>its</u> own traditions and values.

(A few indefinite pronouns are plural; others can be singular or plural.)

 PRONOUN-ANTECEDENT AGREEMENT

In speech and in informal writing, many people use the plural pronouns *they* or *their* with singular indefinite pronouns that refer to people, such as *someone, everyone,* and *nobody.*

<u>Everyone</u> can present <u>their</u> own viewpoint.

In college writing, however, you should never use a plural pronoun with a singular subject. Instead, you can use both the masculine and the feminine pronoun.

<u>Everyone</u> can present <u>his or her</u> own viewpoint.

Or, you can make the sentence's subject plural.

<u>All participants</u> can present <u>their</u> own viewpoints.

The use of *his* alone to refer to a singular indefinite pronoun (Everyone can present *his* own viewpoint) is considered **<u>sexist language</u>**.

See 14d2

CHAPTER 6

USING VERBS CORRECTLY

6a Using Irregular Verbs

A **regular verb** forms both its past tense and its past participle by adding *-d* or *-ed* to the **base form** of the verb (the present tense form of the verb that is used with *I*).

PRINCIPAL PARTS OF REGULAR VERBS

Base Form	*Past Tense Form*	*Past Participle*
smile	smiled	smiled
talk	talked	talked

Irregular verbs do not follow this pattern. The chart that follows lists the principal parts of the most frequently used irregular verbs.

FREQUENTLY USED IRREGULAR VERBS

Base Form	*Past Tense Form*	*Past Participle*
arise	arose	arisen
awake	awoke, awaked	awoke, awaked
be	was/were	been
beat	beat	beaten
begin	began	begun
bend	bent	bent
bet	bet, betted	bet
bite	bit	bitten
blow	blew	blown
break	broke	broken
bring	brought	brought
build	built	built
burst	burst	burst
buy	bought	bought
catch	caught	caught
choose	chose	chosen
cling	clung	clung

continued on the following page

---

continued from the previous page

Base Form	Past Tense Form	Past Participle
come	came	come
cost	cost	cost
deal	dealt	dealt
dig	dug	dug
dive	dived, dove	dived
do	did	done
drag	dragged	dragged
draw	drew	drawn
drink	drank	drunk
drive	drove	driven
eat	ate	eaten
fall	fell	fallen
fight	fought	fought
find	found	found
fly	flew	flown
forget	forgot	forgotten, forgot
freeze	froze	frozen
get	got	gotten
give	gave	given
go	went	gone
grow	grew	grown
hang (suspend)	hung	hung
have	had	had
hear	heard	heard
keep	kept	kept
know	knew	known
lay	laid	laid
lead	led	led
lend	lent	lent
let	let	let
lie (recline)	lay	lain
make	made	made
prove	proved	proved, proven
read	read	read
ride	rode	ridden
ring	rang	rung
rise	rose	risen
run	ran	run
say	said	said
see	saw	seen
set (place)	set	set
shake	shook	shaken

continued on the following page

continued from the previous page

Base Form	Past Tense Form	Past Participle
shrink	shrank, shrunk	shrunk, shrunken
sing	sang	sung
sink	sank	sunk
sit	sat	sat
speak	spoke	spoken
speed	sped, speeded	sped, speeded
spin	spun	spun
spring	sprang	sprung
stand	stood	stood
steal	stole	stolen
strike	struck	struck, stricken
swear	swore	sworn
swim	swam	swum
swing	swung	swung
take	took	taken
teach	taught	taught
throw	threw	thrown
wake	woke, waked	waked, woken
wear	wore	worn
wring	wrung	wrung
write	wrote	written

CLOSE-UP

IRREGULAR VERBS: *LIE/LAY* AND *SIT/SET*

Lie means "to recline" and does not take an object ("He likes to *lie* on the floor"); *lay* means "to place" or "to put" and does take an object ("He wants to *lay* a rug on the floor"):

Base Form	Past Tense Form	Past Participle
lie	lay	lain
lay	laid	laid

Sit means "to assume a seated position" and does not take an object ("She wants to *sit* on the table"); set means "to place" or "to put" and usually takes an object ("She wants to *set* a vase on the table"):

Base Form	Past Tense Form	Past Participle
sit	sat	sat
set	set	set

6b Understanding Tense

Tense is the form a verb takes to indicate when an action occurred or when a condition existed.

ENGLISH VERB TENSES

Simple Tenses
Present (I *finish*, he or she *finishes*)
Past (I *finished*)
Future (I *will finish*)

Perfect Tenses
Present perfect (I *have finished*, he or she *has finished*)
Past perfect (I *had finished*)
Future perfect (I *will have finished*)

Progressive Tenses
Present progressive (I *am finishing*, he or she *is finishing*)
Past progressive (I *was finishing*)
Future progressive (I *will be finishing*)
Present perfect progressive (I *have been finishing*)
Past perfect progressive (I *had been finishing*)
Future perfect progressive (I *will have been finishing*)

---

(1) Using the Simple Tenses

The **simple tenses** include *present, past,* and *future.*

The **present tense** usually indicates an action that is taking place at the time it is expressed in speech or writing or an action that occurs regularly.

I <u>see</u> your point. (an action taking place when it is expressed)

We <u>wear</u> wool in the winter. (an action that occurs regularly)

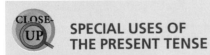

SPECIAL USES OF THE PRESENT TENSE

The present tense has four special uses.

TO INDICATE FUTURE TIME: The grades <u>arrive</u> next Thursday.

TO STATE A GENERALLY HELD BELIEF: Studying <u>pays</u> off.

continued on the following page

continued from the previous page

To State a Scientific Truth: An object at rest <u>tends</u> to stay at rest.

To Discuss a Literary Work: *Family Installments* <u>tells</u> the story of a Puerto Rican family.

The **past tense** indicates that an action has already taken place.

John Glenn <u>orbited</u> the Earth three times on February 20, 1962. (an action completed in the past)

As a young man, Mark Twain <u>traveled</u> through the Southwest. (an action that occurred once or many times in the past but did not extend into the present)

The **future tense** indicates that an action will or is likely to take place.

Halley's Comet <u>will reappear</u> in 2061. (a future action that will definitely occur)

The land boom in Nevada <u>will</u> probably <u>continue</u>. (a future action that is likely to occur)

(2) Using the Perfect Tenses

The **perfect tenses** designate actions that were or will be completed before other actions or conditions. The perfect tenses are formed with the appropriate tense form of the auxiliary verb *have* plus the past participle.

The **present perfect** tense can indicate two types of continuing action beginning in the past.

Dr. Kim <u>has finished</u> studying the effects of BHA on rats. (an action that began in the past and is finished at the present time)

My mother <u>has invested</u> her money wisely. (an action that began in the past and extends into the present)

The **past perfect** tense indicates an action occurring before a certain time in the past.

By 1946, engineers <u>had built</u> the first electronic digital computer.

The **future perfect** tense indicates that an action will be finished by a certain future time.

By Tuesday, the transit authority <u>will have run</u> out of money.

(3) Using the Progressive Tenses

The **progressive tenses** express continuing action. They are formed with the appropriate tense of the verb *be* plus the present participle.

The **present progressive** tense indicates that something is happening at the time it is expressed in speech or writing.

> The volcano <u>is erupting</u>, and lava <u>is flowing</u> toward the town.

The **past progressive** tense indicates two kinds of past action.

> Roderick Usher's actions <u>were becoming</u> increasingly bizarre. (a continuing action in the past)

> The French revolutionary Marat was stabbed to death while he <u>was bathing</u>. (an action occurring at the same time in the past as another action)

The **future progressive** tense indicates a continuing action in the future.

> The treasury secretary <u>will be monitoring</u> the money supply very carefully.

The **present perfect progressive** tense indicates action continuing from the past into the present and possibly into the future.

> Rescuers <u>have been working</u> around the clock.

The **past perfect progressive** tense indicates that a past action went on until another one occurred.

> Before President Kennedy was assassinated, he <u>had been working</u> on civil rights legislation.

The **future perfect progressive** tense indicates that an action will continue until a certain future time.

> By eleven o'clock we <u>will have been driving</u> for seven hours.

6c Understanding Mood

Mood is the form a verb takes to indicate whether a writer is making a statement, asking a question, giving a command, or expressing a wish or a contrary-to-fact statement. There are three moods in English: the *indicative,* the *imperative,* and the *subjunctive.*

The **indicative** mood states a fact, expresses an opinion, or asks a question: Jackie Robinson <u>had</u> a great impact on professional baseball.

The **imperative** mood is used in commands and direct requests: <u>Use</u> a dictionary.

The **subjunctive** mood causes the greatest difficulty for writers.

The **present subjunctive** uses the base form of the verb, regardless of the subject.

Dr. Gorman suggested that he <u>study</u> the Cambrian period.

The present subjunctive is used in *that* clauses after words such as *ask, suggest, require, recommend,* and *demand.*

The report recommended that doctors <u>be</u> more flexible.

Captain Ahab insisted that his crew <u>hunt</u> the white whale.

The **past subjunctive** has the same form as the past tense of the verb.

He wished he <u>had</u> more time.

The past subjunctive is used in **conditional statements** (statements beginning with *if, as if,* or *as though* that are contrary to fact and statements that express a wish).

If John <u>went</u> home, he could see Marsha. (John is not home.)

The father acted as if he <u>were</u> having the baby. (The father couldn't be having the baby.)

I wish I <u>were</u> more organized. (expresses a wish)

NOTE: In the past subjunctive, the verb *be* takes the form *were* (not *was*) even with a singular subject.

6d Understanding Voice

Voice is the form a verb takes to indicate whether its subject acts or is acted upon. When the subject of a verb does something—that is, acts—the verb is in the **active voice.** When the subject of a verb receives the action—that is, is acted upon—the verb is in the **passive voice.**

ACTIVE VOICE: Hart Crane <u>wrote</u> *The Bridge.*

PASSIVE VOICE: *The Bridge* <u>was written</u> by Hart Crane.

NOTE: Because the active voice emphasizes the doer of an action, it is usually clearer and more emphatic than the passive voice. Whenever possible, use active voice in your college writing.

CHAPTER 7

USING PRONOUNS CORRECTLY

7a Understanding Pronoun Case

Pronouns change **case** to indicate their function in a sentence. English has three cases: *subjective, objective,* and *possessive.*

PRONOUN CASE FORMS

Subjective

I	he, she	it	we	you	they	who	whoever

Objective

me	him, her	it	us	you	them	whom	whomever

Possessive

my	his, her	its	our	your	their	whose
mine	hers		ours	yours	theirs	

---

(1) Subjective Case

A pronoun takes the **subjective case** in the following situations.

SUBJECT OF A VERB: I bought a new mountain bike.

SUBJECT COMPLEMENT: It was he for whom the men were looking.

(2) Objective Case

A pronoun takes the **objective case** in these situations.

DIRECT OBJECT: Our sociology teacher asked Adam and me to work on the project.

INDIRECT OBJECT: The plumber's bill gave him quite a shock.

OBJECT OF A PREPOSITION: Between us we own ten shares of stock.

PRONOUN CASE IN COMPOUND CONSTRUCTIONS

I is not necessarily more appropriate than *me*. In compound constructions like the following, *me* is correct.

Just between you and <u>me</u> [not *I*], I think the data are incomplete. (*Me* is the object of the preposition *between*.)

(3) Possessive Case

A pronoun takes the **possessive case** when it indicates ownership (*our* car, *your* book). The possessive case is also used before a **gerund**.

See A1.3

Napoleon approved of <u>their</u> [not *them*] ruling Naples. (*Ruling* is a gerund.)

7b Determining Pronoun Case in Special Situations

(1) Comparisons with *Than* or *As*

When a comparison ends with a pronoun, the pronoun's function in the sentence dictates your choice of pronoun case. If the pronoun functions as a subject, use the subjective case; if it functions as an object, use the objective case.

Darcy likes John more than <u>I</u>. (*I* is the subject: more than *I* like John)

Darcy likes John more than <u>me</u>. (*me* is the object: more than she likes *me*)

(2) *Who* and *Whom*

The case of the pronouns *who* and *whom* depends on their function *within their own clause*. When a pronoun serves as the subject of its clause, use *who* or *whoever*; when it functions as an object, use *whom* or *whomever*.

The Salvation Army gives food and shelter to <u>whoever</u> is in need. (*Whoever* is the subject of a dependent clause.)

I wonder <u>whom</u> jazz musician Miles Davis influenced.
(*Whom* is the object of *influenced* in the dependent
clause.)

 PRONOUN CASE IN QUESTIONS

To determine the case of *who* at the beginning of a
question, use a personal pronoun to answer the question.
The case of *who* should be the same as the case of the personal pronoun.

<u>Who</u> wrote *The Age of Innocence?* (<u>She</u> wrote it—sub-
ject)

<u>Whom</u> do you support for mayor? (I support <u>her</u>—
object)

(3) Appositives

An **appositive** is a noun or noun phrase that identifies or renames an adjacent noun or pronoun. The case of a pronoun in
an appositive depends on the function of the word the appositive identifies.

We heard two Motown recording artists, Smokey Robinson
and <u>him</u>. (*Artists* is the object of the verb *heard*, so the pronoun in the appositive *Smokey Robinson and him* takes the
objective case.)

Two Motown recording artists, Smokey Robinson and <u>he</u>,
recorded for Motown Records. (*Artists* is the subject of the
sentence, so the pronoun in the appositive *Smokey Robinson
and he* takes the subjective case.)

(4) *We* and *Us* before a Noun

When a first-person plural pronoun precedes a noun, the
case of the pronoun depends on the way the noun functions in
the sentence.

<u>We</u> women must stick together. (*Women* is the subject of
the sentence, so the pronoun *we* must be in the subjective
case.)

Teachers make learning easy for <u>us</u> students. (*Students* is the
object of the preposition *for*, so the pronoun *us* must be in
the objective case.)

7c Revising Common Errors of Pronoun Reference

An **antecedent** is the word or word group to which a pronoun refers. The connection between a pronoun and its antecedent should always be clear.

(1) Ambiguous Antecedents

Sometimes a pronoun—for example, *this, that, which,* or *it*—appears to refer to more than one antecedent. In such cases, substitute a noun for the pronoun.

The accountant took out his calculator and completed the tax return. Then, he put ~~it~~ the calculator into his briefcase.

Sometimes a pronoun does not seem to refer to any specific antecedent. In such cases, supply a noun to clarify the reference.

Some one-celled organisms contain chlorophyll yet are considered animals. This paradox illustrates the difficulty of classifying single-celled organisms.

(2) Remote Antecedents

The farther a pronoun is from its antecedent, the more difficult it is for readers to make a connection between them. If a pronoun's antecedent is far away from it, replace the pronoun with a noun.

During the mid-1800s, many Czechs began to immigrate to America. By 1860, about 23,000 Czechs had left their country. By 1900, 13,000 Czech immigrants were coming to ~~its~~ America's shores each year.

(3) Nonexistent Antecedents

Sometimes a pronoun refers to a nonexistent antecedent. In such cases, replace the pronoun with a noun.

Our township has decided to build a computer lab in the elementary school. ~~They~~ Teachers feel that fourth-graders should begin using computers.

WHO, WHICH, AND THAT

In general, *who* refers to people or to animals that have names. *Which* and *that* refer to objects, events, or unnamed animals. When referring to an antecedent, be sure to choose the appropriate pronoun (*who, which,* or *that*).

David Henry Hwang, <u>who</u> wrote the Tony Award-winning play *M. Butterfly,* also wrote *Family Devotions* and *FOB.*

The spotted owl, <u>which</u> lives in old-growth forests, is in danger of extinction.

Houses <u>that</u> are built today are usually more energy efficient than those built twenty years ago.

CHAPTER 8

USING ADJECTIVES AND ADVERBS CORRECTLY

Adjectives modify nouns and pronouns. **Adverbs** modify verbs, adjectives, or other adverbs—or entire phrases, clauses, or sentences.

The *function* of a word, not its *form,* determines whether it is an adjective or an adverb. Although many adverbs (such as *immediately* and *hopelessly*) end in *-ly,* others (such as *almost* and *very*) do not. Moreover, some words that end in *-ly* (such as *lively*) are adjectives.

8a Using Adjectives as Subject Complements

See
A1.3
Be sure to use an adjective, not an adverb, as a subject complement. A <u>**subject complement**</u> is a word that follows a linking verb and modifies the sentence's subject, not its verb. A **linking verb** does not show physical or emotional action. *Seem, appear, believe, become, grow, turn, remain, prove, look, sound, smell, taste, feel,* and the forms of the verb *be* are or can be used as linking verbs.

> Michelle seemed <u>brave</u>. (*Seemed* shows no action and is therefore a linking verb. Because *brave* is a subject complement that modifies the noun *Michelle,* it takes the adjective form.)

> Michelle smiled <u>bravely</u>. (*Smiled* shows action, so it is not a linking verb. *Bravely* modifies *smiled,* so it takes the adverb form.)

NOTE: Sometimes the same verb can function as either a linking verb or an action verb.

> He looked <u>hungry</u>. (*Looked* is a linking verb; *hungry* modifies the subject.)

> He looked <u>hungrily</u> at the sandwich. (*Looked* is an action verb; *hungrily* modifies the verb.)

8b Using Adverbs Appropriately

Be sure to use an adverb, not an adjective, to modify verbs, adjectives, or other adverbs—or entire phrases, clauses, or sentences.

Most students did ~~great~~ ^{very well} on the midterm.

My parents dress a lot more conservative_∧^{ly} than my friends do.

 USING ADJECTIVES AND ADVERBS

In informal speech, adjective forms such as *good, bad, sure, real, slow, quick,* and *loud* are often used to modify verbs, adjectives, and adverbs. Avoid these informal modifiers in college writing.

The program ran ~~real good~~ ^{really well} the first time we tried it, but the new system performed ~~bad~~ ^{badly}.

Using Comparative and Superlative Forms

COMPARATIVE AND SUPERLATIVE FORMS

Form	*Function*	*Example*
Positive	Describes a quality; indicates no comparisons	big
Comparative	Indicates comparisons between *two* qualities (greater or lesser)	bigger
Superlative	Indicates comparisons among *more than two* qualities (greatest or least)	biggest

NOTE: Some adverbs, particularly those indicating time, place, and degree (*almost, very, here, yesterday,* and *immediately*), do not have comparative or superlative forms.

---

(1) Regular Comparatives and Superlatives

To form the comparative and superlative, all one-syllable adjectives and many two-syllable adjectives (particularly those that end in *-y, -ly, -le, -er,* and *-ow*) add *-er* or *-est:* slow<u>er</u>, funn<u>i</u>er; slow<u>est</u>, funn<u>i</u>est. (Note that a final *y* becomes *i* before the *-er* or *-est* is added.)

Other two-syllable adjectives and all long adjectives form the comparative with *more* and the superlative with *most:* <u>more</u> famous, <u>more</u> incredible; <u>most</u> famous, <u>most</u> incredible.

Adverbs ending in *-ly* also form the comparative with *more* and the superlative with *most:* <u>more</u> slowly; <u>most</u> slowly. Other adverbs use the *-er* and *-est* endings: soon<u>er</u>; soon<u>est</u>.

All adjectives and adverbs indicate a lesser degree with *less* (<u>less</u> lovely; <u>less</u> slowly) and the least degree with *least* (<u>least</u> lovely; <u>least</u> slowly).

USING COMPARATIVES AND SUPERLATIVES

Never use both *more* and *-er* to form the comparative, and never use both *most* and *-est* to form the superlative.

Nothing could have been ~~more~~ easier.

Jack is the ~~most~~ meanest person in town.

Never use the superlative when comparing only two things.

Stacy is the ~~oldest~~ older of the two sisters.

Never use the comparative when comparing more than two things.

We chose the ~~earlier~~ earliest of the four appointments.

(2) Irregular Comparatives and Superlatives

Some adjectives and adverbs have irregular comparative and superlative forms.

IRREGULAR COMPARATIVES AND SUPERLATIVES

	Positive	*Comparative*	*Superlative*
Adjectives:	good	better	best
	bad	worse	worst
	a little	less	least
	many, some, much	more	most
Adverbs:	well	better	best
	badly	worse	worst

ILLOGICAL COMPARISONS

Many adjectives and adverbs can logically exist only in the positive degree. For example, words such as *perfect, unique, empty, excellent, impossible, parallel,* and *dead* cannot have comparative or superlative forms.

I read ~~the most~~ *an* excellent story.

The vase in her collection was ~~very~~ unique.

PART 3

WRITING EFFECTIVE SENTENCES

CHAPTER 9

WRITING VARIED SENTENCES

9a Using Compound and Complex Sentences

Paragraphs that mix <u>simple sentences</u> with compound and ^{See} ^{A2.2} complex sentences are more varied—and therefore more interesting—than those that do not.

(1) Compound Sentences

A **compound sentence** is created when two or more independent clauses are joined with *coordinating conjunctions, transitional words and phrases, correlative conjunctions, semicolons,* or *colons.*

Coordinating Conjunctions

The pianist made some mistakes, <u>but</u> the concert was a success.

NOTE: Use a comma before a coordinating conjunction—*and, or, nor, but, for, so,* and *yet*—that joins two **independent clauses**. ^{See} ^{A1.7}

Transitional Words and Phrases

The saxophone does not belong to the brass family; <u>in fact</u>, it is a member of the woodwind family.

NOTE: Use a semicolon—not a comma—before a transitional word or phrase that joins two independent clauses. Frequently used **transitional words and phrases** include conjunctive adverbs like *consequently, finally, still,* and *thus* as well as expressions like *for example, in fact,* and *for instance.* ^{See} ^{2b}

Correlative Conjunctions

<u>Either</u> he left his coat in his locker, <u>or</u> he left it on the bus.

Semicolons

Alaska is the largest state; Rhode Island is the smallest.

Colons

He got his orders: he was to leave for France on Sunday.

(2) Complex Sentences

A **complex sentence** consists of one independent clause and at least one **dependent clause**. A **subordinating conjunction** or **relative pronoun** links the independent and dependent clauses and indicates the relationship between them. ^{See} ^{A1.7}

49

(dependent clause)   (independent clause)
[After the town was evacuated], [the hurricane began].

(independent clause)   (dependent clause)
[Officials watched the storm], [which threatened to destroy the town].

(dependent clause)
Town officials, [who were very concerned], watched the storm.

FREQUENTLY USED SUBORDINATING CONJUNCTIONS

after	before	until
although	if	when
as	once	whenever
as if	since	where
as though	that	wherever
because	unless	while

RELATIVE PRONOUNS

that	whatever	who (whose, whom)
what	which	whoever (whomever)

9b Varying Sentence Length

Strings of short simple sentences can be tedious—and sometimes hard to follow, as the following paragraph indicates.

> John Peter Zenger was a newspaper editor. He waged and won an important battle for freedom of the press in America. He criticized the policies of the British governor. He was charged with criminal libel as a result. Zenger's lawyers were disbarred by the governor. Andrew Hamilton defended him. Hamilton convinced the jury that Zenger's criticisms were true. Therefore, the statements were not libelous.

You can revise choppy sentences like these by using *coordination, subordination,* or *embedding* to combine them with adjacent sentences.

Coordination pairs similar elements—words, phrases, or clauses—giving equal weight to each.

Two choppy sentences linked with *and,* creating compound sentence

> John Peter Zenger was a newspaper editor. He waged and won an important battle for freedom of the press in America. <u>He criticized the policies of the British governor, and he was charged with criminal libel as a result.</u> Zenger's lawyers were disbarred by the governor. Andrew Hamilton defended him. Hamilton convinced the jury that Zenger's criticisms were true. Therefore, the statements were not libelous.

Subordination places the more important idea in an independent clause and the less important idea in a dependent clause.

> John Peter Zenger was a newspaper editor who waged and won an important battle for freedom of the press in America. He criticized the policies of the British governor, and he was charged with criminal libel as a result. When Zenger's lawyers were disbarred by the governor, Andrew Hamilton defended him. Hamilton convinced the jury that Zenger's criticisms were true. Therefore, the statements were not libelous.

Simple sentences become dependent clauses, creating two complex sentences

Embedding is the working of additional words and phrases into sentences.

> John Peter Zenger was a newspaper editor who waged and won an important battle for freedom of the press in America. He criticized the policies of the British governor, and he was charged with criminal libel as a result. When Zenger's lawyers were disbarred by the governor, Andrew Hamilton defended him, convincing the jury that Zenger's criticisms were true. Therefore, the statements were not libelous.

The sentence Hamilton convinced the jury . . . *becomes the phrase* convincing the jury

This final revision of the original string of choppy sentences uses coordination, subordination, and embedding to vary sentence length, retaining the final short simple sentence for emphasis.

9c Varying Sentence Types

Another way to achieve sentence variety is to mix <u>**declarative**</u> sentences (statements) with occasional <u>**imperative**</u> sentences (commands or requests), <u>**exclamatory**</u> sentences, and **rhetorical questions** (questions that the reader is not expected to answer).

See A2.2

> Local television newscasts seem to be delivering less and less news. Although we tune in to be updated on local, national, and world events, only about 30 percent of most newscasts is devoted to news. The remaining time is spent on feature stories, advertising, weather, sports, and casual conversation between anchors. Given this focus on "soft" material, what options do those of us wishing to find out what happened in the world have? [**rhetorical question**] Critics of local television have a few suggestions. First, write to your local station's management voicing your concern; then, try to get others to sign a petition. [**imperatives**] If changes are not made, you can turn off your television. Better yet, read the newspaper! [**exclamation**]

9d Varying Sentence Openings

Rather than beginning every sentence with the subject, begin with modifying words, phrases, or clauses.

Words

<u>Proud</u> and <u>relieved</u>, they watched their daughter receive her diploma. (adjectives)

Phrases

<u>For better or worse</u>, credit cards are now widely available to college students. (prepositional phrase)

<u>Located on the west coast of Great Britain</u>, Wales is part of the United Kingdom. (participial phrase)

<u>His interests widening</u>, Picasso designed ballet sets and illustrated books. (absolute phrase)

Clauses

<u>After Woodrow Wilson was incapacitated by a stroke</u>, his wife unofficially performed many presidential duties. (adverb clause)

9e Varying Standard Word Order

(1) Inverting Word Order

You can vary standard subject-verb-object (or complement) word order by placing the complement or direct object *before* the verb instead of in its conventional position or by placing the verb *before* the subject instead of after it.

 (object) (verb)
A cheery smile he had for everyone.
      (subject)

(complement)
Hardest hit were the coastal areas.
      (verb)   (subject)

Inverting word order draws attention to the word or word group that appears in an unexpected place—but inverted word order can be distracting, so use it in moderation.

(2) Separating Subject from Verb

You can also vary conventional word order by placing words or phrases between the subject and verb—but be sure that the word group does not obscure the connection between subject and verb or create an **agreement** error.

See
5a1

 (subject)   (verb)
Many <u>states</u>, hoping to reduce needless fatalities, <u>require</u> that children ride in government-approved child safety seats.

CHAPTER 10

WRITING CONCISE SENTENCES

A sentence is not concise simply because it is short; a concise sentence contains only the words necessary to make its point.

10a Eliminating Nonessential Words

Whenever possible, delete nonessential words—*deadwood, utility words,* and *circumlocution*—from your writing.

(1) Eliminating Deadwood

Deadwood is a term used for unnecessary phrases that simply take up space and add nothing to meaning.

~~There were many~~ Many factors ~~that~~ influenced his decision to become a priest.

Shoppers ~~who are~~ looking for bargains often go to outlets.

They played ~~a~~ an exhausting racquetball game ~~that was exhausting~~.

~~In this~~ This article ~~it~~ discusses lead poisoning.

Deadwood also includes unnecessary statements of opinion, such as *I feel, it seems to me,* and *in my opinion.*

~~In my opinion, I believe the~~ The characters seem undeveloped.

~~As far as I'm concerned, this~~ This course looks interesting.

(2) Eliminating Utility Words

Utility words are fillers; they contribute nothing to a sentence. Utility words include nouns with imprecise meanings (*factor, situation, type, aspect,* and so on); adjectives so general that they are almost meaningless (*good, bad, important*); and common adverbs denoting degree (*basically, actually, quite, very, definitely*). Often you can just delete a utility word; if you cannot, replace it with a more precise word.

~~The registration situation~~ Registration was disorganized.

The scholarship ~~basically~~ offered Fran ~~a good~~ *an* opportunity to study Spanish.

It was ~~actually~~ a worthwhile book, but I didn't ~~completely~~ finish it.

(3) Eliminating Circumlocution

Taking a roundabout way to say something (using ten words when five will do) is called **circumlocution.** Instead of complicated constructions, use concise, specific words and phrases that come right to the point.

~~It is not unlikely that the~~ *The* trend toward lower consumer spending will *probably* continue.

Joel was in the army ~~during the same time that~~ *while* I was in college.

 REVISING WORDY PHRASES

If you cannot edit a wordy construction, substitute a more concise, more direct term.

Wordy	*Concise*
at the present time	now
due to the fact that	because
in the vicinity of	near
have the ability to	be able to

Eliminating Unnecessary Repetition

Unnecessary repetition and redundant word groups (repeated words or phrases that say the same thing) can annoy readers and obscure your meaning. Correct unnecessary repetition by using one of the following strategies.

(1) Deleting Redundancy

People's clothing ~~attire~~ can reveal a good deal about their personalities.

(2) Substituting a Pronoun

Fictional detective Miss Marple has solved many crimes. *The Murder at the Vicarage* was one of ~~Miss Marple's~~ *her* most challenging cases.

(3) Creating an Appositive

Red Barber, ~~was~~ a sportscaster, ~~He~~ was known for his colorful
expressions.

(4) Creating a Compound

John F. Kennedy was the youngest man ever elected president, *and* ~~He was~~ also the first Catholic to hold this office.

(5) Creating a Complex Sentence

Americans value freedom of speech, *which* ~~Freedom of speech~~ is
guaranteed by the First Amendment.

10c Tightening Rambling Sentences

The combination of nonessential words, unnecessary repetition, and complicated syntax creates **rambling sentences.** Revising rambling sentences frequently requires extensive editing.

(1) Eliminating Excessive Coordination

When you string a series of clauses together with coordinating conjunctions, you create a rambling, unfocused **compound** See 9a1
sentence. To revise such sentences, first identify the main idea
or ideas, and then subordinate the supporting details.

Benjamin Franklin, ~~was~~ the son of a candlemaker, ~~but he~~
later apprenticed with his half-brother as a printer, *an* ~~and this~~
that experience, ~~led~~ to his buying *The Pennsylvania Gazette,* *which* ~~and~~
he managed ~~this periodical~~ with great success.

(2) Eliminating Adjective Clauses

A series of **adjective clauses** is also likely to produce a ram- See A2.3
bling sentence. To revise, substitute concise modifying words or
phrases for adjective clauses.

Moby-Dick, ~~which is~~ a novel about a white whale, was writ-
ten by Herman Melville, who *revised the first draft at the urging of his* ~~was~~ friendl~~y with~~ Nathaniel
Hawthorne. ~~who urged him to revise the first draft.~~

(3) Eliminating Passive Constructions

See 6d

Excessive use of the <u>passive voice</u> can create rambling sentences. Correct this problem by changing passive voice to active voice.

> Concerned Americans are organizing
> ∧"Buy American" rallies, ~~are being organized by concerned~~
>   hoping ∧
> ~~Americans who hope~~ that ~~jobs can be saved by~~ such gatherings⹁ can save jobs.

(4) Eliminating Wordy Prepositional Phrases

See A2.3

When you revise, substitute adjectives or adverbs for wordy <u>prepositional phrases</u>.

>   dangerous   exciting
> The trip was ~~one of danger~~ but also ~~one of excitement~~.
>   confidently   authoritatively
> He spoke ~~in a confident manner~~ and ~~with a lot of authority~~.

(5) Eliminating Wordy Noun Constructions

See A2.3

Substitute strong verbs for wordy <u>noun phrases</u>.

>   decided
> We have ~~made the decision~~ to postpone the meeting until ~~the~~
> ~~appearance of~~ all the board members. appear
>   ∧

CHAPTER 11

REVISING AWKWARD
OR CONFUSING SENTENCES

The most common causes of awkward or confusing sentences are *unwarranted shifts, mixed constructions, faulty predication,* and *illogical comparisons.*

11a Revising Unwarranted Shifts

(1) Shifts in Tense

Verb <u>tense</u> in a sentence or in a related group of sentences should not shift without good reason—to indicate changes of time, for example.

> *The Wizard of Oz* <u>is</u> a classic film that <u>was made</u> in 1939.
> (acceptable shift from present to past)

Unwarranted shifts in tense can be confusing.

> I registered for the advanced philosophy seminar because I wanted a challenge. However, by the first week I ~~start~~ started having trouble understanding the reading.

> Jack Kerouac's novel *On the Road* follows a group of friends who ~~drove~~ drive across the United States in the 1950s.

(2) Shifts in Voice

Unwarranted shifts from active to passive <u>voice</u> (or from passive to active) can be confusing. In the following sentence, for instance, the shift from active (*wrote*) to passive (*was written*) makes it unclear who wrote *The Great Gatsby.*

> F. Scott Fitzgerald wrote *This Side of Paradise,* and later wrote *The Great Gatsby.* ~~was written.~~

NOTE: Sometimes a shift from active to passive voice within a sentence may be necessary to give the sentence proper emphasis.

Even though consumers <u>protested</u>, the sales tax <u>was increased</u>. (To say *the legislature increased the sales tax* would draw the emphasis away from *consumers*.)

(3) Shifts in Mood

See
6c

Unnecessary shifts in **<u>mood</u>** can also create awkward sentences.

Next, heat the mixture in a test tube, and ~~you should make~~ ^{be}

sure it does not boil. (shift from imperative to indicative)

(4) Shifts in Person and Number

Person indicates who is speaking (first person—*I, we*), who is spoken to (second person—*you*), and who is spoken about (third person—*he, she, it,* and *they*). Unwarranted shifts between the second and the third person are most often responsible for awkward sentences.

When ~~someone~~ look*s* for a car loan, you compare the inter- ^{you}

est rates of several banks. (shift from third to second person)

Number indicates one (singular—*novel, it*) or more than one (plural—*novels, they, them*). Unwarranted shifts in number can create awkward sentences, so be sure singular pronouns refer to singular **<u>antecedents</u>** and plural pronouns to plural antecedents.

See
5b

If a person does not study regularly, ~~they~~ will have a difficult ^{he or she}

time passing Spanish. (shift from singular to plural)

11b Revising Mixed Constructions

A **mixed construction** is created when a dependent clause, prepositional phrase, or independent clause is incorrectly used as the subject of a sentence.

Because she studies every day, ~~explains why~~ she gets good

grades. (dependent clause used as subject)

By calling for information, ~~is the way to~~ learn more about the ^{, you can}

benefits of ROTC. (prepositional phrase used as subject)

58

Being
~~He was~~ late ~~was what~~ made him miss Act 1. (independent

clause used as subject)

11c Revising Faulty Predication

Faulty predication occurs when a sentence's predicate does not logically complete its subject. Faulty predication is especially common in sentences that contain a linking verb—a form of the verb *be*, for example—and a subject complement.

caused
Mounting costs and decreasing revenues ~~were~~ the downfall of the hospital.

Faulty predication also occurs in sentences that contain a construction like *is where* or *is when. Is* must be preceded and followed by a noun or noun phrase.

the construction of
Taxidermy is ~~where you construct~~ a lifelike representation of an animal from its preserved skin.

Faulty predication also occurs when the phrase *the reason is* precedes *because.* In this situation, *because* (which means "for the reason that") is redundant and can be deleted.

that
The reason we drive is ~~because~~ we are afraid to fly.

CHAPTER 12

USING PARALLELISM

Parallelism—the use of matching words, phrases, clauses, or sentence structures to express equivalent ideas—adds unity, balance, and force to your writing. Remember, however, that although effective parallelism can help you write clearer sentences, faulty parallelism can create awkward sentences that obscure your meaning and confuse readers.

12a Using Parallelism Effectively

(1) With Items in a Series

<u>Eat</u>, <u>drink</u>, and <u>be</u> merry.

<u>Baby food consumption</u>, <u>toy production</u>, and <u>marijuana use</u> are likely to decline as the U.S. population ages.

(2) With Paired Items

Paired words, phrases, or clauses should be presented in parallel terms.

The thank-you note was <u>short</u> but <u>sweet</u>.

<u>Ask not what your country can do for you</u>; <u>ask what you can do for your country</u>. (John F. Kennedy, *inaugural address*)

Paired items linked by **correlative conjunctions** (such as *not only . . . but also* and *either . . . or*) should always be parallel.

The designer paid attention not only <u>to color</u> but also <u>to texture</u>.

Either <u>repeat physics</u> or <u>take calculus</u>.

Parallelism is also used with paired elements linked by *than* or *as*.

Richard Wright and James Baldwin chose <u>to live in Paris</u> rather than <u>to remain in the United States</u>.

See 27e1, 34b **NOTE:** Elements in <u>lists</u> and <u>outlines</u> should also be parallel.

12b Revising Faulty Parallelism

Faulty parallelism occurs when elements that have the same function in a sentence are not presented in parallel terms.

Many developing countries lack sufficient housing, sufficient food, and ~~their~~ sufficient health-care facilities ~~are also insufficient.~~

To correct faulty parallelism, match nouns with nouns, verbs with verbs, and phrases or clauses with similarly constructed phrases or clauses.

Popular exercises for men and women include spinning, weight ~~lifters,~~ lifting and jogging.

I look forward to hearing from you and to ~~have~~ having an opportunity to tell you more about myself.

 CLOSE-UP   **REPEATING KEY WORDS**

Although the use of similar grammatical structures may be enough to convey parallelism, sometimes sentences are even clearer if certain key words (for example, prepositions that introduce items in a series) are also parallel. In the following sentence, repeating the preposition *by* makes it clear that *not* applies only to the first phase.

Computerization has helped industry by not allowing labor costs to skyrocket, by increasing the speed of production, and by improving efficiency.

CHAPTER 13

PLACING MODIFIERS CAREFULLY

A **modifier** is a word, phrase, or clause that describes, limits, or qualifies another word or word group in the sentence. A modifier should be placed close to its **headword,** the word or phrase it modifies. **Faulty modification** is the confusing placement of modifiers or the modification of nonexistent words.

13a Revising Misplaced Modifiers

A **misplaced modifier** is a word or word group whose placement suggests that it modifies one word or phrase when it is intended to modify another.

Wendy watched the storm, dark
∧ ~~Dark~~ and threatening, ~~Wendy watched the storm.~~ (Was Wendy dark and threatening?)

(1) Placing Modifying Words Precisely

Limiting modifiers such as *almost, only, even,* and *just* should immediately precede the words they modify. A different placement will change the meaning of a sentence.

Nick *just* set up camp at the edge of town. (He did it just now.)

Just Nick set up camp at the edge of town. (He did it alone.)

Nick set up camp *just* at the edge of town. (His camp was precisely at the edge.)

When a limiting modifier is placed so that it is not clear whether it modifies a word before it or one after it, it is called a *squinting modifier.*

The life that everyone thought would fulfill her <u>totally</u> bored her.

To correct a squinting modifier, place the modifier so that it clearly modifies its headword.

The life that everyone thought would <u>totally</u> fulfill her bored her. (She was expected to be totally fulfilled.)

The life that everyone thought would fulfill her bored her <u>totally</u>. (She was totally bored.)

(2) Relocating Misplaced Phrases

When you revise, relocate misplaced verbal phrases, placing them directly before or directly after the words or word groups they modify.

Roller-skating along the shore,
Λ Jane watched the boats. ~~roller-skating along the shore.~~

Place prepositional phrase modifiers immediately after the words they modify.

　　　　　　　　　　with no arms
Venus de Milo is a statueΛcreated by a famous artist. ~~with no arms~~.

(3) Relocating Misplaced Dependent Clauses

An adjective clause usually appears immediately after the word it modifies.

　　　　　, which will benefit everyone,
This diet programΛwill limit the consumption of possible carcinogens,̶ ~~which will benefit everyone~~.

An adverb clause may appear in various positions, but its relationship to its headword must be clear and logical.

After they had a glass of wine, the
~~The~~ parents checked to see that the children were sleeping. ~~after they had a glass of wine~~.

13b Revising Intrusive Modifiers

An **intrusive modifier** interrupts a sentence, making the sentence difficult to understand.

Revise when a long modifying phrase comes between an auxiliary verb and a main verb.

Without
~~She had, without~~ giving it a second thought or considering
　　　　　　　she had
the consequences, planned to reenlist.
　　　　　　　　Λ

Revise when modifiers awkwardly interrupt an <u>infinitive</u>, ^See A1.3^ coming between the word *to* and the base form of the verb.

　　　defeat his opponent
He hoped <u>to</u> quickly and easily. ~~defeat his opponent~~.
　　　Λ

13c Revising Dangling Modifiers

A **dangling modifier** is a word or phrase that cannot logically modify any word or word group in the sentence.

<u>Using this drug</u>, many undesirable side effects are experienced.

One way to correct this dangling modifier is to create a new subject by adding a word or word group that *using this drug* can modify.

Using this drug, <u>patients</u> experience many undesirable side effects.

Another way to correct the dangling modifier is to change it into a dependent clause.

Many undesirable side effects are experienced <u>when this drug is used</u>.

DANGLING MODIFIERS AND THE PASSIVE VOICE

See 6d

Most sentences that include dangling modifiers do not include a headword because they are in the passive voice. Changing the <u>passive voice</u> to the <u>active voice</u> corrects the dangling modifier by changing the subject of the sentence's main clause (*side effects*) to a word that the dangling modifier can logically modify (*patients*).

CHAPTER 14

CHOOSING THE RIGHT WORD

14a Avoiding Jargon

Jargon, the specialized or technical vocabulary of a trade, profession, or academic discipline, is useful for communicating in the field for which it was developed, but outside that field it can be confusing.

The patient had an ~~acute myocardial infarction~~ *a heart attack*.

When you write, use vocabulary that is appropriate for your audience and purpose.

14b Avoiding Pretentious Diction

Good writing is clear writing, and pompous or flowery language is no substitute for clarity. Revise to eliminate **pretentious diction,** inappropriately elevated and wordy language.

As I fell ~~into slumber~~ *asleep*, I ~~cogitated~~ *thought* about my day ~~ambling~~ *hiking* through ~~the splendor of~~ the Appalachian Mountains.

14c Avoiding Clichés

Clichés are trite expressions that have lost all meaning because they have been so overused. Familiar sayings like "happy as a clam," and "what goes around comes around," for example, do little to enhance your writing. Avoid the temptation to use clichés in your college writing. Take the time to think of fresh language.

14d Avoiding Biased Language

(1) Offensive Labels

When referring to a racial, ethnic, or religious group, use words with neutral connotations or words that the group itself uses in *formal* speech or writing. Also avoid potentially offensive labels related to age, class, occupation, physical ability, or sexual orientation.

(2) Sexist Language

Sexist language entails much more than the use of derogatory words such as *hunk* and *bimbo*. Assuming that some professions are exclusive to one gender—for instance, that *nurse* denotes only women or that *engineer* denotes only men—is also sexist. So is the use of job titles such as *postman* for *letter carrier* and *stewardess* for *flight attendant*.

Sexist language also occurs when a writer fails to apply the same terminology to both men and women. For example, you should refer to two scientists with Ph.D.s not as Dr. Sagan and Mrs. Yallow, but as Dr. Sagan and Dr. Yallow.

In your writing, always use *women*—not *girls* or *ladies*—when referring to adult females. Also avoid using the generic *he* or *him* when your subject could be either male or female. Instead, use the third-person plural or the phrase *he or she* (not *he/she*).

SEXIST: Before boarding, each <u>passenger</u> should make certain that <u>he</u> has <u>his</u> ticket.

REVISED: Before boarding, <u>passengers</u> should make certain that <u>they</u> have <u>their</u> tickets.

REVISED: Before boarding, each <u>passenger</u> should make certain that <u>he or she</u> has a ticket.

NOTE: Be careful not to use *they* or *their* to refer to a singular antecedent.

   Drivers
~~Any driver~~ caught speeding should have their driving privileges suspended.

✔ ELIMINATING SEXIST LANGUAGE

SEXIST USAGE	POSSIBLE REVISIONS
1. Mankind	People, human beings
Man's accomplishments	Human accomplishments
Man-made	Synthetic
2. Female engineer (lawyer, accountant, etc.), male model	Engineer (lawyer, accountant, etc.), model

continued on the following page

continued from the previous page

SEXIST USAGE	**POSSIBLE REVISIONS**
3. Policeman/woman Salesman/woman/girl Businessman/woman	Police officer Salesperson/representative Businessperson, executive
4. <u>Everyone</u> should complete <u>his</u> application by Tuesday.	Everyone should complete <u>his or her</u> application by Tuesday. <u>All students</u> should complete <u>their</u> applications by Tuesday.

PART 4

UNDERSTANDING PUNCTUATION

CHAPTER 15

END PUNCTUATION

15a Using Periods

Use a period to signal the end of most sentences, including indirect questions.

Something is rotten in Denmark.

They wondered whether the water was safe to drink.

Also use periods in most abbreviations.

Mr. Spock	Aug.	Dr. Livingstone
9 p.m.	etc.	1600 Pennsylvania Ave.

If an abbreviation ends the sentence, do not add another period.

He promised to be there at 6 a.m.

However, add a question mark if the sentence is a question.

Did he arrive at 6 p.m.?

If the abbreviation falls *within* a sentence, use normal punctuation after the period.

He promised to be there at 6 p.m., but he forgot.

 CLOSE-UP

ABBREVIATIONS WITHOUT PERIODS

Abbreviations composed of all capital letters do not usually require periods unless they stand for initials of people's names (E. B. White).

MD   RN   BC

Familiar abbreviations of names of corporations or government agencies and scientific and technical terms do not require periods.

CD-ROM   NYU   DNA   CIA   WCAU-FM

continued on the following page

continued from the previous page

Acronyms—new words formed from the initial letters or first few letters of a series of words—do not include periods.

hazmat   AIDS   NAFTA   CAT scan

Clipped forms (commonly accepted shortened forms of words, such as *gym, dorm, math,* and *fax*) do not use periods.

Postal abbreviations do not include periods.

TX   CA   MS   PA   FL   NY

Use periods to mark divisions in dramatic, poetic, and biblical references.

Hamlet 2.2.1–5 (act, scene, lines)
Paradise Lost 7.163–167 (book, lines)
Judges 4.14 (chapter, verse)

ELECTRONIC ADDRESSES

Periods, along with other punctuation marks (such as slashes and colons), are used in electronic addresses (URLs).

g.mckay@smu.edu
http://www.nwu.org/nwu

NOTE: When you type an electronic address, do not end it with a period or add spaces after periods within the address.

15b Using Question Marks

Use a question mark to signal the end of a direct question.

Who was that masked man?

Use a question mark in parentheses to indicate that a date or number is uncertain.

Aristophanes, the Greek playwright, was born in 448 (?) BC and died in 380 (?) BC.

EDITING MISUSED QUESTION MARKS

Use a period, not a question mark, with an indirect question.

The personnel officer asked whether he knew how to type~~?~~.

Do not use a question mark to convey sarcasm. Instead, suggest your attitude through your choice of words.

I refused his *not very* generous (?) offer.

15c Using Exclamation Points

An exclamation point is used to signal the end of an emotional or emphatic statement, an emphatic interjection, or a forceful command.

Remember the Maine!

"No! Don't leave!," he cried.

EDITING MISUSED EXCLAMATION POINTS

Except for when you are recording dialogue, do not use exclamation points in college writing. Even in informal writing, use exclamation points sparingly.

CHAPTER 16

THE COMMA

16a Setting Off Independent Clauses

Use a comma when you form a compound sentence by linking two independent clauses with a **coordinating conjunction**
(and, but, or, nor, for, yet, so) or a pair of **correlative conjunctions**.

See
A1.7

The House approved the bill, <u>but</u> the Senate rejected it.

<u>Either</u> the hard drive is full, <u>or</u> the modem is too slow.

NOTE: You may omit the comma if two clauses connected by a
coordinating conjunction are very short: Love it or leave it.

16b Setting Off Items in a Series

Use commas between items in a series of three or more **coordinate elements** (words, phrases, or clauses joined by a coordinating conjunction).

Chipmunk, *raccoon*, and *Mugwump* are Native American
words.

You may pay <u>by check</u>, <u>with a credit card</u>, or <u>in cash</u>.

<u>Brazilians speak Portuguese</u>, <u>Colombians speak Spanish</u>,
and <u>Haitians speak French and Creole</u>.

NOTE: To avoid ambiguity, always use a comma before the coordinating conjunction that separates the last two items in a
series.

Do not use a comma to introduce or to close a series.

Three important criteria are, fat content, salt content, and
taste.

The provinces Quebec, Ontario, and Alberta, are in Canada.

Use a comma between items in a series of two or more **coordinate adjectives**—adjectives that modify the same word or
word group—unless they are joined by a conjunction.

She brushed her <u>long</u>, <u>shining</u> hair.

The baby was <u>tired</u> and <u>cranky</u> and <u>wet</u>. (no comma required)

✔ CHECKLIST: PUNCTUATING ADJECTIVES IN A SERIES

✔ If you can reverse the order of the adjectives or insert *and* between the adjectives without changing the meaning, the adjectives are coordinate, and you should use a comma.

She brushed her long, shining hair.

She brushed her shining, long hair.

She brushed her long [and] shining hair.

✔ If you cannot, the adjectives are not coordinate, and you should not use a comma.

Ten red balloons fell from the ceiling.

Red ten balloons fell from the ceiling.

Ten [and] red balloons fell from the ceiling.

NOTE: Numbers—such as *ten*—are not coordinate with other adjectives.

16c Setting Off Introductory Elements

An introductory dependent clause, verbal phrase, or prepositional phrase is generally set off from the rest of the sentence by a comma.

<u>Although the CIA used to call undercover agents *penetration agents*</u>, they now routinely refer to them as *moles*. (dependent clause)

<u>Pushing onward</u>, Scott struggled toward the South Pole. (verbal phrase)

<u>During the Depression</u>, movie attendance rose. (prepositional phrase)

If the clause or phrase is short, you may omit the comma—*provided that the sentence will be clear without it.*

<u>When I exercise</u> I drink plenty of water.

<u>After the exam</u> I took a four-hour nap.

TRANSITIONAL WORDS AND PHRASES

When a <u>transitional word or phrase</u> begins a sentence, it is usually set off with a comma.

<u>However</u>, any plan that is enacted must be fair.

<u>In other words</u>, we cannot act hastily.

16d Setting Off Nonessential Material

Use commas to set off nonessential material whether it appears at the beginning, in the middle, or at the end of a sentence.

(1) Nonrestrictive Modifiers

Do *not* use commas to set off **restrictive modifiers,** which supply information essential to the meaning of the word or word group they modify. However, *do* use commas to set off **nonrestrictive modifiers,** which supply information that is not essential to the meaning of the word or word group they modify.

> **RESTRICTIVE** (no commas):
> Actors <u>who have inflated egos</u> are often insecure. (Only those actors with inflated egos—not all actors—are insecure.)
>
> **NONESTRICTIVE** (commas required):
> Actors<u>, who have inflated egos,</u> are often insecure. (*All* actors—not just those with inflated egos—are insecure.)

In the following examples, commas set off only nonrestrictive modifiers—those that supply nonessential information—but not restrictive modifiers, which supply essential information.

> *Adjective Clauses*
> **RESTRICTIVE:** Speaking in public is something <u>that most people fear</u>.
>
> **NONRESTRICTIVE:** He ran for the bus<u>, which was late as usual</u>.

> *Prepositional Phrases*
> **RESTRICTIVE:** The man <u>with the gun</u> demanded their money.
>
> **NONRESTRICTIVE:** The clerk<u>, with a nod,</u> dismissed me.

> *Verbal Phrases*
> **RESTRICTIVE:** The candidates <u>running for mayor</u> have agreed to a debate.

NONRESTRICTIVE: The marathoner, <u>running his fastest</u>, beat his previous record.

Appositives
RESTRICTIVE: The film <u>*Citizen Kane*</u> made Orson Welles famous.

NONRESTRICTIVE: *Citizen Kane*, <u>Orson Welles's first film</u>, made him famous.

✔ CHECKLIST: RESTRICTIVE AND NONRESTRICTIVE MODIFIERS

To determine whether a modifier is restrictive or non-restrictive, answer these questions.

✔ Is the modifier essential to the meaning of the noun it modifies (*The man with the gun,* not just any man)? If so, it is restrictive and does not take commas.

✔ Is the modifier introduced by *that* (*something that most people fear*)? If so, it is restrictive. *That* cannot introduce a nonrestrictive clause.

✔ Can you delete the relative pronoun without causing ambiguity or confusion (*something [that] most people fear*)? If so, the clause is restrictive.

✔ Is the appositive more specific than the noun that precedes it (*the film* Citizen Kane)? If so, it is restrictive.

USING COMMAS WITH *THAT* AND *WHICH*

That is used to introduce only restrictive clauses; *which* can be used to introduce both restrictive and nonrestrictive clauses. Many writers, however, prefer to use *which* only to introduce nonrestrictive clauses.

(2) Transitional Words and Phrases

<u>Transitional words and phrases</u> qualify, clarify, and make connections. However, they are not essential to meaning. For

See 2b

this reason, they are always set off by commas when they inter-rupt or come at the end of a clause (as well as when they begin a sentence).

> The Outward Bound program, _for example_, is extremely safe.

> Other programs are not so safe, _however_.

TRANSITIONAL WORDS AND PHRASES

When a transitional word or phrase joins two inde-pendent clauses, it must be preceded by a semicolon and followed by a comma.

Laughter is the best medicine; _of course_, penicillin also comes in handy sometimes.

---

(3) Contradictory Phrases and Absolute Phrases

A phrase that expresses a contradiction is usually set off by commas.

> This medicine is taken after meals, _never on an empty stomach_.

> Mark McGwire, _not Sammy Sosa_, was the first to break Roger Maris's home-run record.

An **absolute phrase,** which usually consists of a noun plus a participle, is always set off by commas from the sentence it modifies.

> _His fear increasing_, he waited to enter the haunted house.

(4) Miscellaneous Nonessential Elements

Other nonessential elements usually set off by commas in-clude tag questions, names in direct address, mild interjections, and *yes* and *no*.

> This is your first day on the job, _isn't it?_

> I wonder, _Mr. Honeywell_, whether Mr. Albright deserves a raise.

> _Well_, it's about time.

> _Yes_, we have no bananas.

16e Using Commas in Other Conventional Contexts

(1) With Direct Quotations

In most cases, use commas to set off a direct quotation from the **identifying tag** (*he said, she answered,* and so on).

Emerson said◉ "I greet you at the beginning of a great career."

"I greet you at the beginning of a great career◉" Emerson said.

"I greet you◉" Emerson said◉ "at the beginning of a great career."

When the identifying tag comes between two complete sentences, however, the tag is introduced by a comma but followed by a period.

"Winning isn't everything◉" Vince Lombardi said. "It's the only thing."

(2) With Titles or Degrees Following a Name

Michael Crichton◉ MD◉ wrote *Jurassic Park*.

Hamlet◉ Prince of Denmark◉ is Shakespeare's most famous character.

(3) In Dates and Addresses

On August 30◉ 1983◉ the space shuttle *Challenger* was launched.

Her address is 600 West End Avenue◉ New York◉ NY 10024.

NOTE: When only the month and year are given, no commas are used (May 1968). No comma separates the street number from the street or the state name from the zip code.

16f Using Commas to Prevent Misreading

In some cases, a comma is used to prevent ambiguity. For example, consider the following sentence.

Those who can, sprint the final lap.

Without the comma, *can* appears to be an auxiliary verb ("Those who can sprint. . . ."), and the sentence seems incomplete. The comma tells readers to pause and thereby prevents confusion.

Also use a comma to acknowledge the omission of a repeated word, usually a verb, and to separate words repeated consecutively.

Pam carried the box; Tim, the suitcase.

Everything bad that could have happened, happened.

16g Editing Misused Commas

Do not use commas in the following situations.

(1) To Set Off Restrictive Modifiers

The film, *Malcolm X*, was directed by Spike Lee.

They planned a picnic, in the park.

(2) Between a Subject and Its Predicate

A woman with dark red hair, opened the door.

(3) Between a Verb and an Indirect Quotation or Indirect Question

General Douglas MacArthur vowed, that he would return.

The landlord asked, if we would sign a two-year lease.

(4) In Compounds That Are Not Composed of Independent Clauses

During the 1400s plagues, and pestilence were common.
(compound subject)

Many women thirty-five and older are returning to college, and tend to be good students. (compound predicate)

(5) Before a Dependent Clause at the End of a Sentence

Jane Addams founded Hull House, because she wanted to help Chicago's poor.

CHAPTER 17

THE SEMICOLON

The **semicolon** is used only between items of equal grammatical rank: two independent clauses, two phrases, and so on.

17a Separating Independent Clauses

Use a semicolon between closely related independent clauses that convey parallel or contrasting information but are not joined by a coordinating conjunction.

> Paul Revere's *The Boston Massacre* is an early example of American protest art ; Edward Hicks's later "primitive" paintings are socially conscious art with a religious strain.

 CLOSE-UP **USING SEMICOLONS**

Using only a comma or no punctuation at all between independent clauses creates a <u>comma splice</u> or a <u>fused sentence</u>.

See Ch. 3

Use a semicolon between two independent clauses when the second clause is introduced by a transitional word or phrase (the transitional element is followed by a comma).

> Thomas Jefferson brought two hundred vanilla beans and a recipe for vanilla ice cream back from France ; <u>thus</u>, he gave America its all-time favorite ice cream flavor.

17b Separating Items in a Series

Use semicolons between items in a series when one or more of these items include commas.

> Three papers are posted on the bulletin board outside the building: a description of the exams ; a list of appeal procedures for students who fail ; and an employment ad from an automobile factory, addressed specifically to candidates whose appeals are turned down. (Andrea Lee, *Russian Journal*)

Laramie, Wyoming; Wyoming, Delaware; and Delaware, Ohio, were three of the places they visited.

17c Editing Misused Semicolons

Do not use semicolons in the following situations.

(1) Between a Dependent and an Independent Clause

Because drugs can now suppress the body's immune reaction; fewer organ transplants are rejected.

(2) To Introduce a List

Despite the presence of CNN and FOX News, the evening news remains a battleground for the three major television networks; CBS, NBC, and ABC.

(3) To Introduce a Direct Quotation

Marie Antoinette may not have said; "Let them eat cake."

CHAPTER 18

THE APOSTROPHE

Use an apostrophe to form the possessive case, to indicate omissions in contractions, and to form certain plurals.

18a Forming the Possessive Case

The possessive case indicates ownership. In English, the possessive case of nouns and indefinite pronouns is indicated either with a phrase that includes the word *of* (the hands *of* the clock) or with an apostrophe and, in most cases, an *s* (the clock's hands).

(1) Singular Nouns and Indefinite Pronouns

To form the possessive case of singular nouns and indefinite pronouns, add '*s*.

> "The Monk's Tale" is one of Chaucer's *Canterbury Tales*.

> When we would arrive was anyone's guess.

NOTE: With some singular nouns that end in -*s*, pronouncing the possessive ending as a separate syllable can sound awkward. In such cases, it is acceptable to use just an apostrophe: Crispus Attucks' death, Aristophanes' *Lysistrata*.

(2) Plural Nouns

To form the possessive case of regular plural nouns (those that end in -*s* or -*es*), add only an apostrophe.

> Laid-off employees received two weeks' severance pay and three months' medical benefits.

> The Lopezes' three children are triplets.

To form the possessive case of nouns that have irregular plurals, add '*s*.

> *The Children's Hour* is a play by Lillian Hellman.

(3) Compound Nouns or Groups of Words

To form the possessive case of compound words or of groups of words, add '*s* to the last word.

> The Secretary of State's resignation was accepted under protest.

> This is someone else's responsibility.

(4) Two or More Items

To indicate individual ownership of two or more items, add 's to each item.

Ernest Hemingway's and Gertrude Stein's writing styles have some similarities.

To indicate joint ownership, add 's only to the last item.

We studied Lewis and Clark's expedition.

APOSTROPHES WITH PLURAL NOUNS AND PERSONAL PRONOUNS

Do not use apostrophes with plural nouns that are not possessive.

The Thompson's are out.

These down vest's are very warm.

The Philadelphia Seventy Sixer's have some outstanding players.

Do not use apostrophes to form the possessive case of personal pronouns.

This ticket must be your's or her's.

The next turn is their's.

The doll lost it's right eye.

The next great moment in history is our's.

See 18b
Be especially careful not to confuse **contractions** (which always include apostrophes) with the possessive forms of personal pronouns (which never include apostrophes).

Contraction	*Possessive Form*
Who's on first?	Whose book is this?
They're playing our song.	Their team is winning.
It's raining.	Its paws were muddy.
You're a real pal.	Your résumé is very impressive.

18b Indicating Omissions in Contractions

Apostrophes replace omitted letters in contractions that combine a pronoun and a verb (*he + will = he'll*) or the elements of a verb phrase (*do + not = don't*).

FREQUENTLY USED CONTRACTIONS

it's (it is)   let's (let us)
we've (we have)   isn't (is not)
they're (they are)   wouldn't (would not)
we'll (we will)   don't (do not)
I'm (I am)   won't (will not)

In informal writing, an apostrophe may also be used to represent the century in a year: Class of '97, the '60s. In college writing, however, write out the year in full.

18c Forming Plurals

In a few special situations, add 's to form plurals.

FORMING PLURALS WITH APOSTROPHES

Plurals of Letters

The Italian language has no *j*'s or *k*'s.

Plurals of Words Referred to as Words

The supervisor would accept no *if*'s, *and*'s, or *but*'s.

NOTE: <u>Elements spoken of as themselves</u> (letters, numerals, or words) are set in italic type; the plural ending, however, is not.

See
23c

CHAPTER 19

QUOTATION MARKS

Use quotation marks to set off brief passages of quoted speech or writing, to set off titles, and to set off words used in special ways. Do not use quotation marks when quoting long passages of prose or poetry.

19a Setting Off Quoted Speech or Writing

When you quote a word, phrase, or brief passage of someone's speech or writing, enclose the quoted material in a pair of quotation marks.

Gloria Steinem observed, **"**We are becoming the men we once hoped to marry.**"**

Galsworthy describes Aunt Juley as **"**prostrated by the blow**"** (329). (Note that the end punctuation follows the parenthetical documentation.)

Special rules govern the punctuation of a quotation when it is used with an **identifying tag**—a phrase (such as *he said*) that identifies the speaker or writer.

(1) Identifying Tag in the Middle of a Quoted Passage

Use a pair of commas to set off an identifying tag that interrupts a quoted passage.

"In the future**,**" pop artist Andy Warhol once said**,** "everyone will be world famous for fifteen minutes."

If the identifying tag follows a completed sentence but the quoted passage continues, use a period after the tag, and begin the new sentence with a capital letter and quotation marks.

"Be careful**,**" Erin warned**.** "Reptiles can be tricky**.**"

(2) Identifying Tag at the Beginning of a Quoted Passage

Use a comma after an identifying tag that introduces quoted speech or writing.

The Raven repeated**,** "Nevermore."

Use a <u>**colon**</u> instead of a comma before a quotation if the ^{See 20a} identifying tag is a complete sentence.

She gave her final answer:"No."

(3) Identifying Tag at the End of a Quoted Passage

Use a comma to set off a quotation from an identifying tag that follows it.

"Be careful out there," the sergeant warned.

If the quotation ends with a question mark or an exclamation point, use that punctuation mark instead of the comma. In this situation, the tag begins with a lowercase letter even though it follows end punctuation.

"Is Ankara the capital of Turkey?" she asked.

"Oh boy!" he cried.

NOTE: Commas and periods are always placed inside quotation marks. For information on placement of other punctuation marks with quotation marks, see 19d.

NOTE: When you record **dialogue** (conversation between two or more people), enclose the quoted words in quotation marks. Begin a new paragraph each time a new speaker is introduced. When you are quoting several paragraphs of dialogue by one speaker, begin each new paragraph with quotation marks. However, use closing quotation marks only at the end of the entire passage (not at the end of each paragraph).

QUOTING LONG PROSE PASSAGES

Do *not* enclose a **long prose passage** (more than four lines) in quotation marks. Instead, set it off by indenting the entire passage one inch (or ten spaces) from the left-hand margin. Double-space above and below the quoted passage, and double-space between lines within it. Introduce the passage with a colon, and place parenthetical documentation one space *after* the end punctuation.

The following portrait of Aunt Juley illustrates several of the devices Galsworthy uses throughout <u>The Forsyte</u>

continued on the following page

continued from the previous page

Saga, such as a journalistic detachment, a sense of the grotesque and an ironic stance:

> Aunt Juley stayed in her room, prostrated by the blow. Her face, discoloured by tears, was divided into compartments by the little ridges of pouting flesh which had swollen with emotion [. . .]. Her warm heart could not bear the thought that Ann was lying there so cold. (329)

Similar characterizations appear throughout the novel although not every passage includes so many different stylistic devices.

When quoting a long prose passage that is a single paragraph, do not indent the first line. When quoting two or more paragraphs, however, indent the first line of each paragraph (including the first) *three* additional spaces. If the first sentence of the quoted passage does not begin a paragraph in the source, do not indent it—but do indent the first line of each subsequent paragraph.

See
32b

NOTE: <u>APA guidelines</u> differ from those set forth here, which conform to MLA style.

 QUOTING POETRY

Treat one line of poetry like a short prose passage: enclose it in quotation marks and run it into the text. If you quote two or three lines of poetry, separate the lines with <u>**slashes**</u>, and run the quotation into the text. If you quote more than three lines of poetry, set them off like a long prose passage. (For special emphasis, you may set off fewer lines in this way.) Be sure to reproduce *exactly* the spelling, capitalization, and indentation of the quoted lines.

See
20e

Wilfred Owen, a poet who was killed in action in World War I, expressed the horrors of war with vivid imagery:

> Bent double, like old beggars under sacks.
> Knock-kneed, coughing like hags, we cursed
>   through sludge.
> Till on the haunting flares we turned our backs
> And towards our distant rest began to trudge. (1–4)

19b Setting Off Titles

<u>Titles</u> of short works and titles of parts of long works are ^{See 23a} enclosed in quotation marks. Other titles are italicized.

NOTE: MLA style recommends underlining to indicate italics.

TITLES REQUIRING QUOTATION MARKS

Articles in Magazines, Newspapers, and Professional Journals
"Why Johnny Can't Write" (*Newsweek*)

Essays, Short Stories, Short Poems, and Songs
"Fenimore Cooper's Literary Offenses"
"Flying Home"
"The Road Not Taken"
"The Star-Spangled Banner"

Chapters or Sections of Books
"Miss Sharp Begins to Make Friends" (Chapter 10 of *Vanity Fair*)

Episodes of Radio or Television Series
"Lucy Goes to the Hospital" (*I Love Lucy*)

19c Setting Off Words Used in Special Ways

Enclose a word used in a special or unusual way in quotation marks. (If you use *so-called* before the word, do not use quotation marks as well.)

It was clear that adults approved of children who were "readers," but it was not at all clear why this was so. (Annie Dillard)

Also enclose a **coinage**—an invented word—in quotation marks.

After the twins were born, the minivan became a "baby-mobile."

19d Using Quotation Marks with Other Punctuation

Place quotation marks *after* the comma or period at the end of a quotation.

Many, like poet Robert Frost, think about "the road not taken," but not many have taken "the one less traveled by."

Place quotation marks *before* a semicolon or colon at the end of a quotation.

Students who do not pass the test receive "certificates of completion"; those who pass are awarded diplomas.

Taxpayers were pleased with the first of the candidate's promised "sweeping new reforms": a balanced budget.

If a question mark, exclamation point, or dash is part of the quotation, place the quotation marks *after* the punctuation.

"Who's there?" she demanded.

"Stop!" he cried.

"Should we leave now, or —" Vicki paused, unable to continue.

If a question mark, exclamation point, or dash is not part of the quotation, place the quotation marks *before* the punctuation.

Did you finish reading "The Black Cat"?

Whatever you do, don't yell "Uncle"!

The first story—Updike's "*A & P*"—provoked discussion.

 CLOSE-UP **QUOTATIONS WITHIN QUOTATIONS**

Use *single* quotation marks to enclose a quotation within a quotation.

Claire noted, "Liberace always said, 'I cried all the way to the bank.'"

Also use single quotation marks within a quotation to indicate a title that would normally be enclosed in double quotation marks.

I think what she said was, "Play it, Sam. Play 'As Time Goes By.'"

See 19a Use double quotation marks around quotations or titles within a <u>long prose passage</u>.

19e Editing Misused Quotation Marks

Do not use quotation marks to set off indirect quotations (someone else's written or spoken words that are not quoted exactly).

Freud wondered ~~"~~what women wanted~~."~~

Do not use quotation marks to set off slang or technical terms.

Dawn is ~~"~~into~~"~~ running.

~~"~~Biofeedback~~"~~ is sometimes used to treat migraines.

 CLOSE-UP **TITLES OF YOUR OWN PAPERS**

Do not use quotation marks (or italics) to set off the title of your own paper.

CHAPTER 20

OTHER PUNCTUATION MARKS

20a Using Colons

The **colon** is a strong punctuation mark that points readers ahead to the rest of the sentence. When a colon introduces a list or series, explanatory material, or a quotation, it must be preceded by a complete sentence.

(1) Introducing Lists or Series

Use colons to set off lists or series, including those introduced by phrases like *the following* or *as follows*.

Waiting tables requires three skills: memory, speed, and balance.

(2) Introducing Explanatory Material

Use colons to introduce material that explains, exemplifies, or summarizes.

She had one dream: to play professional basketball.

Sometimes a colon separates two independent clauses, the second illustrating or clarifying the first.

The survey presents an interesting finding: Americans do not trust the news media.

 USING COLONS

When a complete sentence follows a colon, the sentence may begin with either a capital or a lowercase letter. However, if the sentence is a quotation, the first word is always capitalized (unless it was not capitalized in the source).

(3) Introducing Quotations

See 19a

When you quote a **long prose passage**, always introduce it with a colon. Also use a colon before a short quotation when it is introduced by a complete independent clause.

With dignity, Bartleby repeated the words again: "I prefer not to."

OTHER CONVENTIONAL USES OF COLONS

To Separate Titles from Subtitles
Family Installments : *Memories of Growing Up Hispanic*

To Separate Minutes from Hours
6:15 a.m.

After Salutations in <u>business letters</u>
Dear Dr. Evans:

To Separate Place of Publication from Name of Publisher in a <u>Works Cited list</u>
Boston: Heinle, 2003.

See
35a

See
31a

---

(4) Editing Misused Colons

Do not use colons after expressions such as *namely, for example, such as,* or *that is.*

The Eye Institute treats patients with a wide variety of conditions, such as: myopia, glaucoma, and cataracts.

Do not place colons between verbs and their objects or complements or between prepositions and their objects.

James Michener wrote: *Hawaii, Centennial, Space,* and *Poland.*

Hitler's armies marched through: the Netherlands, Belgium, and France.

20b Using Dashes

(1) Setting Off Nonessential Material

Like commas, **dashes** can set off <u>nonessential material</u>, but unlike commas, dashes call attention to the material they set off. When you type, you indicate a dash with two unspaced hyphens (which most word processing programs will convert to a dash).

See
16d

For emphasis, you may use dashes to set off explanations, qualifications, examples, definitions, and appositives.

Neither of the boys—both nine-year-olds—had any history of violence.

Too many parents learn the dangers of swimming pools the hard way—after their toddler has drowned.

(2) Introducing a Summary

Use a dash to introduce a statement that summarizes a list or series that appears before it.

"Study hard," "Respect your elders," "Don't talk with your mouth full"—Sharon had often heard her parents say these things.

(3) Indicating an Interruption

In dialogue, a dash may indicate a hesitation or an unfinished thought.

"I think—no, I know—this is the worst day of my life," Julie sighed.

(4) Editing Overused Dashes

Because too many dashes can make a passage seem disorganized and out of control, dashes should not be overused.

Registration was a nightmare—most of the courses I wanted to take—geology and conversational Spanish, for instance— met at inconvenient times—or were closed by the time I tried to sign up for them.

20c Using Parentheses

(1) Setting Off Nonessential Material

Use parentheses to enclose material that is relatively unimportant in a sentence—for example, material that expands, clarifies, illustrates, or supplements.

In some European countries (notably Sweden and France), superb daycare is offered at little or no cost to parents.

Also use parentheses to set off digressions and afterthoughts.

Last Sunday we went to the new stadium (it was only half-filled) to see the game.

When a complete sentence set off by parentheses falls within another sentence, it should not begin with a capital letter or end with a period.

The area is so cold (temperatures average in the low twenties) that it is virtually uninhabitable.

If the parenthetical sentence does *not* fall within another sentence, however, it must begin with a capital letter and end with appropriate punctuation.

The region is very cold. (Temperatures average in the low twenties.)

(2) Using Parentheses in Other Situations

Use parentheses around letters and numbers that identify points on a list, dates, cross references, and documentation.

All reports must include the following components: (1) an opening summary, (2) a background statement, and (3) a list of conclusions.

Russia defeated Sweden in the Great Northern War (1700–1721).

Other scholars also make this point (see p. 54).

One critic has called the novel "puerile" (Arvin 72).

20d Using Brackets

Brackets within quotations tell readers that the enclosed words are yours and not those of your source. You can bracket an explanation, a clarification, a correction, or an opinion.

"Even at Princeton he [F. Scott Fitzgerald] felt like an outsider."

If a quotation contains an error, indicate that the error is not yours by following the error with the italicized Latin word *sic* ("thus") in brackets.

"The octopuss [*sic*] is a cephalopod mollusk with eight arms."

NOTE: Use brackets to indicate parentheses that fall within parentheses.

USING BRACKETS TO EDIT QUOTATIONS

Use brackets to indicate changes that enable you to fit a **quotation** smoothly into your sentence. If you use **ellipses** to indicate that you have omitted words from a quotation, MLA requires that you enclose the ellipses in brackets.

See 30a1
See 20f

20e Using Slashes

(1) Separating One Option from Another

The either / or fallacy is a common error in logic.

Writer / director M. Night Shyamalan spoke at the film festival.

Note that in this case there is no space before or after the slash.

(2) Separating Lines of Poetry Run into the Text

The poet James Schevill writes, "I study my defects **/** And learn how to perfect them."

In this case, leave one space before and one space after the slash.

20f Using Ellipses

Use an **ellipsis**—three *spaced* periods—to indicate that you have omitted words (or even entire sentences) from a quotation. MLA style recommends that you enclose the ellipsis in brackets to distinguish ellipses you have added from ellipses that might have appeared in the original quotation. (If you are not following MLA style, do not use brackets.) When deleting material from a quotation, be very careful not to change the meaning of the original passage.

> **ORIGINAL:** "When I was a young man, being anxious to distinguish myself, I was perpetually starting new propositions." (Samuel Johnson)

> **WITH OMISSION:** "When I was a young man, [. . .] I was perpetually starting new propositions."

Note that when you delete words immediately after an internal punctuation mark (such as a comma), you retain the punctuation before the ellipsis.

When you delete words *at the end of a sentence,* place the sentence's period or other end punctuation after the bracketed ellipsis.

> According to humorist Dave Barry, "from outer space Europe appears to be shaped like a large ketchup stain[. . .]."

NOTE: Never begin a quoted passage with an ellipsis.

When you delete material from a quotation of more than one sentence, where to place the end punctuation—before or after the bracketed ellipsis—is determined by where you have deleted material.

Deletion from Middle of One Sentence to End of Another

According to Donald Hall, "Everywhere one meets the idea that reading is an activity desirable in itself [. . .]. People surround the idea of reading with piety and do not take into account the purpose of reading."

Deletion from Middle of One Sentence to Middle of Another

"When I was a young man, [ ] I found that generally what was new was false." (Samuel Johnson)

NOTE: An ellipsis in the middle of a quoted passage can indicate the omission of a word, a sentence or two, or even a whole paragraph or more.

CLOSE-UP   **USING ELLIPSES**

If a quotation ending with an ellipsis is followed by parenthetical documentation, the final punctuation *follows* the documentation.

As Jarman argues, "Compromise was impossible[...]" (161).

PART 5

SPELLING AND MECHANICS

CHAPTER 21

SPELLING

21a Understanding Spelling and Pronunciation

Because pronunciation in English often provides few clues to spelling, you must memorize the spellings of many words and use a dictionary or spell checker regularly.

(1) Vowels in Unstressed Positions

Many unstressed vowels sound exactly alike. For instance, the unstressed vowels *a, e,* and *i* are impossible to distinguish by pronunciation alone in the suffixes -*able* and -*ible*, -*ance* and -*ence*, and -*ant* and -*ent*.

comfort<u>able</u>	brilli<u>ance</u>	serv<u>ant</u>
compat<u>ible</u>	excell<u>ence</u>	independ<u>ent</u>

(2) Silent Letters

Some English words contain silent letters, such as the *b* in *climb* and the *t* in *mortgage*.

ai<u>s</u>le	depo<u>t</u>
condem<u>n</u>	k<u>n</u>ight
des<u>c</u>end	<u>p</u>neumonia

(3) Words That Are Often Pronounced Carelessly

Words like the following are often misspelled because when we pronounce them, we add, omit, or transpose letters.

can<u>d</u>idate	nu<u>c</u>lear	recognize
environ<u>m</u>ent	lib<u>r</u>ary	suppose<u>d</u> to
Feb<u>r</u>uary	quan<u>t</u>ity	use<u>d</u> to

(4) Homophones

Homophones are words—such as *accept* and *except*—that are pronounced alike but spelled differently. For a list of homophones, along with their meanings and sentences illustrating their use, consult **Appendix B,** "Usage Review."

21b Learning Spelling Rules

Memorizing a few reliable spelling rules can help you overcome some of the problems caused by inconsistencies between pronunciation and spelling.

(1) The *ie/ei* Combinations

Use *i* before *e* (*belief, chief*) except after *c* (*ceiling, receive*) or when pronounced *ay*, as in *neighbor* or *weigh*. **Exceptions:** *either, neither, foreign, leisure, weird,* and *seize*. In addition, if the *ie* combination is not pronounced as a unit, the rule does not apply: *atheist, science*.

(2) Doubling Final Consonants

The only words that double their consonants before a suffix that begins with a vowel (*-ed* or *-ing*) are those that pass the following three tests.

1. They have one syllable or are stressed on the last syllable.
2. They have only one vowel in the last syllable.
3. They end in a single consonant.

The word *tap* satisfies all three conditions: it has only one syllable, it has only one vowel (*a*), and it ends in a single consonant (*p*). Therefore, the final consonant doubles before a suffix beginning with a vowel (*tapped, tapping*).

(3) Silent *e* before a Suffix

When a suffix that begins with a consonant is added to a word ending in a silent *e*, the *e* is generally kept: *hope/hopeful.* **Exceptions:** *argument, truly, ninth, judgment,* and *abridgment.*

When a suffix that begins with a vowel is added to a word ending in a silent *e*, the *e* is generally dropped: *hope/hoping.* **Exceptions:** *changeable, noticeable,* and *courageous.*

(4) *y* before a Suffix

When a word ends in a consonant plus *y*, the *y* generally changes to an *i* when a suffix is added (*beauty + ful = beautiful*). The *y* is kept, however, when the suffix *-ing* is added (*tally + ing = tallying*) and in some one-syllable words (*dry + ness = dryness*).

When a word ends in a vowel plus *y*, the *y* is kept (*joy + ful = joyful*). **Exception:** *day + ly = daily.*

(5) *seed* Endings

Endings with the sound *seed* are nearly always spelled *cede*, as in *precede.* **Exceptions:** *supersede, exceed, proceed,* and *succeed.*

(6) *-able, -ible*

If the root of a word is itself a word, the suffix *-able* is most commonly used (*comfortable, agreeable*). If the root of a word is not a word, the suffix *-ible* is most often used (*compatible, incredible*).

(7) Plurals

Most nouns form plurals by adding *s: tortilla/tortillas, boat/boats.* There are, however, a number of exceptions.

- Some words ending in *-f* or *-fe* form plurals by changing the *f* to *v* and adding *es* or *s: life/lives, self/selves.* Others add just *s: belief/beliefs, safe/safes.*
- Most words that end in a consonant followed by *y* form plurals by changing the *y* to *i* and adding *es: baby/babies.* **Exceptions:** proper nouns such as *Kennedy* (plural *Kennedys*).
- Most words that end in a consonant followed by *o* add *es* to form the plural: *tomato/tomatoes, hero/heroes.* **Exceptions:** *silo/silos, piano/pianos, memo/memos, soprano/sopranos.*
- Words ending in *-s, -sh, -ch, -x,* and *-z* form plurals by adding *es: Jones/Joneses, rash/rashes, lunch/lunches, box/boxes, buzz/buzzes.* **Exceptions:** Some one-syllable words that end in *-s* or *-z* double their final consonants when forming plurals: *quiz/quizzes.*
- Hyphenated compound nouns whose first element is more important than the others form the plural with the first element: *sister-in-law/sisters-in-law.*
- Some words, especially those borrowed from Latin or Greek, keep their foreign plurals.

Singular	*Plural*
criterion	criteria
datum	data
memorandum	memoranda
stimulus	stimuli

RUNNING A SPELL CHECK

If you use a computer spell checker, remember that it will not identify a word that is spelled correctly but used incorrectly—*then* for *than* or *its* for *it's*, for example—or a typo that creates another word, such as *form* for *from*. Even after you run a spell check, you still need to proofread your papers .

CHAPTER 22

CAPITALIZATION

In addition to capitalizing the first word of a sentence (including a quoted sentence) and the pronoun *I*, always capitalize proper nouns and important words in titles.

22a Capitalizing Proper Nouns

Proper nouns—the names of specific persons, places, or things—are capitalized, and so are adjectives formed from proper nouns.

(1) Specific People's Names

Eleanor Roosevelt   Medgar Evers

Capitalize a title when it precedes a person's name or replaces the name (Senator Barbara Boxer, Dad). Do not capitalize titles that *follow* names or that refer to the general position, not to the particular person who holds it (Barbara Boxer, the senator), except for very high-ranking positions: President of the United States. Never capitalize a title denoting a family relationship when it follows an article or a possessive pronoun: an aunt, my uncle.

Capitalize titles or abbreviations of academic degrees, even when they follow a name: Dr. Benjamin Spock, Benjamin Spock, MD

(2) Names of Particular Structures, Special Events, Monuments, and so on

the *Titanic*   the World Series
the Brooklyn Bridge   Mount Rushmore

(3) Places and Geographical Regions

Saturn   the Straits of Magellan
Budapest   the Western Hemisphere

Capitalize *north, east, south,* and *west* when they denote particular geographical regions (the West), but not when they designate directions (west of town).

(4) Days of the Week, Months, and Holidays

Saturday   Rosh Hashanah
January   Ramadan

(5) Historical Periods and Events, Documents, and Names of Legal Cases

the Battle of Gettysburg   Romanticism
Brown v Board of Education   the Treaty of Versailles

(6) Races, Ethnic Groups, Nationalities, and Languages

African-American   Korean
Latino/Latina   Dutch

NOTE: When the words *black* and *white* refer to races, they have traditionally not been capitalized. Current usage is divided on whether to capitalize *black*.

(7) Religions and Their Followers; Sacred Books and Figures

Jews   the Talmud   Buddha
Islam   God   the Scriptures

(8) Specific Organizations

the New York Yankees   the American Bar Association
League of Women Voters   the Anti-Defamation League

(9) Businesses, Government Agencies, and Other Institutions

Congress   Lincoln High School
the Environmental Protection   the University of
 Agency   Maryland

(10) Brand Names and Words Formed from Them

Coke   Astroturf   Rollerblades   Post-it

(11) Specific Academic Courses and Departments

Sociology 201   Department of English

NOTE: Do not capitalize a general subject area (sociology, zoology) unless it is the name of a language (French).

(12) Adjectives Formed from Proper Nouns

Keynesian economics   Elizabethan era
Freudian slip   Shakespearean sonnet

When words derived from proper nouns have lost their specialized meanings, do not capitalize them: *china* pattern, *french* fries.

22b Capitalizing Important Words in Titles

In general, capitalize all words in titles with the exception of articles (*a, an,* and *the*), prepositions, coordinating conjunctions, and the *to* in infinitives. If an article, preposition, or coordinating conjunction is the *first* or *last* word in the title, however, do capitalize it.

The Declaration of Independence   *A Man and a Woman*
Across the River and into the Trees   *What Friends Are For*

 EDITING MISUSED CAPITALS

Do not capitalize the following.

- Seasons (summer, fall, winter, spring)
- Names of centuries (the twenty-first century)
- Names of general historical periods (the automobile age)
- Diseases and other medical terms (unless a proper noun is part of the name): mumps, smallpox, polio

CHAPTER 23

ITALICS

23a Setting Off Titles and Names

Use italics for the titles and names in the box below. All other titles are set off with **quotation marks**.

See 19b

TITLES AND NAMES SET IN ITALICS

BOOKS: *David Copperfield, The Bluest Eye*

NEWSPAPERS: the *Washington Post,* the *Philadelphia Inquirer*

(Articles and names of cities are italicized only when they are part of a title.)

MAGAZINES AND JOURNALS: *Rolling Stone, Scientific American, PMLA*

ONLINE MAGAZINES AND JOURNALS *salon.com, theonion.com*

WEBSITES OR HOME PAGES: *urbanlegends.com, movie-mistakes.com*

PAMPHLETS: *Common Sense*

FILMS: *Casablanca, Citizen Kane*

TELEVISION PROGRAMS: *Law & Order, 60 Minutes, The Simpsons*

RADIO PROGRAMS: *All Things Considered, A Prairie Home Companion*

LONG POEMS: *John Brown's Body, The Faerie Queen*

PLAYS: *Macbeth, A Raisin in the Sun*

LONG MUSICAL WORKS: *Rigoletto, Eroica*

SOFTWARE PROGRAMS: *Word, PowerPoint*

PAINTINGS AND SCULPTURE: *Guernica, Pietà*

SHIPS: *Lusitania,* U.S.S. *Saratoga*

(S.S. and U.S.S. are not italicized.)

continued on the following page

---

continued from the previous page

TRAINS: *City of New Orleans, The Orient Express*

AIRCRAFT: *The Hindenburg, Enola Gay*

(Only particular aircraft, not makes or types such as Piper Cub and Boeing 757, are italicized.)

SPACECRAFT: *Challenger, Enterprise*

NOTE: Names of sacred books, such as the Bible, and well-known documents, such as the Constitution and the Declaration of Independence, are neither italicized nor placed within quotation marks.

USING ITALICS

MLA style recommends that you underline to indicate italics. However, you may italicize if your instructor gives you permission to do so.

23b Setting Off Foreign Words and Phrases

Use italics to set off foreign words and phrases that have not become part of the English language.

"C'est la vie," Madeleine said when she saw the long line for basketball tickets.

Spirochaeta plicatilis is a corkscrew-like bacterium.

If you are not sure whether a foreign word has been assimilated into English, consult a dictionary.

23c Setting Off Elements Spoken of as Themselves and Terms Being Defined

Use italics to set off letters, numerals, and words that refer to the letters, numerals, and words themselves.

Is that a *p* or a *g*?

I forget the exact address, but I know it has a *3* in it.

Does *through* rhyme with *cough?*

Italics also set off words and phrases that you go on to define.

A *closet drama* is a play meant to be read, not performed.

NOTE: When you quote a dictionary definition, put the words you are defining in italics and the definition itself in quotation marks.

To *infer* means "to draw a conclusion"; to *imply* means "to suggest."

23d Using Italics for Emphasis

Italics can occasionally be used for emphasis.

Initially, poetry might be defined as a kind of language that says *more* and says it *more intensely* than does ordinary language. (Lawrence Perrine, *Sound and Sense*)

However, overuse of italics is distracting. Instead of italicizing, indicate emphasis with word choice and sentence structure.

CHAPTER 24

HYPHENS

Hyphens have two conventional uses: to break a word at the end of a typed or handwritten line and to link words in certain compounds.

24a Breaking a Word at the End of a Line

A computer never breaks a word at the end of a line; if the full word will not fit, it is brought down to the next line. Sometimes, however, you will want to break a word with a hyphen—for example, to fill in space at the end of a line. When you break a word at the end of a line, divide it only between syllables, consulting a dictionary if necessary. Never divide a word at the end of a page, and never hyphenate one-syllable words. In addition, never leave a single letter at the end of a line or carry only one or two letters to the next line.

See 24b If you divide a **compound word** at the end of a line, put the hyphen between the elements of the compound (*snow-mobile,* not *snowmo-bile*).

DIVIDING ELECTRONIC ADDRESSES

Do not insert a hyphen when dividing a long electronic address at the end of a line. (A hyphen at this point could confuse readers, making them think it is part of the address.) Instead, simply break the address in a logical place—before or after a slash or a period, for example—or avoid the problem entirely by putting the entire address on one line.

24b Dividing Compound Words

A **compound word** is composed of two or more words. Some familiar compound words are always hyphenated: *no-hitter, helter-skelter.* Other compounds are always written as one word (*fireplace*) and others as two separate words (*bunk bed*). Your dictionary can tell you whether a particular compound requires a hyphen.

Hyphens are generally used in the following compounds.

(1) In Compound Adjectives

A **compound adjective** is a series of two or more words that function together as an adjective. When a compound adjective comes before the noun it modifies, use hyphens to join its elements.

The research team tried to use <u>nineteenth-century</u> technology to design a <u>space-age</u> project.

When a compound adjective *follows* the noun it modifies, do not use hyphens to join its elements.

The three government-operated programs were run smoothly, but the one that was not <u>government operated</u> was short of funds.

NOTE: A compound adjective formed with an adverb ending in *-ly* is not hyphenated even when it precedes the noun.

Many <u>upwardly mobile</u> families are on tight budgets.

Use **suspended hyphens**—hyphens followed by a space or by appropriate punctuation and a space—in a series of compounds that have the same principal elements.

The <u>three-, four-,</u> and <u>five-year-old</u> children ate lunch together.

(2) With Certain Prefixes or Suffixes

Use a hyphen between a prefix and a proper noun or adjective.

mid-July   pre-Columbian

Use a hyphen to connect the prefixes *all-, ex-, half-, quarter-, quasi-,* and *self-* and the suffix *-elect* to a noun.

ex-senator   self-centered
quarter-moon   president-elect

Also hyphenate to avoid certain hard-to-read combinations, such as two *i*'s (*semi-illiterate*) or more than two of the same consonant (*shell-less*).

(3) In Compound Numerals and Fractions

Hyphenate compounds that represent numbers below one hundred, even if they are part of a larger number.

the <u>twenty-first</u> century   three hundred <u>sixty-five</u> days

Also hyphenate the written form of a fraction when it modifies a noun.

a <u>two-thirds</u> share of the business

CHAPTER 25

ABBREVIATIONS

Generally speaking, **abbreviations** are not appropriate in college writing except in tables, charts, and Works Cited lists. Some abbreviations are acceptable only in scientific, technical, or business writing or only in a particular discipline. If you have questions about the appropriateness of a particular abbreviation, check a style manual in your field.

25a Abbreviating Titles

Titles before and after proper names are usually abbreviated.

Mr. Homer Simpson   Rep. Chaka Fattah
Henry Kissinger, PhD   Dr. Martin Luther King, Jr.

Do not, however, use an abbreviated title without a name.

The ~~Dr.~~ doctor diagnosed hepatitis.

25b Abbreviating Organization Names and Technical Terms

Well-known businesses and government, social, and civic organizations are commonly referred to by capitalized initials. These **abbreviations** fall into two categories: those in which the initials are pronounced as separate units (MTV) and **acronyms,** in which the initials are pronounced as a word (NATO).

See 15a

To save space, you may use accepted abbreviations for complex technical terms that are not well known, but be sure to spell out the full term the first time you mention it, followed by the abbreviation in parentheses.

Citrus farmers have been using ethylene dibromide (EDB), a chemical pesticide, for more than twenty years. Now, however, EDB has contaminated water supplies.

25c Abbreviating Dates, Times of Day, Temperatures, and Numbers

50 BC (BC follows the date)   AD 432 (AD precedes the date)
3:03 p.m. (lowercase)   180° F (Fahrenheit)

Always capitalize BC and AD. (The alternatives BCE, for "before the Common Era," and CE, for "Common Era," are also capitalized.) The abbreviations a.m. and p.m. are used only when they are accompanied by numbers.

I'll see you in the ~~a.m.~~ morning.

Avoid the abbreviation *no.* except in technical writing, and then use it only before a specific number: *The unidentified substance was labeled no. 52.*

ABBREVIATIONS IN MLA DOCUMENTATION

MLA DOcumentation Style requires abbreviations of publishers' company names—for example, *Columbia UP* for *Columbia University Press.* Do not, however, use such abbreviations in the body of your paper. MLA style also permits the use of abbreviations that designate parts of written works (*ch. 3, sec. 7*), but only in the Works Cited list and parenthetical documentation.

25d Editing Misused Abbreviations

In college writing, abbreviations are not used in the following cases.

(1) Latin Expressions

Poe wrote "The Gold Bug," "The Tell-Tale Heart," ~~etc.~~ and so on.

Many musicians (~~e.g.,~~ for example, Bruce Springsteen) have been influenced by Bob Dylan.

(2) Names of Days, Months, or Holidays

On ~~Sat., Dec.~~ Saturday, December 23, I started my ~~Xmas~~ Christmas shopping.

(3) Names of Streets and Places

He lives on Riverside ~~Dr.~~ Drive in ~~NYC.~~ New York City.

Exceptions: The abbreviations *U.S.* (*U.S. Coast Guard*), *St.* (*St. Albans*), *and Mt.* (*Mt. Etna*) are acceptable, as is *DC* in *Washington, DC.*

(4) Names of Academic Subjects

Psychology   literature
~~Psych.~~ and English ~~lit.~~ are required courses.

(5) Units of Measurement

In technical writing, some units of measurement are abbreviated when preceded by a numeral.

The hurricane had winds of 35 mph.

Our new Honda gets over 50 mpg.

In college writing, however, write out such expressions, and spell out words such as *inches, feet, years, miles, pints, quarts,* and *gallons.*

(6) Symbols

The symbols %, =, +, #, and ¢ are acceptable in technical and scientific writing but not in nontechnical college writing. The symbol *$* is acceptable before specific numbers ($15,000) but not as a substitute for the words *money* and *dollars.*

CHAPTER 26

NUMBERS

Convention determines when to use a **numeral** (22) and when to spell out a number (twenty-two). Numerals are commonly used in scientific and technical writing and in journalism, but less often in academic or literary writing.

NOTE: The guidelines in this chapter are based on the *MLA Handbook for Writers of Research Papers*. **APA style** requires See Ch. 32 that all numbers below ten be spelled out if they do not represent specific measurements and that numbers ten and above be expressed as numerals.

26a Spelled-Out Numbers versus Numerals

Unless a number falls into one of the categories listed in **26b,** spell it out *if you can do so in one or two words.*

The Hawaiian alphabet has only <u>twelve</u> letters.

Class size stabilized at <u>twenty-eight</u> students.

The subsidies are expected to total about <u>two million</u> dollars.

Numbers *more than two words* long are expressed in figures.

The dietitian prepared <u>125</u> sample menus.

The developer of the community purchased <u>300,000</u> doorknobs, <u>153,000</u> faucets, and <u>4,000</u> manhole covers.

NOTE: Numerals and spelled-out numbers should generally not be mixed in the same passage. For consistency, then, the number 4,000 in the preceding example is expressed in figures even though it could be written in just two words.

 NUMBERS AS SENTENCE OPENERS

Never begin a sentence with a numeral. Spell out the number, or reword the sentence.

continued on the following page

115

continued from the previous page

INCORRECT: 250 students are currently enrolled in World History 101.

REVISED: Two-hundred fifty students are currently enrolled in World History 101.

REVISED: Current enrollment in World History 101 is 250 students.

26b Conventional Uses of Numerals

- **Addresses:** 111 Fifth Avenue, New York, NY 10003
- **Dates:** January 15, 1929   1914–1919
- **Exact Times:** 9:16   10 a.m. or 10:00 a.m. (but spell out times of day when they are used with *o'clock:* ten o'clock)
- **Exact Sums of Money:** $25.11 $6,752.00
- **Divisions of Works:** Act 5   lines 17–28   page 42
- **Percentages:** 80 percent (or 80%)
- **Decimals and Fractions:** 3.14   6¾
- **Measurements with Symbols or Abbreviations:** 32°   15 cc
- **Ratios and Statistics:** 20 to 1   average age of 40
- **Scores:** a lead of 6 to 0
- **Identification Numbers:** Route 66   Track 8   Channel 12

PART 6

WRITING WITH SOURCES

CHAPTER 27

WRITING RESEARCH PAPERS

Research is the systematic investigation of a topic outside your own knowledge and experience. However, doing research means more than just reading about other people's ideas. When you undertake a research project, you become involved in a process that requires you to think critically, evaluating and interpreting the ideas explored in your sources and formulating ideas of your own.

Not so long ago, searching for source material meant spending long hours in the library flipping through card catalogs, examining heavy reference volumes, and hunting for books in the stacks. Technology, however, has dramatically changed the way research is conducted. The wiring of school and community libraries means that today, students and professionals engaged in research find themselves spending a great deal of time in front of a computer, particularly during the exploratory stage of the research process. Note, however, that although the way in which research materials are located and accessed has changed, the research process itself has not. Whether you are working with **print sources** (books, journals, magazines) or <u>**electronic resources**</u> (online catalogs, databases, the Internet), in the library or at your home computer, you need to follow a systematic process.

See 28a2

✔ CHECKLIST: THE RESEARCH PROCESS

- ✔ Choose a topic **(See 27a)**
- ✔ Do exploratory research and formulate a research question **(See 27b)**
- ✔ Assemble a working bibliography **(See 27c)**
- ✔ Develop a tentative thesis **(See 27d)**
- ✔ Do focused research **(See 27e)**
- ✔ Take notes **(See 27f)**
- ✔ Decide on a thesis **(See 27g)**
- ✔ Outline your paper **(See 27h1)**
- ✔ Draft your paper **(See 27h2)**
- ✔ Revise your paper **(See 27h3)**

27a   Choosing a Topic

The first step in the research process is finding a topic to write about. In many cases, your instructor will help you to choose a topic, either by providing a list of suitable topics or by suggesting a general subject area—for example, a famous trial, an event that happened on the day you were born, or a social problem on college campuses. Even in these instances, you will still need to choose one of the topics or narrow the subject area—deciding, for example, on one trial, one event, or one problem.

If your instructor prefers that you select a topic on your own, you must consider a number of possible topics and weigh both their suitability for research and your interest in them. You decide on a topic for your research paper in much the same way in which you decide on a topic for a short essay: you read, brainstorm, talk to people, and ask questions. Specifically, you talk to friends and family members, co-workers, and perhaps your instructor; you read magazines and newspapers; you take stock of your interests; you consider possible topics suggested by your other courses—historical events, scientific developments, and so on; and, of course, you search the Internet. (Your search engine's <u>subject guides</u> can be particularly helpful as you look for a promising topic or narrow a broad subject.)

See
29a

As you look for a suitable topic, keep the following guidelines in mind.

✔ CHECKLIST: CHOOSING A RESEARCH TOPIC

✔ **Are you genuinely interested in your research topic?** Be sure the topic you select is one that will hold your interest.

✔ **Is your topic suitable for research?** Be sure your paper will not depend on your personal experiences or value judgments.

✔ **Is your topic too broad? too narrow?** Be sure the boundaries of your research topic are appropriate.

✔ **Can your topic be researched in a library to which you have access?** Be sure that your school library has the sources you need (or that you can access those sources on the Internet).

27b   Doing Exploratory Research and Formulating a Research Question

Doing **exploratory research**—searching the Internet and looking through general reference works such as encyclopedias, bibliographies, and specialized dictionaries (either in print or online)—helps you to get an overview of your topic. Your goal is to formulate a **research question,** the question you want your research paper to answer. A research question helps you to decide which sources to seek out, which to examine first, which to examine in depth, and which to skip entirely. (The answer to your research question will be your paper's <u>thesis statement</u>.)

See 1c

27c Assembling a Working Bibliography

As soon as you start your exploratory research, you begin to assemble a **working bibliography** for your paper. (This working bibliography will be the basis for your <u>Works Cited list</u>, which will include all the sources you cite in your paper.)

See 31a

As you consider each potential source, record full and accurate bibliographic information—author, title, pages numbers, and complete publication information—in a separate computer file designated "Bibliography" or, if you prefer, on individual index cards. (See Figures 1 and 2.) Keep records of interviews (including telephone and e-mail interviews), meetings, lectures, films, and electronic sources as well as of books and articles. For each source, include not only basic identifying details—such as the date of an interview, the call number of a library book, the address (URL) of an Internet source, or the author of an article accessed from a database—but also a brief evaluation that includes comments about the kind of information the source contains, the amount of information offered, its relevance to your topic, and its limitations.

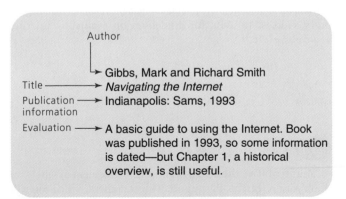

*Figure 1 Information for Working Bibliography
           (in computer file)*

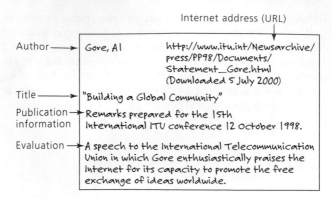

Internet address (URL)

Author ──► Gore, Al   http://www.itu.int/Newsarchive/
                             press/PP98/Documents/
                             Statement__Gore.html
                             (Downloaded 5 July 2000)

Title ──► "Building a Global Community"

Publication ──► Remarks prepared for the 15th
information   International ITU conference 12 October 1998.

Evaluation ──► A speech to the International Telecommunication
               Union in which Gore enthusiastically praises the
               Internet for its capacity to promote the free
               exchange of ideas worldwide.

*Figure 2 Information for Working Bibliography
          (on index card)*

As you go about collecting sources and building your working bibliography, monitor the quality and relevance of all the materials you examine. Making informed choices early in the research process will save you a lot of time in the long run, so don't collect a large number of sources first and assess their usefulness later. Before you check a book out of the library, photocopy a journal article, or download a text, take the time to consider its relevance to your topic. Resist the temptation to check out every book that mentions your subject, photocopy page after page of marginally useful articles, or download material from every electronic source to which you have access. After all, you will eventually have to read all these sources and take detailed notes on them. If you have too many sources, you will be overwhelmed, unable to remember why a particular idea or a certain article seemed important. (For more on evaluating library sources, see **28b**; for guidelines on evaluating Internet sources, see **29c**.)

27d Developing a Tentative Thesis

Your **tentative thesis** is a preliminary statement of what you think your research will support. This statement, which you will eventually refine into a **thesis statement**, should be the tentative answer to your research question.

See
27g

DEVELOPING A TENTATIVE THESIS

Subject Area	Topic	Research Question	Tentative Thesis
Computers and Society	The Internet's effect on American society	Do all Americans have equal access to the Internet?	Not all Americans have equal access to the Internet, and this is a potentially serious problem.

Because it suggests the specific direction your research will take as well as the scope and emphasis of your argument, the tentative thesis you come up with at this point can help you generate a list of the main ideas you plan to develop in your paper. This list of points can help you to narrow the focus of your research so that you can zero in on a few specific categories to explore as you read and take notes.

Tentative Thesis: Not all Americans have equal access to the Internet, and this is a potentially serious problem.

- Give background about Internet; tell why it's important.
- Identify groups that do not have access to Internet.
- Explain problems this creates.
- Suggest possible solutions.

27e Doing Focused Research

Once you have decided on a tentative thesis and made a list of the points you plan to discuss in your paper, you are ready to begin your focused research. When you do **focused research,** you look for the specific information—facts, examples, statistics, definitions, quotations—you need to support your points.

(1) Reading Sources

As you look for information, try to explore as many sources, and as many different viewpoints, as possible. It makes sense to examine more sources than you actually intend to use. This strategy will enable you to proceed even if one or more of your sources turns out to be biased, outdated, unreliable, superficial, or irrelevant—in other words, unusable. Exploring different viewpoints is just as important. After all, if you read only those sources that agree on a particular issue, it will be difficult for you to develop a viewpoint of your own.

As you explore various sources, try not to waste time reading irrelevant material; instead, try to evaluate each source's potential usefulness to you as quickly as possible. For example, if your source is a book, skim the table of contents and the index; if your source is a journal article, read the abstract. Then, if an article or a section of a book seems potentially useful, photocopy it for future reference. Similarly, when you find an online source that looks promising, resist the temptation to paste it directly into a section of your paper-in-progress. Instead, print it out (or send it to yourself as an e-mail) so that you can evaluate it further later on. (For information on evaluating library sources, see **28b**; for information on evaluating Internet sources, see **29c.**)

(2) Balancing Primary and Secondary Sources

In the course of your focused research, you will encounter both **primary sources** (original documents and observations) and **secondary sources** (interpretations of original documents and observations).

PRIMARY AND SECONDARY SOURCES

Primary Source	Secondary Source
Novel, poem, play, film	Criticism
Diary, autobiography	Biography
Letter, historical document, speech, oral history	Historical analysis
Newspaper article	Editorial
Raw data from questionnaires or interviews	Social science article; case study
Observation/experiment	Scientific article

Primary sources are essential for many research projects, but secondary sources, which provide scholars' insights and interpretations, are also valuable. Remember, though, that the further you get from the primary source, the more chances exist for inaccuracies introduced by researchers' inadvertent misinterpretations or distortions.

27f Taking Notes

As you locate information in the library and on the Internet, you take notes to keep a record of exactly what you found and where you found it. Each piece of information that you record in your notes (whether summarized, paraphrased, or quoted from your sources) should be accompanied by a short descriptive heading that indicates its relevance to one of the points you will develop in your paper. Also include a brief comment that makes clear your reasons for recording the information and identifies what you think it will contribute to your paper. This comment (enclosed in brackets so you will know it expresses your own ideas, not those of your source) should establish the purpose of your note—what you think it can explain, support, clarify, describe, or contradict—and perhaps suggest its relationship to other notes or other sources. Any questions you have about the information or its source can also be included in your comment. Finally, each note should fully and accurately identify the source of the information you are recording.

(1) Managing Source Information

When you take notes, your goal is flexibility: you want to be able to arrange and rearrange information easily and efficiently as your paper takes shape. If you take notes on your computer, type each piece of information under a specific heading on a separate page; don't list all information from a single source under one general heading. If you take notes by hand, you may decide to use the time-honored index card system. If you do, write on only one side of the card, and be sure to use a separate index card for each piece of information rather than running several ideas together on a single card. (See Figures 3 and 4.)

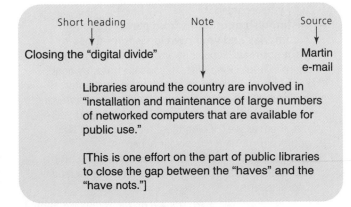

Short heading   Note   Source

Closing the "digital divide"   Martin e-mail

Libraries around the country are involved in "installation and maintenance of large numbers of networked computers that are available for public use."

[This is one effort on the part of public libraries to close the gap between the "haves" and the "have nots."]

Figure 3 Note (in computer file)

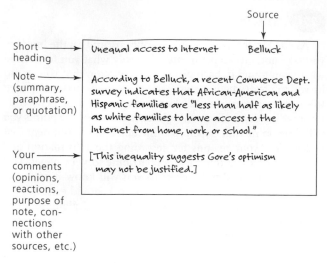

Source

Short ——→   Unequal access to Internet   Belluck
heading

Note ——→   According to Belluck, a recent Commerce Dept.
(summary,   survey indicates that African-American and
paraphrase,   Hispanic families are "less than half as likely
or quotation) as white families to have access to the
              Internet from home, work, or school."

Your ——→   [This inequality suggests Gore's optimism
comments   may not be justified.]
(opinions,
reactions,
purpose of
note, con-
nections
with other
sources, etc.)

Figure 4 Note (on index card)

✔ CHECKLIST: TAKING NOTES

✔ **Identify the source of each piece of information
   clearly and completely**—even if the source is sitting on your bookshelf or stored in your computer's
   hard drive.

✔ **Include everything now that you will need later**
   to understand your note—names, dates, places,
   connections with other notes—and to remember
   why you recorded it.

✔ **Distinguish quotations from paraphrases and
   summaries and your own ideas from those of
   your sources.** If you copy a source's words, place
   them in quotation marks. (If you take notes by hand,
   circle the quotation marks; if you type your notes,
   boldface the quotation marks.) If you write down your
   own ideas, bracket them and, if you are typing, italicize them as well. (Using these techniques will help
   you avoid **plagarism** in your paper.)

See
Ch.
30

✔ **Copy each author's comments accurately,** using
   the exact words, spelling, punctuation marks, and
   capitalization.

continued on the following page

continued from the previous page

✔ **Put an author's comments into your own words whenever possible,** summarizing and paraphrasing material as well as adding your own observations and analysis.

PHOTOCOPIES AND COMPUTER PRINTOUTS

Making photocopies and printing out sections of electronic sources that you have downloaded can be useful, time-saving strategies, but photocopies and computer printouts are no substitute for notes. In fact, copying information is only the first step in the process of taking thorough, careful notes on a source. You should be especially careful not to allow the ease and efficiency of copying to encourage you to postpone decisions about the usefulness of your information. Remember, you can easily accumulate so many pages that it will be almost impossible to keep track of all your information.

Also keep in mind that photocopies and printouts do not have the flexibility of notes you take yourself because a single page of text may include information that should be earmarked for several different sections of your paper. This lack of flexibility makes it difficult for you to arrange source material into any meaningful order.

Finally, remember that the annotations you make on photocopies and printouts are usually not focused or polished enough to be incorporated directly into your paper. You will still have to paraphrase and summarize your source's ideas and make connections among them. Therefore, you should approach a photocopy or printout just as you approach any other print source—as material that you will read, highlight, annotate, and then take notes about.

✔ CHECKLIST: WORKING WITH PHOTOCOPIES AND COMPUTER PRINTOUTS

✔ Record full and accurate source information, including the inclusive page numbers, electronic address (URL), and any other relevant information, on the first page of each copy. *continued on the following page*

> *continued from the previous page*
>
> ✔ Clip or staple together consecutive pages of a single source.
> ✔ Do not copy a source without reminding yourself—*in writing*—why you are doing so. In pencil or on removable self-stick notes, record your initial responses to the source's ideas, jot down cross references to other works or notes, and highlight important sections.
> ✔ Photocopying can be time-consuming and expensive, so try to avoid copying material that is only marginally relevant to your paper.
> ✔ Keep photocopies and printouts in a file so you will be able to find them when you need them.

(2) Summarizing, Paraphrasing, and Quoting

Summarizing Sources A **summary** is a brief restatement in your own words of a source's main idea. When you summarize a source, you condense the author's ideas into a few concise sentences. You do *not* include your own opinions or interpretations of the writer's ideas.

Original Source

Today, the First Amendment faces challenges from groups who seek to limit expressions of racism and bigotry. A growing number of legislatures have passed rules against "hate speech"—[speech] that is offensive on the basis of race, ethnicity, gender, or sexual orientation. The rules are intended to promote respect for all people and protect the targets of hurtful words, gestures, or actions.

Legal experts fear these rules may wind up diminishing the rights of all citizens. "The bedrock principle [of our society] is that government may never suppress free speech simply because it goes against what the community would like to hear," says Nadine Strossen, president of the American Civil Liberties Union and professor of constitutional law at New York University Law School. In recent years, for example, the courts have upheld the right of neo-Nazis to march in Jewish neighborhoods; protected cross-burning as a form of free expression; and allowed protesters to burn the American flag. The offensive, ugly, distasteful, or repugnant nature of expression is not reason enough to ban it, courts have said.

But advocates of limits on hate speech note that certain kinds of expression fall outside of First Amendment protection. Courts have ruled that "fighting words"—words intended to provoke immediate violence—or speech that creates a clear and present danger are not protected forms of expression. As the classic argument goes, freedom of speech does not give you the right to yell "Fire!" in a crowded theater. (Sudo, Phil. "Freedom of Hate Speech?" *Scholastic Update* 124.14 [1992]: 17–20.)

Summary The right to freedom of speech, guaranteed by the First Amendment, is becoming more difficult to defend. Some people think stronger laws against the use of "hate speech" weaken the First Amendment, but others argue that some kinds of speech remain exempt from this protection (Sudo 17).

✔ CHECKLIST: SUMMARIZING A SOURCE

- ✔ Reread your source until you understand its main idea.
- ✔ Write your summary, using your own words and phrasing. If you quote a distinctive word or phrase, use quotation marks.
- ✔ Add appropriate documentation.

Paraphrasing Sources A summary conveys just the essence of a source; a **paraphrase** is a *detailed* restatement, in your own words, of all a source's important ideas—but not your opinions or interpretations of those ideas. In a paraphrase, you indicate not only the source's main points but also its order, tone, and emphasis. Consequently, a paraphrase can sometimes be as long as the source itself.

Compare the following paraphrase with the summary of the same source above.

Paraphrase

Many groups want to limit the right of free speech guaranteed by the First Amendment to the Constitution. They believe this is necessary to protect certain groups of people from "hate speech." Women, people of color, and gay men and lesbians, for example, may find that hate speech is used to intimidate them. Legal scholars are afraid that even though the rules against hate speech are well intentioned, such rules undermine our freedom of speech. As Nadine Strossen, president of the American Civil Liberties Union, says, "The bedrock principle [of our society] is that government may never suppress free speech simply because it goes against what the community would like to hear" (qtd. in Sudo 17). People who support speech codes point out, however, that certain types of speech are not protected by the First Amendment—for example, words that create a "clear and present danger" or that would lead directly to violence (Sudo 17).

✔ CHECKLIST: PARAPHRASING A SOURCE

✔ Reread your source until you understand its key points.

✔ List the key points in the order in which they appear in the source.

✔ Write your paraphrase, following the order, tone, and emphasis of the original. Use your own words and phrasing; if you quote a distinctive word or phrase, use quotation marks.

✔ Add appropriate documentation.

SUMMARIZING AND PARAPHRASING SOURCES

When you summarize or paraphrase, be sure to familiarize yourself with your source before you begin to write, and then try not to look at it again until you are finished. Use language and syntax that come naturally to you, and be careful not to duplicate the wording or sentence structure of the source. If you cannot think of a synonym for an important word or phrase that appears in the source, place it in quotation marks.

Quoting Sources When you **quote,** you copy an author's remarks exactly as they appear in a source, word for word and punctuation mark for punctuation mark, enclosing the borrowed words in quotation marks. As a rule, you should not quote extensively in a research paper. The use of numerous quotations interrupts the flow of your discussion and gives readers the impression that your paper is just an unassimilated collection of other people's ideas.

WHEN TO QUOTE

• Quote when a source's wording or phrasing is so distinctive that a summary or paraphrase would diminish its impact.

continued on the following page

continued from the previous page

- Quote when a source's words—particularly those of a recognized expert on your subject—will lend authority to your paper.
- Quote when paraphrasing would create a long, clumsy, or incoherent phrase or would change the meaning of the original.
- Quote when you plan to disagree with a source. Using a source's exact words helps to assure readers that you are being fair.

27g Deciding on a Thesis

After you have finished your focused research and note taking, you must refine your tentative thesis into a carefully worded statement that expresses a conclusion that your research can support. This **thesis statement** should be more detailed than your tentative thesis, accurately conveying the direction, emphasis, and scope of your paper.

See 1b

DECIDING ON A THESIS

Tentative Thesis
Not all Americans have equal access to the Internet, and this is a potentially serious problem.

Thesis Statement
Although the Internet has changed our world for the better, it threatens to create two distinct classes: those who have access and those who do not.

27h Outlining, Drafting, and Revising

Keeping your thesis in mind, you are now ready to outline your supporting points and draft your paper.

(1) Outlining

Before you write your rough draft, you should make an outline. At this point, you need to make some sense out of all the notes you have accumulated, and you do this by sorting and organizing them. By identifying categories and subcategories of information, you begin to see your paper take shape and are able to construct an outline that reflects this shape. A **formal outline** indicates not only the exact order in which you will present your ideas but also the relationship between main ideas and supporting details.

NOTE: The outline you construct at this stage is only a guide for you to follow as you draft your paper; it is likely to change as you draft and revise. The final outline, written after your paper is complete, will reflect what you have written and serve as a guide for your readers. An example of a formal outline appears with the sample MLA research paper in **31a.**

✔ CHECKLIST: PREPARING A FORMAL OUTLINE

✔ Write your thesis statement at the top of the page.

✔ Review your notes to make sure that each note expresses only one general idea. If this is not the case, recopy any unrelated information, creating a separate note.

✔ Check that the heading for each note specifically characterizes the note's information. If it does not, change the heading.

✔ Sort your notes by their headings, keeping a miscellaneous pile for notes that do not seem to fit into any category. Irrelevant notes—those unrelated to your paper's thesis—should be set aside (but not discarded).

✔ Check your categories for balance. If most of your notes fall into one or two categories, rewrite some of your headings to create narrower, more focused categories. If you have only one or two notes in a category, you will need to do additional research or treat that topic only briefly (or not at all).

✔ Organize the individual notes within each group, adding more specific subheads as needed. Arrange your notes in an order that highlights the most important points and subordinates lesser ones.

✔ Decide on a logical order in which to discuss your paper's major points.

✔ Construct your formal outline, using divisions and subdivisions that correspond to your headings. (Outline only the body of your paper, not your introduction and conclusion.) Be sure each heading has at least two subheadings; if one does not, combine it with another heading. Follow outline format strictly.

continued on the following page

continued from the previous page

I. First major point of your paper
   A. First subpoint
   B. Next subpoint
      1. First supporting example
      2. Next supporting example
         a. First specific detail
         b. Next specific detail
II. Second major point

✔ Review your completed outline to make sure you have not placed too much emphasis on a relatively unimportant idea, ordered ideas illogically, or created sections that overlap with others.

OUTLINING

Before you begin writing, create a separate file for each major section of your outline. Then, copy your notes into these files in the order in which you intend to use them. You can print out each file as you need it and use it for a guide as you write.

(2) Drafting

See 1d1

When you are ready to write your **rough draft**, arrange your notes in the order in which you intend to use them. Follow your outline as you write, using your notes as needed. As you draft, jot down questions to yourself, and identify points that need further clarification (you can bracket those ideas or print them in boldface on a typed draft, or you can write them on self-stick notes). Leave space for material you plan to add, and bracket phrases or whole sections that you think you may later decide to move or delete. In other words, lay the groundwork for a major revision. Remember that even though you are guided by an outline and notes, you are not bound to follow their content or sequence exactly. As you write, new ideas or new connections among ideas may occur to you. If you find yourself wandering from your thesis or outline, check to see whether the departure is justified.

As your draft takes shape, you will probably find that each paragraph corresponds to one major point on your outline. Be sure to supply transitions between sentences and paragraphs to show how your points are related. To make it easy for you to revise later on, triple-space your draft. Be careful to copy source information fully and accurately on this and every subsequent draft, placing the documentation as close as possible to the material it identifies.

DRAFTING

See 30b

You can use a split screen or multiple windows to view your notes as you draft your paper. You can also copy the material that you need from your notes and then insert it into the text of your paper. (As you copy, be especially careful that you do not unintentionally commit **plagiarism**).

Shaping the Parts of Your Paper Like any other essay, a research paper has an introduction, a body, and a conclusion. In your rough draft, as in your outline, you focus on the body of your paper. You should not spend time planning an introduction or a conclusion at this stage; your ideas will change as you write, and you will want to revise your opening and closing paragraphs later to reflect those changes.

See 2d

In your **introduction,** you identify your topic and establish how you will approach it. Your **introduction** also includes your thesis statement, which expresses the position you will support in the rest of the paper. Sometimes the introductory paragraphs briefly summarize your major supporting points (the major divisions of your outline) in the order in which you will present them. Such a preview of your thesis and support provides a smooth transition into the body of your paper. Your introduction can also present an overview of the problem you will discuss, or it can summarize research already done on your topic. In your rough draft, however, an undeveloped introduction is perfectly acceptable; in fact, your thesis statement alone can serve as a placeholder for the more polished introduction that you will write later.

See 2a

As you draft the **body** of your paper, indicate its direction with strong **topic sentences** that correspond to the divisions of your outline.

> Today, many people believe the Internet has ushered in a new age, one in which this instant communication will bring people closer together and eventually even eliminate national boundaries.

You can also use **headings** if they are a convention of the disci- _{See} pline in which you are writing. _{34a}

> Reactions from Public Officials
>
>   Many public officials recognize the potential danger of
>
>   the "digital divide," and they are taking steps to narrow
>
>   the gap.

Even in your rough draft, carefully worded headings and topic sentences will help you keep your discussion under control.

The **conclusion** of a research paper often restates the thesis. This is especially important in a long paper, because by the time your readers get to the end, they may have lost sight of your paper's main idea. Your **conclusion** can also include a sum- _{See} mary of your key points, a call for action, or perhaps an apt _{2d} quotation. In your rough draft, however, your concluding paragraph is usually very brief.

Working Source Material into Your Paper In the body of your paper, you evaluate and interpret your sources, comparing different ideas and assessing conflicting points of view. As a writer, your job is to draw your own conclusions, blending information from various sources into a paper that coherently and forcefully presents your own original viewpoint to your readers.

Your source material must be smoothly integrated into your paper, and the relationships among various sources (and between those sources' ideas and your own) must be clearly and accurately identified. If two sources present conflicting interpretations, you must be especially careful to use precise language and accurate transitions to make the contrast apparent (for instance, "Although Gore is optimistic, recent studies suggest . . ."). When two sources agree, you should make this clear (for example, "Like Belluck, Gates believes . . ." or "Commerce Department statistics confirm Gates's point"). Such phrasing will provide a context for your own comments and conclusions. If different sources present complementary information about a subject, blend details from the sources *carefully,* keeping track of which details come from which source.

(3) Revising

A good way to start revising is to check to see that your thesis statement still accurately expresses your paper's central focus. Then, make an outline of your draft, and compare it with the outline you made before you began the draft. If you find significant differences, you will have to revise your thesis statement or rewrite sections of your paper. The checklists in **1d2** can guide your revision of your paper's overall structure and its individual paragraphs, sentences, and words.

✔ CHECKLIST: REVISING A RESEARCH PAPER

- ✔ Should you do more research to find support for certain points?
- ✔ Do you need to reorder the major sections of your paper?
- ✔ Should you rearrange the order in which you present your points within those sections?
- ✔ Do you need to add section headings? transitional paragraphs?
- ✔ Have you **integrated your notes** smoothly into your paper?
- ✔ Do you introduce source material with **identifying tags**?
- ✔ Are quotations blended with paraphrase, summary, and your own observations and reactions?
- ✔ Have you avoided **plagiarism** by carefully documenting all borrowed ideas?
- ✔ Have you analyzed and interpreted the ideas of others rather than simply stringing those ideas together?
- ✔ Do your own ideas—not those of your sources—dominate your discussion?

See
30a

See
30a1

See
30b

 REVISING

When you finish revising your paper, copy the file that contains your working bibliography, and insert it at the end of your paper. Delete any irrelevant entries, and then compile your Works Cited list. (Make sure that the format of the entries on your Works Cited list conforms to the documentation style you are using.)

PREPARING A FINAL DRAFT

Before you print out the final version of your paper, **edit and proofread** not just the paper itself but also your outline and your Works Cited list. Next, consider (or reconsider) your paper's **title.** It should be descriptive enough to tell your readers what your paper is about, and it should create interest in your subject. Your title should also be consistent with the purpose and tone of your paper. (You would hardly want a humorous title for a paper about the death penalty or world hunger.) Finally, your title should be engaging and to the point—and perhaps even provocative. Often a quotation from one of your sources will suggest a likely title.

See 1e

When you are satisfied with your title, read your paper through one last time, proofreading for any grammar, spelling, or typing errors you may have missed. Pay particular attention to parenthetical documentation and Works Cited entries. (Remember that every error undermines your credibility.) Finally, make sure your paper's format conforms to your instructor's guidelines. Once you are satisfied that your paper is as accurate as you can make it, print it out. Then, fasten the pages with a paper clip (do not staple the pages or fold the corners together), and hand it in.

CHAPTER 28

USING AND EVALUATING
LIBRARY SOURCES

28a Using LIbrary Sources

Even though the Internet has changed the nature of research, the library is still the best place to begin a research project. With its wide variety of print and electronic resources—some suitable for **exploratory research**, others for **focused research**—the library gives you access to material that you cannot get anywhere else.

See
27b

See
27e

(1) Using the Online Catalog

Most college and other libraries have abandoned print catalog systems in favor of **online catalogs**—computer databases that list all the books, journals, and other materials held by the library.

You access the online catalog (as well as the other electronic resources of the library) by using computer terminals located throughout the library. Typing in certain words or phrases—*search terms*—enables you to find the information you need. When you search an online catalog for information about a topic, you can conduct either a *keyword search* or a *subject search.*

Conducting a Keyword Search When you carry out a keyword search, you enter into the online catalog a term or terms associated with your topic. The computer then retrieves catalog entries that contain those words. The more precise your search terms, the more specific and useful the information you will receive. (Combining search terms with AND, OR, and NOT enables you to narrow or broaden your search. This technique is called conducting a **Boolean search**.)

See
29a2

Conducting a Subject Search When you carry out a subject search, you enter specific subject headings into the online catalog. The subject headings in the library are most often arranged according to headings listed in the five-volume manual *Library of Congress Subject Headings,* which is held at the reference desk of your library. Although it may be possible to guess at a subject heading, your search will be more successful if you consult these volumes to identify the exact words you need.

(2) Using Electronic Resources

Today's college libraries have electronic resources that enable you to find a wide variety of sources. Many of the print sources located in the library are also available in electronic format. For example, **periodical indexes** such as *Readers' Guide to Periodical Literature* and *Expanded Academic ASAP* offer bibliographic See 28a6 citations, abstracts, and full articles in journals, magazines, and newspapers. Other online databases enable you to access general reference works, such as encyclopedias and bibliographies, as well as indexes for specific disciplines, such as *Humanities Index* and *Social Science Index.* Often, the same computer terminals that enable you to access the online catalog also allow you to access online databases. Information stored on CD-ROM and DVD is accessed on computers located in the reference section of the library.

NOTE: In general, the electronic resources of the library enable you to access more specialized databases than you can access on the Internet. For this reason, be sure to use these resources whenever you are assigned a research project.

(3) Consulting General Reference Works

During your exploratory research, general reference works can provide a broad overview of a particular subject. The following reference works, available in electronic form as well as in print, are useful for exploratory research.

General Encyclopedias General multivolume encyclopedias are available both in electronic format and in print. For example, *The New Encyclopaedia Britannica* is available on CD-ROM and DVD, as well as on the World Wide Web at <http://www.britannica.com>.

Specialized Encyclopedias, Dictionaries, and Bibliographies These specialized reference works contain in-depth articles focusing on a single subject area.

General Bibliographies General bibliographies list books available in a wide variety of fields.

> *Books in Print.* An index of authors and titles of books in print in the United States. The *Subject Guide to Books in Print* indexes books according to subject area.

> *The Bibliographic Index.* A tool for locating bibliographies.

Biographical References Biographical reference books provide information about people's lives as well as bibliographic listings.

> *Living Persons*
> *Who's Who in America.* Gives concise biographical information about prominent Americans.

> *Who's Who.* Collects concise biographical facts about notable British men and women.

Current Biography. Includes articles on people of many na-
tionalities.

Deceased Persons
Dictionary of American Biography. Considered the best of
American biographical dictionaries. Includes articles on
over 13,000 Americans.

Dictionary of National Biography. The most important reference work for British biography.

Webster's Biographical Dictionary. Perhaps the most widely
used biographical reference work. Includes people from
all periods and places.

(4) Consulting Specialized Reference Works

More specialized reference works can help you find facts, examples, statistics, definitions, and quotations. The following
reference works—many of which are available on CD-ROM, on
DVD, or online as well as in print versions—are most useful for
focused research.

Unabridged Dictionaries   Unabridged dictionaries, such as
the *Oxford English Dictionary,* are comprehensive works that
give detailed information about words.

Special Dictionaries   These dictionaries focus on such topics as usage, synonyms, slang and idioms, etymologies, and foreign terms; some focus on specific disciplines, such as
accounting or law.

Yearbooks and Almanacs   A **yearbook** is an annual publication that updates factual and statistical information already
published in a reference source. An **almanac** provides lists,
charts, and statistics about a wide variety of subjects.

World Almanac. Includes statistics about government, population, sports, and many other subjects. Published annually since 1868.

Information Please Almanac. Includes information unavail-
able in the *World Almanac.* Published annually since 1947.

Facts on File. Covering 1940 to the present, this work offers
digests of important news stories from metropolitan
newspapers.

Editorials on File. Reprints important editorials from American and Canadian newspapers.

Atlases   An **atlas** contains maps and charts as well as historical, cultural, political, and economic information.

National Geographic Society. *National Geographic Atlas of the World*. The most up-to-date atlas available.

Rand McNally Cosmopolitan World Atlas. A modern and extremely legible medium-sized atlas.

We the People: An Atlas of America's Ethnic Diversity. Presents information about specific ethnic groups. Maps show immigration routes and settlement patterns.

Quotation Books A **quotation book** contains numerous quotations on a wide variety of subjects. Such quotations can be especially useful for your paper's introductory and concluding paragraphs.

Bartlett's Familiar Quotations. Quotations are arranged chronologically by author.

The Home Book of Quotations. Quotations are arranged by subject. An author index and a keyword index are also included.

(5) Finding Books

The online catalog gives you the call numbers you need for locating specific titles. A **call number** is like a book's address in the library: it tells you exactly where to find the book you are looking for.

> AUTHOR: Smith, Richard J.
> TITLE: Navigating the Internet / Richard J. Smith, Mark Gibbs
> EDITION: 1st ed.
> CALL NUMBER: 796.06073S
> PUBLISHED: Carmel, IN: Sams Publishing, c1993
> DESCRIPTION: xxiii, 500p.: ill.; 23cm.
> NOTES: "Includes the Internet gazetteer: a complete directory to over 600 locations, groups and other Internet resources dealing with subjects from A to Z"--Cover.
> Includes index.
> SUBJECTS: Internet (computer network)
> OTHER AUTHORS: Gibbs, Mark
> ISBN: 0-67230-362-0
> OCLC Number: 28642785

Figure 1 Online Catalog Entry

(6) Finding Articles

A **periodical** is a newspaper, magazine, scholarly journal, or other publication that is published at regular intervals (weekly, monthly, or quarterly). **Periodical indexes** list articles from a selected group of magazines, newspapers, or scholarly journals.

These indexes may be available in your library in bound volumes, on microfilm or microfiche, on CD-ROM or DVD, or online. Choosing the right index for your research saves you time and energy by allowing you to easily find articles written about your subject.

NOTE: Articles in scholarly journals provide current information and are written by experts in the field. Because these journals focus on a particular subject area, they can provide in-depth analysis.

 PERIODICAL INDEXES FOR SPECIFIC DISCIPLINES

Category	Description
Social Science Index	Political science, psychology, sociology, history, sports
Humanities Index	Music, literature, film, arts
General Science Index	Science, nursing, medicine, health
Business Index	Business
Biology and Agricultural Index	Agriculture, ecology, forestry

 FREQUENTLY USED PERIODICAL INDEXES

Index	Description
Dow Jones Interactive	Full text of articles from U.S. newspapers and trade journals
Ebscohost	Database system for thousands of periodical articles
ERIC	Largest index of education-related journal articles and reports in the world
FirstSearch	Abstracts and some full-text files in news and current events
Expanded Academic ASAP	Full-text articles from many popular and scholarly periodicals.

continued on the following page

continued from the previous page

Index	Description
LexisNexis Academic	Wide range of local, national, and international publications on law and business
New York Times Index	Article summaries, from 1918 to the present
Readers' Guide to Periodical Literature	General index to all topics
Reuters Business Briefings	Full-text articles from newspapers, newswires, and magazines
InfoTrac SearchBank	General reference and academic topic databases
Uncover	Tables of contents for 14,000 periodicals
Wall Street Journal Index	Article citations, 1955–1992 (continued by Dow Jones Interactive)

NOTE: Not all libraries will provide access to these indexes from outside the library.

Microfilm and Microfiche Extremely small images of pages of a periodical may be stored on microfilm. (You need a microfilm scanner to read or photocopy the pages.) Microfiche is similar to microfilm, but images are on a 5-by-7-inch sheet of film and are scanned with a microfiche reader.

(7) Using Special Library Services

As you do focused research, consult a librarian if you plan to use any of the following special services.

SPECIAL LIBRARY SERVICES

- **Interlibrary Loans**　Your library may be part of a library system that allows loans of books from one location to another. Check with your librarian.

continued on the following page

continued from the previous page

- **Special Collections**   Your library may house special collections of books, manuscripts, or documents.
- **Government Documents**   A large university library may have a separate government documents area with its own catalog or index.
- **Vertical File**   The vertical file includes pamphlets from a variety of organizations and interest groups, newspaper clippings, and other material collected by librarians.

28b Evaluating Library Sources

Whenever you find information in the library (print or electronic), you should take the time to **evaluate** it—to assess its usefulness and its reliability. To determine the usefulness of a library source, you should ask yourself the following questions.

Does the Source Treat Your Topic in Enough Detail? To be useful, your source should treat your topic in detail. Skim the book's table of contents and index for references to your topic. To be of any real help, a book should include a section or chapter on your topic, not simply a footnote of brief reference. For articles, read the abstract, or skim the entire article for key facts, looking closely at section headings, information set in boldface type, and topic sentences. An article should have your topic as its central subject, or at least one of its main concerns.

Is the Source Current? The date of publication tells you whether the information in a book or article is up-to-date. A source's currency is particularly important for scientific and technological subjects. But even in the humanities, new discoveries and new ways of thinking lead scholars to reevaluate and modify their ideas. Be sure to check with your instructor to see if he or she prefers sources that have been published after a particular date.

Is the Source Respected? A contemporary review of a source can help you make this assessment. *Book Review Digest,* available in the reference section of your library, lists popular books that have been reviewed in at least three newspapers or magazines and includes excerpts from representative reviews. Book reviews are also available from the *New York Times Book Review's* Web site <http://www.nytimes. com/books>, which includes text and of book reviews the newspaper has published since 1980.

Is the Source Reliable? Is a piece of writing largely fact or unsubstantiated opinion? Does the author support his or her conclusions? Does the author include documentation? Is the supporting information balanced? Is the author objective, or does he or she have a particular agenda to advance? Is the author associated with a special interest group that may affect his or her view of the issue?

In general, **scholarly publications**—books and journals aimed at an audience of expert readers—are more respected and reliable than **popular publications**—books, magazines, and newspapers aimed at an audience of general readers. Assuming they are current and written by reputable authors, however, articles from popular publications may be appropriate for your research. But remember that not all popular publications adhere to the same rigorous standards as scholarly publications. For example, although some popular periodicals (such as *Atlantic Monthly* and *Harper's*) generally contain articles that are reliable and carefully researched, other periodicals do not. For this reason, before you use information from popular sources such as *Newsweek* or *Sports Illustrated,* check with your instructor.

The following box summarizes the differences between scholarly and popular publications.

SCHOLARLY AND POPULAR PUBLICATIONS

Scholarly Publications	Popular Publications
Scholarly publications report the results of research.	Popular publications entertain and inform.
Scholarly publications are frequently published by a university press or have some connection with a university or academic organization.	Popular publications are published by commercial presses.
Scholarly publications are **refereed;** that is, an editorial board or group of expert reviewers determines what will be published.	Popular publications are usually not refereed.
Scholarly publications are usually written by someone who is a recognized authority in the field about which he or she is writing.	Popular publications may be written by experts in a particular field, but more often they are written by staff or freelance writers.

continued on the following page

145

continued from previous page

Scholarly publications are written for a scholarly audience, so they often contain a highly technical vocabulary and challengeing content.	Popular publications are written for general readers, so they usually use accessible language and do not have very challenging content.
Scholarly publications nearly always contain extensive documentation as well as a bibliography of works consulted.	Popular publications rarely cite sources or use documentation.
Scholarly publications are published primarily because they make a contribution to a particular field of study.	Popular publications are published primarily to make a profit.

CHAPTER 29

USING AND EVALUATING INTERNET SOURCES

The **Internet** is a vast system of networks that links millions of computers. Because of its size and diversity, the Internet allows people from all over the world to communicate quickly and easily.

Furthermore, because it is inexpensive to publish text, pictures, and sound online (via the Internet), businesses, government agencies, libraries, and universities are able to make available vast amounts of information: years' worth of newspaper articles, hundreds of thousands of pages of scientific or technical papers, government reports, images of all the paintings in a museum, virtual tours of historically significant buildings or sites—even an entire library of literature.

29a Using the World Wide Web for Research

When most people refer to the Internet, they actually mean the **World Wide Web,** which is just a part of the Internet. (See **29b** for other components of the Internet that you can use in your research.) The Web relies on **hypertext links,** key words highlighted in blue. By clicking your mouse on these links, you can move easily from one part of a document to another or from one Web site to another. The Web has become a powerful tool that can give you access to a great deal of print information as well as graphics, sound, animation, film clips, and even live video.

The Web enables you to connect to a vast variety of documents. For example, you can call up a **home page** or **Web page** (an individual document), or a **Web site** (a collection of Web pages). Government agencies, businesses, universities, libraries, newspapers and magazines, journals, and public interest groups, as well as individuals, all operate their own Web sites. Each of these sites contains hypertext links that can take you to other relevant sites. By using these links, you can "surf the Net," following your interests and moving from one document to another.

To carry out a Web search, you need a **Web browser,** a tool that enables you to find information on the Web. Two of the most popular browsers—*Netscape Navigator* and *Microsoft*

Internet Explorer—display the full range of text, photos, sound, and video available in Web documents. Most new computers come with one of these browsers already installed.

Before you can access the Web, you have to be **online,** connected to an Internet service provider (ISP). Most colleges and universities provide Internet access to students free of charge. Once you are online, you have to use your browser to connect to a **search engine,** a program that helps you retrieve information by searching the documents that are available on the Internet.

 MOST POPULAR SEARCH ENGINES

AltaVista (www.altavista.com): Good engine for precise searches. Fast and easy to use.

Ask Jeeves (www.askjeeves.com): Good beginner's site. Allows you to narrow your search by asking questions, such as *Are dogs smarter than pigs?*

Excite (www.excite.com): Good for general topics. Because it searches over 250 million Web sites, you often get more information than you need.

Hotbot (www.hotbot.com): Excellent, fast search engine for locating specific information. Good search options allow you to fine-tune your searches.

Infoseek (www.infoseek.com): Enables you to access information in a directory of reviewed sites, news stories, and Usenet groups.

Lycos (www.lycos.com): Enables you to search for specific media (graphics, for example). A somewhat small index of Web pages.

Magellan (www.magellan.excite.com): Enables you to search sites that have been evaluated for content.

Northern Light (www.northernlight.com): Searches Web pages but also lists pay-for-view articles not always listed by other search engines. Arranges results under subject headings.

WebCrawler (www.webcrawler.com): Good for beginners. Easy to use and very forgiving.

Yahoo! (www.yahoo.com): Enables you to search using both subject headings and keywords. Searches its own indexes as well as the Web.

SPECIALIZED SEARCH ENGINES

Bizbot (business search engine)
http://www.bizbot.net/

FedWorld (U.S. government database and report search engine)
http://www.fedworld.gov/

FindLaw (legal search engine)
http://www.findlaw.com/

HealthFinder (health, nutrition, and disease information for consumers)
http://www.heathfinder.gov/

The Internet Movie Database (search engine and database for film facts, reviews, and so on)
http://www.imdb.com

Newsbot (news search engine)
http://www.lycos.com/news/

Pilot-Search.com (literary search engine)
http://www.Pilot-Search.com/

SportQuest (sports search engine)
http://www.sportquest.com/

Voice of the Shuttle (humanities search engine)
http://www.vos.ucsb.edu/

Because even the best search engines search only a fraction of what is on the Web, you should also carry out a metasearch using a **metacrawler,** a search engine that searches several search engines simultaneously. Dogpile <www.dogpile.com>, Google <www.googlc.com>, and Metacrawler <www.metacrawler. com> are useful tools for finding out the full range of online sources that are available.

There are three ways to use search engines to find the information you want.

(1) Entering an Electronic Address

The most basic way to access information on the Web is to go directly to a specific electronic address. Search engines and Web browsers display a box that enables you to enter the electronic address (URL) of a specific Web site. Once you type in an address and click on *search* (or hit *enter* or the return key), you will be connected to the Web site you want. Make sure that you type the electronic address exactly as it appears, without adding spaces or adding or deleting punctuation marks. Remember that omitting just a single letter or punctuation mark will send you to the wrong site—or to no site at all.

(2) Doing a Keyword Search

Search engines also enable you to do a keyword search. On the first page of the search engine that you have chosen, you will find a box in which you can enter a keyword (or keywords). When you hit *enter* or the return key, the search engine retrieves and displays all the Web pages that contain your keywords.

Keep in mind that a search engine identifies any site in which the keyword or keywords that you have typed appear. (These sites are called *hits.*) Thus, a general keyword such as *Baltimore* could result in over a million hits. Because examining all these sites would be impossible, you need to focus your search, just as you would with your library's online catalog. By carrying out a **Boolean search,** combining keywords with AND, OR, or NOT (typed in capital letters), you can eliminate irrelevant hits from your search. For example, to find Web pages that have to do with Baltimore's economy, type *Baltimore* AND *economy.* Some search engines allow you to search using three or four key-words—*Baltimore* AND *economy* NOT *agriculture,* for example. Focusing your searches in this way will enable you to retrieve information quickly and easily.

(3) Using Subject Guides

Some search engines, such as Yahoo!, About.com, and Look Smart, contain a **subject guide**—a list of general categories (*The Humanities, The Arts, Entertainment, Business,* and so on) from which you can choose. Each of these categories will lead you to more specific lists of categories and subcategories, until eventually you get to the topic you want. For example, clicking on *The Humanities* would lead you to *History,* which in turn would lead you to *American History* and eventually to *Vietnam War.* Although this is a time-consuming strategy for finding specific information, it can be an excellent tool for finding or narrowing a topic.

✔ CHECKLIST: TIPS FOR EFFECTIVE WEB SEARCHES

✔ **Choose the Right Search Engine**   No one all-pur-pose search engine exists. Use a subject guide, such as the one available on Yahoo!, for exploratory re-search, and use a search engine, such as AltaVista, for more focused research.

continued on the following page

continued from the previous page

✔ **Choose Your Keywords Carefully** A search engine is only as good as the keywords you use. Choose keywords carefully.

✔ **Narrow Your Search** Carry out a Boolean search to make your searches more productive.

✔ **Check Your Spelling** If your search does not yield the results you expect, check to make sure you have spelled your search terms correctly. Even a one-letter mistake can confuse a search engine and cause it to retrieve the wrong information—or no information at all.

✔ **Include Enough Terms** If you are looking for information on housing, for example, search for several different variations of your keyword: *housing, houses, home buyer, buying houses, residential real estate*, and so on.

✔ **Consult the Help Screen** Most search engines have a help screen. If you have trouble with your search, do not hesitate to consult it. A little time spent here can save you a lot of time later.

✔ **Use More Than One Subject Guide or Search Engine** Different subject guides and search engines index different sites.

✔ **Add Useful Sites to Your Bookmark or Favorites List** Whenever you find a particularly useful Web site, **bookmark** it by selecting this option on the menu bar of your browser (with some browsers, such as *Microsoft Explorer,* this option is called *Favorites*). When you add a site to your bookmark list, you can return to the site whenever you want to by opening the bookmark menu and selecting it.

29b Using Other Internet Tools

In addition to the World Wide Web, the Internet contains a number of other components that you can use to gather and share information for your research.

(1) Using E-Mail

E-mail can be very useful to you as you do research. You can exchange ideas with classmates, ask questions of your instructors, and even conduct long-distance interviews. You can follow e-mail links in Web documents, and you can also transfer word-processing documents or other files (as e-mail attachments) from one computer to another.

(2) Using Listservs

Listservs, (sometimes called **discussion lists**), electronic mailing lists to which you must subscribe, enable you to communicate with groups of people interested in particular topics (board games or salt-water aquariums, for example). Individuals in a listserv send e-mails to a main e-mail address, and these messages are routed to all members in the group. Many listserv subscribers are experts who will often answer legitimate queries. Keep in mind, however, that anyone can join a listserv, so make sure you <u>evaluate</u> the information you get before you use it in your research.

See 29c

(3) Using Newsgroups

Like listservs, **newsgroups** are discussion groups. Unlike listserv messages, which are sent to you as e-mail, newsgroup messages are collected on the **Usenet** system, a global collection of news servers, where anyone can access them. In a sense, newsgroups function as gigantic bulletin boards where users post messages that others can read and respond to. Thus, newsgroups can be a source of specific information as well as suggestions about where to look for further information. Just as you would with a listserv, evaluate information you get from a newsgroup before you use it.

(4) Using Gopher, FTP, and Telnet

At one time, you needed special software to access gopher, telnet, and FTP. Now they can be accessed with most programs that access the Web.

Gopher is a tool that organizes textual information into hierarchical menus. You follow one menu to another until you get the information you want. Gopher gives you access to information about business, medicine, and engineering as well as access to archived newsgroups and electronic books and magazines.

FTP (file transfer protocol) enables you to transfer documents at high speed from one computer on the Internet to another. With FTP, you can get full text of books and articles as well as pictures. The most common use for FTP is for downloading updates from computer software manufacturers.

Telnet is a program that enables you to make a connection via telephone to another computer on the Internet. With telnet you can download anything from another host computer.

(5) Using MUDS, MOOS, and IRCS (Synchronous Communication)

With e-mails and listservs, there is a delay between the time a message is sent and the time it is received. **MUDS, MOOS,** and **IRCS** enable you to send and receive messages in real time. Communication is **synchronous;** that is, messages are sent and received as they are typed. Synchronous communication programs are being used more and more in college settings—for class discussions, online workshops, and collaborative projects.

29c Evaluating Internet Sites

Using the Web for your research has many advantages: it is easy, it is convenient, and it can yield a great deal of information, some of which you can get nowhere else. Even with these advantages, using the Web as a research tool can have some significant disadvantages.

DISADVANTAGES OF USING THE WEB

- A Web search can yield more information than you can reasonably handle or properly evaluate.
- Because it is so convenient, Web research can cause you to ignore the resources in your college library. Many important and useful publications are available only in print and on library databases, not on the Web.
- A Web document may be unstable. Unlike print sources, Web documents can be altered at any time. For this reason, you cannot be sure that the information you see on a Web site will be there when you try to access it at a later date. (MLA recommends that you keep copies of all Web documents that you use in your research.)
- Anyone can publish on the Web, so Web sites can vary greatly in reliability.
- Authorship and affiliation can sometimes be difficult or impossible to determine.

Because of these disadvantages, critical evaluation of Web site material is even more important than evaluation of more traditional print sources of information, such as books and journal articles. For this reason, you should carefully evaluate the content of any Web site for *accuracy, credibility, objectivity, currency, coverage* or *scope*, and *stability.*

Accuracy Accuracy refers to the reliability of the material itself and to the use of proper documentation. Keep in mind that factual error—especially errors in facts that are central to the main point of the source—should cause you to question the reliability of the material you are reading.

- Is the text free of basic grammatical and mechanical errors?
- Does the site contain factual errors?
- Does the site provide a list of references?
- Are links available to other references?
- Can information be verified with print or other resources?

Credibility *Credibility* refers to the credentials of the person or organization responsible for the site. Web sites operated by well-known institutions (the Smithsonian or the U.S. Department of Health and Human Services, for example) have built-in credibility. Those operated by individuals (private Web pages, for example) are often less reliable.

* Does the site list an author?
* Is the author a recognized authority in his or her field?
* Is the site **refereed?** That is, does an editorial board or a group of experts determine what material appears on the Web site?
* Does the organization sponsoring the Web site exist apart from its Web presence?
* Can you determine how long the Web site has existed?

✔ CHECKLIST: DETERMINING THE LEGITIMACY OF AN ANONYMOUS OR QUESTIONABLE WEB SOURCE

When a Web source is anonymous (or has an author whose name is not familiar to you), you have to take special measures to determine its legitimacy.

✔ *Post a query.* If you subscribe to a newsgroup or listserv, ask others in the group what they know about the source and its author.

✔ *Follow the links.* Follow the hypertext links in a document to other documents. If the links take you to legitimate sources, you know that the author is aware of these sources of information.

✔ *Do a keyword search.* Do a search using the name of the sponsoring organization or the article as key-words. Other documents (or citations in other works) may identify the author.

✔ *Look at the URL.* The last part of a Web site's URL can tell you whether the site is sponsored by a com-mercial entity (*.com*), a nonprofit organization (*.org*), an educational institution (*.edu*), the military (*.mil*), or a government agency (*.gov*). Knowing this infor-mation can tell you whether an organization is trying to sell you something (*.com*) or just providing infor-mation (*.edu* or *.org*).

Objectivity or Reasonableness *Objectivity* or *reasonableness* refers to the degree of bias that a Web site exhibits. Some Web sites make no secret of their biases. They openly advocate a particular point of view or action, or they are clearly trying to sell something. Other Web sites may hide their biases. For example, a Web site may present itself as a source of factual information when it is actually advocating a political point of view.

- Does advertising appear in the text?
- Does a business, a political organization, or a special interest group sponsor the site?
- Are links provided to sites with a political agenda?
- Does the site express a particular viewpoint?
- Does the site contain links to other sites that express a particular viewpoint?

Currency Currency refers to how up-to-date the Web site is. The easiest way to assess a site's currency is to determine when it was last updated. Keep in mind, however, that even if the date on the site is current, the information that the site contains may not be.

- Does the site clearly identify the date it was created?
- Is the most recent update displayed?
- Are all the links to other sites still functioning?
- Is the actual information on the page up-to-date?

Coverage or Scope Coverage or *scope* refers to the comprehensiveness of the information on a Web site. More is not necessarily better, but some sites may be scanty or incomplete. Others may provide information that is no more than common knowledge. Still others may present discussions that may not be suitable for college-level research.

- Does the site provide in-depth coverage?
- Does the site provide information that is not available elsewhere?
- Does the site identify a target audience? Does this target audience suggest the site is appropriate for your research needs?

Stability Stability refers to whether or not the site is being maintained. A stable site will be around when you want to access it again. Web sites that are here today and gone tomorrow make it difficult for readers to check your sources or for you to obtain updated information.

- Has the site been active for a long period of time?
- Is the site updated regularly?
- Is the site maintained by a well-known, reliable organization—that is, one that is likely to be committed to financing the site?

29d Useful Web Sites

The Web sites listed here will be useful as you do Internet research.

Humanities Web Sites
- *Art History*
  http://witcombe.sbc.edu/ARTHLinks.com
- *Film*
  http://us.imdb.com
- *History*
  http://www.hyperhistory.com/online_n2/History_n2a.html
- *Literature*
  http://digital.library.upenn.edu/books
- *Philosophy*
  http://plato.stanford.edu
- *Business*
  http://www.ipl.org/ref/RR/static/bus0000.html

Social Sciences Web Sites
- *Education*
  http://www.education-world.com
- *Political Science*
  http://politicalresources.net
- *Psychology*
  http://www.psychcrawler.com
- *Sociology and Social Work*
  http://gwbweb.wustl.edu/websites.html

Natural Sciences Web Sites
- *Biology*
  http://biodiversity.uno.edu
- *Chemistry*
  http://www.ssc.ntu.edu.sg:8000/chemweb/htmlj
- *Engineering*
  http://www.eng-sol.com
- *Mathematics*
  http://mathworld.wolfram.com
- *Physics*
  http://www.physicsweb.org/resources

Other Useful Web Sites
- Guide to Internet Research and Resources
  http://www.miracosta.cc.ca.us/home/gfloren/
  INTNET.HTM
- Information on Evaluating Internet Sources (U. VT)
  http://www.lib.vt.edu/research/libinst/evaluating.html

Useful Web Sites

- Internet Research FAQ
  http://www.purefiction.com/pages/res1.htm
- Internet Tutorials
  http://www.albany.edu/library/internet
- Internet Research Tips
  http://www.albany.edu/library/internet/checklist.html
- Starting Points for Internet Research (Purdue)
  http://owl.english.purdue.edu/internet/tools/research.html
- General Reference Resources (CMU)
  http://eserver.org/reference
- Selected Web Resources by Academic Subject
  (Georgetown U.)
  http://gulib.lausun.georgetown.edu/swr
- (US) Government Information Locator Service
  http://www.fedworld.gov
- Internet Public Library—Serials (Magazines)
  http://www.ipl.org/reading/serials
- Internet Public Library—Newspapers
  http://www.ipl.org/reading/news
- Encyclopaedia Britannica Online
  www.britannica.com
- Citing Electronic Sources (APA and MLA)
  http://www.uvm.edu/~ncrane/estyles
- The World Fact Book
  http://www.odci.gov/cia/publications/factbook
- Library of Congress
  http://lcweb.loc.gov
- Research-It!
  http://www.iTools.com/research-it/research-it.html

CHAPTER 30

INTEGRATING SOURCES AND AVOIDING PLAGIARISM

 **Integrating Source Material into Your Writing**

Weave paraphrases, summaries, and quotations of source material smoothly into your paper, adding your own analysis or explanation to increase coherence and to show the relevance of your sources to the points you are making.

(1) Integrating Quotations

Quotations should never be awkwardly dropped into your paper, leaving the exact relationship between the quotation and your point unclear. Instead, use a brief introductory remark to provide a context for the quotation.

UNACCEPTABLE: For the Amish, the public school system represents a problem. "A serious problem confronting Amish society from the viewpoint of the Amish themselves is the threat of absorption into mass society through the values promoted in the public school system" (Hostetler 193).

ACCEPTABLE: For the Amish, the public school system is a problem because it represents "the threat of absorption into mass society" (Hostetler 193).

Whenever possible, use an **identifying tag** (a phrase that identifies the source) to introduce the quotation.

IDENTIFYING TAG: As John Hostetler points out, the Amish see the public school system as a problem because it represents "the threat of absorption into mass society" (193).

 INTEGRATING SOURCE MATERIAL INTO YOUR WRITING

To make sure all your sentences do not sound the same, experiment with different methods of integrating source material into your paper.

continued on the following page

continued from the previous page

- Vary the verbs you use to introduce a source's words or ideas (instead of repeating *says*).

acknowledges	discloses	implies
suggests	observes	notes
concludes	believes	comments
insists	explains	claims
predicts	summarizes	illustrates
reports	finds	proposes
warns	concurs	speculates
admits	affirms	indicates

- Vary the placement of the identifying tag, putting it sometimes in the middle or at the end of the quoted material instead of always at the beginning.

QUOTATION WITH IDENTIFYING TAG IN MIDDLE: "A serious problem confronting Amish society from the viewpoint of the Amish themselves," observes Hostetler, "is the threat of absorption into mass society through the values promoted in the public school system" (193).

PARAPHRASE WITH IDENTIFYING TAG AT END: The Amish are also concerned about their children's exposure to the public school system's values, notes Hostetler (193).

 CLOSE-UP **PUNCTUATING IDENTIFYING TAGS**

Whether or not you use a comma with an identifying tag depends on where you place it in the sentence. If the identifying tag immediately precedes a quotation, use a comma.

<u>As Hostetler points out</u>, "The Amish are successful in maintaining group identity" (56).

If the identifying tag does not immediately precede a quotation, do not use a comma.

<u>Hostetler points out</u> that the Amish frequently "use severe sanctions to preserve their values" (56).

Substitutions or Additions within Quotations When you make changes or additions to make a quotation fit into your paper, acknowledge your changes by enclosing them in brackets.

ORIGINAL QUOTATION: "Immediately after her wedding, she and her husband followed tradition and went to visit almost everyone who attended the wedding" (Hostetler 122).

QUOTATION REVISED TO SUPPLY AN ANTECEDENT FOR A PRONOUN: "Immediately after her wedding, [Sarah] and her husband followed tradition and went to visit almost everyone who attended the wedding" (Hostetler 122).

QUOTATION REVISED TO CHANGE A CAPITAL TO A LOWERCASE LETTER: The strength of the Amish community is illustrated by the fact that "[i]mmediately after her wedding, she and her husband followed tradition and went to visit almost everyone who attended the wedding" (Hostetler 122).

See 20f

Omissions within Quotations When you delete unnecessary or irrelevant words, substitute an <u>ellipsis</u> (three spaced periods) for the deleted words.

NOTE: MLA style requires brackets around ellipses that you add (to distinguish them from those that appear in the original quotation).

ORIGINAL: "Not only have the Amish built and staffed their own elementary and vocational schools, but they have gradually organized on local, state, and national levels to cope with the task of educating their children" (Hostetler 206).

QUOTATION REVISED TO ELIMINATE UNNECESSARY WORDS: "Not only have the Amish built and staffed their own elementary and vocational schools, but they have gradually organized [. . .] to cope with the task of educating their children" (Hostetler 206).

 OMISSIONS WITHIN QUOTATIONS

Be sure that you do not misrepresent quoted material when you delete words from it. For example, do not say, "the Amish have managed to maintain [. . .] their culture" when the original quotation is "the Amish have managed to maintain *parts of* their culture."

For treatment of long quotations, see **19a.**

(2) Integrating Paraphrases and Summaries

Introduce paraphrases and summaries with identifying tags, and end them with appropriate documentation. Doing so allows readers to differentiate your ideas from the ideas of your sources.

MISLEADING (IDEAS OF SOURCE BLEND WITH IDEAS OF WRITER): Art can be used to uncover many problems that children have at home, in school, or with their friends. For this reason, many therapists use art therapy extensively. Children's views of themselves in society are often reflected by their art style. For example, a cramped, crowded art style using only a portion of the paper shows their limited role (Alschuler 260).

REVISED WITH IDENTIFYING TAG (IDEAS OF SOURCE DIFFERENTIATED FROM IDEAS OF WRITER): Art can be used to uncover many problems that children have at home, in school, or with their friends. For this reason, many therapists use art therapy extensively. <u>According to William Alschuler in *Art and Self-Image*,</u> children's views of themselves in society are often reflected by their art style. For example, a cramped, crowded art style using only a portion of the paper shows their limited role (260).

30b Avoiding Plagiarism

Plagiarism is presenting another person's words or ideas—either accidentally or intentionally—as though they are your own. In general, you must provide <u>**documentation**</u> for all direct quotations, as well as for every opinion, judgment, and insight of someone else that you summarize or paraphrase. You must also document tables, graphs, charts, and statistics taken from a source. See Pt. 7

Of course, certain information need not be documented: **common knowledge** (information that is generally known), familiar sayings and well-known quotations, and the results of your own original research (interviews and surveys, for example). Information that is in dispute or that is one person's original contribution, however, must be acknowledged. For example, you need not document the fact that John F. Kennedy graduated from Harvard in 1949 or that he was elected president in 1960. You must, however, document a historian's evaluation of Kennedy's performance as president or a researcher's recent revelations about Kennedy's private life.

You can avoid plagiarism by using documentation wherever it is required and by following these guidelines.

(1) Enclose Borrowed Words in Quotation Marks

ORIGINAL: DNA profiling begins with the established theory that no two people, except identical twins, have the

161

same genetic makeup. Each cell in the body contains a complete set of genes. (Tucker, William. "DNA in Court." *The American Spectator* Nov. 1994: 26)

PLAGIARISM: William Tucker points out that DNA profiling is based on the premise that genetic makeup differs from person to person and that <u>each cell in the body contains a complete set of genes</u> (26).

Even though the student writer does document the source of his information, he uses the source's exact words without placing them in quotation marks.

CORRECT (BORROWED WORDS IN QUOTATION MARKS): William Tucker points out that DNA profiling is based on the premise that genetic makeup differs from person to person and that <u>"[e]ach cell in the body contains a complete set of genes"</u> (26).

CORRECT (PARAPHRASE): William Tucker points out that DNA profiling is based on the accepted premise that genetic makeup differs from person to person and that <u>every cell includes a full set of an individual's genes</u> (26).

(2) Do Not Imitate a Source's Syntax and Phrasing

ORIGINAL: If there is a garbage crisis, it is that we are treating garbage as an environmental threat and not what it is: a manageable—though admittedly complex—civic issue. (Poore, Patricia. "America's 'Garbage Crisis.'" *Harper's* Mar. 1994: 39)

PLAGIARISM: If a garbage crisis does exist, it is that people see garbage as a menace to the environment and not what it actually is: a controllable—if obviously complicated—public problem (Poore 39).

Although this student does not use the exact words of her source, she closely imitates the original's syntax and phrasing, simply substituting synonyms for the author's words.

CORRECT (PARAPHRASE IN WRITER'S OWN WORDS; ONE DISTINCTIVE PHRASE PLACED IN QUOTATION MARKS): Patricia Poore argues that America's "garbage crisis" is exaggerated; rather than viewing garbage as a serious environmental hazard, she says, we should look at garbage as a public problem that may be complicated but that can be solved (39).

PLAGIARISM AND INTERNET SOURCES

Any time you download text from the Internet, you risk committing plagiarism. To avoid the possibility of plagiarism, follow these guidelines.

- Download information into individual files so that you can keep track of your sources.
- Do not simply cut and paste blocks of downloaded text into your paper; summarize or paraphrase this material first.
- If you do record the exact words of your source, enclose them in quotation marks.
- Whether your information is from e-mails, online discussion groups, listservs, or World Wide Web sites, give proper credit by providing appropriate documentation.

(3) Document Statistics Obtained from a Source

Although many people assume that statistics are common knowledge, statistics are usually the result of original research and must therefore be documented.

> CORRECT: According to one study of 303 accidents recorded, almost one-half took place before the drivers were legally allowed to drive at eighteen (Schuman et al. 1027).

(4) Differentiate Your Words and Ideas from Those of Your Source

> ORIGINAL: At some colleges and universities traditional survey courses of world and English literature [...]. have been scrapped or diluted [...]. What replaces them is sometimes a mere option of electives, sometimes "multicultural" courses introducing material from Third World cultures and thinning out an already thin sampling of Western writings, and sometimes courses geared especially to issues of class, race, and gender. (Howe, Irving. "The Value of the Canon." *The New Republic* 2 Feb. 1991: 40–47).

> PLAGIARISM: At many universities the Western literature survey courses have been edged out by courses that emphasize minority concerns. These courses are "thinning out an already thin sampling of Western writings" in favor of

courses geared especially to issues of "class, race, and gender" (Howe 40).

Because the student writer does not differentiate his ideas from those of his source, it appears that only the quotation in the last sentence is borrowed when, in fact, the first sentence also owes a debt to the original. The student should have clearly identified the boundaries of the borrowed material by introducing it with an identifying tag and ending with documentation. (Note that a quotation always requires separate documentation.)

CORRECT: According to critic Irving Howe, at many universities the Western literature survey courses have been edged out by courses that emphasize minority concerns (41). These courses, says Howe, are "thinning out an already thin sampling of Western writings" in favor of "courses geared especially to issues of class, race, and gender" (40).

PART 7

DOCUMENTING SOURCES

CHAPTER 31
MLA DOCUMENTATION STYLE

CHAPTER 32
APA DOCUMENTATION STYLE

CHAPTER 33
CHICAGO AND OTHER
DOCUMENTATION STYLES

DIRECTORY OF MLA PARENTHETICAL REFERENCES

DIRECTORY OF MLA WORKS CITED LIST ENTRIES

Entries for Books

Entries for Articles

CHAPTER 31

MLA DOCUMENTATION STYLE

Documentation is the formal acknowledgment of the sources you use in your paper. This chapter explains and illustrates the documentation style recommended by the Modern Language Association (MLA). Chapter 32 discusses the documentation style of the American Psychological Association (APA), and Chapter 33 gives an overview of the formats recommended by *The Chicago Manual of Style,* the Council of Biology Editors (CBE), and organizations in other disciplines.

31a Using MLA Style

MLA style* is required by many teachers of English and other languages as well as teachers in other humanities disciplines. MLA documentation has three parts: *parenthetical references in the body of the paper (also known as in-text citations), a Works Cited list, and content notes.*

(1) Parenthetical References

MLA documentation uses parenthetical references in the body of the paper keyed to a Works Cited list at the end of the paper. A typical parenthetical reference consists of the author's last name and a page number.

The colony appealed to many idealists in Europe (Ripley 132).

To distinguish two or more sources by the same author, include an appropriate shortened title after the author's name.

Penn emphasized his religious motivation (Kelley, Colonial Years 116).

If you state the author's name or the title of the work in your discussion, do not include it in the parenthetical reference.

Penn's political motivation is discussed by Joseph J. Kelley in Pennsylvania, The Colonial Years, 1681–1776 (44).

---

*MLA documentation format follows the guidelines set in the *MLA Handbook for Writers of Research Papers,* 5th ed. New York, MLA, 1999.

> ### CLOSE-UP
> ## PUNCTUATING WITH PARENTHETICAL REFERENCES: MLA
>
> *Paraphrases and Summaries* Parenthetical references are placed *before* the sentence's end punctuation.
>
> Penn's writings epitomize seventeenth-century religious thought (Dengler and Curtis 72).
>
> *Quotations Run In with the Text* Parenthetical references are placed *after* the quotation but *before* the end punctuation.
>
> As Ross says, "Penn followed his conscience in all matters" (127).
>
> According to Williams, "Penn's utopian vision was informed by his Quaker beliefs [. . .]" (72).
>
> *Quotations Set Off from the Text* When you quote a **long prose passage** or more than three lines of **poetry,** parenthetical references are placed one space *after* the end punctuation.
>
> According to Arthur Smith, William Penn envisioned a state based on his religious principles:
>> Pennsylvania would be a commonwealth in which all individuals would follow God's truth and develop according to God's law. For Penn this concept of government was self-evident. It would be a mistake to see Pennsylvania as anything but an expression of Penn's religious beliefs. (314)

See 19a

Sample MLA Parenthetical References

1. A Work by a Single Author
Fairy tales reflect the fears of children (Bettelheim 23).

2. A Work by Two or Three Authors
The historian's main job is to search for clues and solve mysteries (Davidson and Lytle 6).

With the advent of behaviorism, psychology began a new phase of inquiry (Cowen, Barbo, and Crum 31–34).

3. A Work by More Than Three Authors List only the first author followed by *et al.* ("and others").
The European powers believed they could change the fundamentals of Moslem existence (Bull et al. 395).

4. A Work in Multiple Volumes If you list more than one volume of a multivolume work in your Works Cited list, include the appropriate volume number as well as the page number. Separate the volume and page numbers with a colon and a space.

The French Revolution had a great influence on William Blake (Raine 1: 52).

5. A Work without a Listed Author Use a shortened version of the title, beginning with the word by which it is alphabetized in the Works Cited list.

In spite of political unrest, Soviet television remained fairly conservative ("Soviet" 3).

6. A One-Page Article Do not include a page reference for a one-page article.

Sixty percent of Arab-Americans work in white-collar jobs (El-Badru).

7. An Indirect Source If you use a statement by one author that is quoted in the work of another author, indicate this with the abbreviation *qtd. in.*

Wagner stated that myth and history stood before him "with opposing claims" (qtd. in Thomas 65).

8. More than One Work

The Brooklyn Bridge has been used as a subject by many American artists (McCullough 144; Tashjian 58).

9. A Literary Work In a parenthetical reference to a prose work, follow the page number with a semicolon and then add any additional information that may be helpful.

In <u>Moby-Dick</u>, Melville refers to a whaling expedition funded by Louis XIV of France (151; ch. 24).

In parenthetical references to long poems, cite both division and line numbers, separating them with a period.

In the <u>Aeneid</u>, Virgil describes the ships as cleaving the "green woods reflected in the calm water" (8.124).

When citing short poems, identify the poem and the poet in the text of the paper, and use line numbers in the citation.

In "A Song in the Front Yard," Brooks says, "I've stayed in the front yard all my life / I want a peek at the back" (lines 1–2).

NOTE: Include the word *line* (or *lines*) only in the first parenthetical reference; use just the numbers in subsequent references.

In citing classic verse plays, include the act, scene, and line numbers, separated by periods (<u>Macbeth</u> 2.2.14–16). In biblical citations, include title, chapter, and verse (Gen. 5.12).

10. An Entire Work   When citing an entire work, include the author's name and the work's title in the text of your paper.

Herbert Gans's <u>The Urban Villagers</u> is a study of an Italian-American neighborhood in Boston.

11. Two or More Authors with the Same Last Name   To distinguish authors with the same last name, include a first initial.

Recent increases in crime have probably caused thousands of urban homeowners to install burglar alarms (Weishoff, R. 115).

12. A Government Document or a Corporate Author   Cite the organization's name followed by the page number (American Automobile Association 34), or work the organization's name into your paper.

According to the President's Commission for the Study of Ethical Problems in Medicine and Biomedical and Behavioral Research, the issues relating to euthanasia are complicated (76).

13. An Electronic Source   If a reference to an electronic source includes paragraph numbers rather than page numbers, use the abbreviation *par.* or *pars.* and the paragraph number or numbers. (If the electronic source has no individual page or paragraph numbers, try to cite the work in your discussion rather than in a parenthetical reference.)

The earliest type of movie censorship came in the form of licensing fees, and in Deer River, Minnesota, "a licensing fee of $200 was deemed not excessive for a town of 1000" (Ernst, par. 20).

(2) Works Cited List

The **Works Cited list,** which appears at the end of your paper, gives publication information for all the research materials you cite. If your instructor tells you to list all the sources you read, whether you actually cited them or not, give this list the title *Works Consulted.*

Sample MLA Works Cited Entries: Books   Book citations include the author's name, book title (underlined), and publication information (place, publisher, date). Capitalize all major words of the title except articles, coordinating conjunctions, prepositions, and the *to* of an infinitive (unless such a word is the first or last word of the title or subtitle). Do not underline the period that follows a book's title.

1. A Book by One Author   Use a short form of the publisher's name. *Alfred A. Knopf, Inc.,* for example, is shortened to *Knopf,* and *Oxford University Press* becomes *Oxford UP.*

Bettelheim, Bruno. <u>The Uses of Enchantment: The Meaning and Importance of Fairy Tales</u>. New York: Knopf, 1976.

Indicate an edition other than the first as follows:

Gans, Herbert J. <u>The Urban Villagers</u>. 2nd ed. New York: Free, 1982.

2. A Book by Two or Three Authors   List the first author last name first. Subsequent authors are listed first name first in the order in which they appear on the title page of the book.

Watson, Jack and Grant McKernie. <u>A Cultural History of the Theatre</u>. New York: Longman, 1993.

3. A Book by More Than Three Authors   List only the first author, followed by *et al.*

Bull, Henry, et al. <u>The Near East</u>. New York: Oxford UP, 1990.

4. Two or More Books by the Same Author   List books by the same author alphabetically by title. After the first entry, use three unspaced hyphens, followed by a period, in place of the author's name.

Thomas, Lewis. <u>The Lives of a Cell: Notes of a Biology Watcher</u>. New York: Viking, 1974.

- - -.   <u>The Medusa and the Snail: More Notes of a Biology Watcher</u>. New York: Viking, 1979.

5. An Edited Book   If your emphasis is on the *author's* work, begin your citation with the author's name. After the title, include the abbreviation *Ed.* ("Edited by") followed by the name of the editor or editors.

Bartram, William. <u>The Travels of William Bartram</u>. Ed. Mark Van Doren. New York: Dover, 1955.

If your emphasis is on the *editor's* work, begin your citation with the editor's name followed by the abbreviation *ed.* ("editor") if there is one editor or *eds.* ("editors") if there is more than one.

Van Doren, Mark, ed. <u>The Travels of William Bartram</u>. By William Bartram. New York: Dover, 1955.

6. A Selection in an Anthology   Supply inclusive page numbers for the entire essay.

Lloyd, G. E. R. "Science and Mathematics." <u>The Legacy of Greece</u>.Ed. Moses I. Finley. New York: Oxford UP, 1981. 256–300.

7. More Than One Essay from the Same Anthology List each essay from the same anthology separately, followed by a cross-reference to the entire anthology. (List complete publication information for the anthology itself.)

Bolgar, Robert R. "The Greek Legacy." Finley 429–72.

Finley, Moses I., ed. <u>The Legacy of Greece</u>. New York: Oxford UP, 1981.

Williams, Bernard. "Philosophy." Finley 202–55.

8. A Multivolume Work   When all volumes of a multivolume work have the same title, include the number of the volume you are using.

Raine, Kathleen. <u>Blake and Tradition</u>. Vol. 1. Princeton: Princeton UP, 1968.

When you use two or more volumes, cite the entire work.

Raine, Kathleen. <u>Blake and Tradition</u>. 2 vols. Princeton: Princeton UP, 1968.

If the volume you are using has an individual title, however, you may cite the title without mentioning any other volumes.

Durant, Will, and Ariel Durant. <u>The Age of Napoleon</u>. New York: Simon, 1975.

9. The Foreword, Preface, or Afterword of a Book
Taylor, Telford. Preface. <u>Less Than Slaves</u>. By Benjamin B. Ferencz. Cambridge: Harvard UP, 1979. xiii–xxii.

10. A Short Story, Play, or Poem in an Anthology
Chopin, Kate. "The Storm." <u>Literature: Reading, Reacting, Writing</u>. Ed. Laurie G. Kirszner and Stephen R. Mandell. Compact 4th ed. Fort Worth: Harcourt, 2000. 138–42.

Shakespeare, William. <u>Othello, The Moor of Venice</u>. <u>Shakespeare: Six Plays and the Sonnets</u>. Ed. Thomas Mard Parrott and Edward Hubler. New York: Scribner's, 1956. 145–91.

11. A Short Story, Play, or Poem in a Collection of an Author's Work
Walcott, Derek. "Nearing La Guaira." <u>Selected Poems</u>. New York: Farrar, 1964. 47–48.

12. A Book with a Title within Its Title   If the book you are citing contains a title that is normally underlined to indicate italics (a novel, play, or long poem, for example), do *not* underline the interior title.

Knoll, Robert E., ed. <u>Storm Over</u> The Waste Land. Chicago: Scott, 1964.

If the book you are citing contains a title that is normally enclosed within quotation marks, keep the quotation marks.

Herzog, Alan, ed. <u>Twentieth Century Interpretations of "To a Skylark."</u>
    Englewood Cliffs: Prentice, 1975.

13. A Translation
García Márquez, Gabriel. <u>One Hundred Years of Solitude</u>. Trans.
    Gregory Rabassa. New York: Avon, 1991.

14. A Republished Book
Wharton, Edith. <u>The House of Mirth</u>. 1905. New York: Scribner's,
    1975.

15. A Dissertation (Published/Unpublished) For dissertations published by University Microfilms International (UMI), include the order number.

Peterson, Shawn. <u>Loving Mothers and Lost Daughters: Images of
    Female Kinship Relations in Selected Novels of Toni Morrison</u>.
    Diss. U of Oregon, 1993. Ann Arbor: UMI, 1994. 9322935.

Use quotation marks for the title of an unpublished dissertation.

Romero, Yolanda Garcia. "The American Frontier Experience in
    Twentieth-Century Northwest Texas." Diss. Texas Tech U, 1993.

16. An Article in a Reference Book (Signed/Unsigned) For a signed article, begin with the author's name.

Drabble, Margaret. "Expressionism." <u>The Oxford Companion to
    English Literature</u>. 5th ed. New York: Oxford UP, 1985.

When citing familiar reference books, do not include publication information. Enter the title of an unsigned article just as it is listed in the reference book.

"Cubism." <u>Encyclopedia Americana</u>. 1994 ed.

17. A Pamphlet If no author is listed, begin with the title (underlined).

<u>Existing Light Photography</u>. Rochester: Kodak, 1989.

18. A Government Publication If the publication has no listed author, begin with the name of the government, followed by the name of the agency.

United States. Office of Consumer Affairs. <u>1999 Consumer's Resource
    Handbook</u>. Washington: GPO, 1999.

Sample MLA Works Cited Entries: Articles Article citations include the author's name, the title of the article (in quotation marks), the title of the periodical (underlined), the month (abbreviated, except for May, June and July) and the year, and the pages on which the full article appears (without the abbreviation *p.* or *pp.*).

19. An Article in a Journal with Continuous Pagination through an Annual Volume   For an article in a journal with continuous pagination—for example, one in which an issue ends on page 172 and the next issue begins with page 173—include the volume number, followed by the date of publication (in parentheses). Follow the publication date with a colon, a space, and the page numbers.

Huntington, John. "Science Fiction and the Future." <u>College English</u>
37 (1975): 340–58.

20. An Article in a Journal with Separate Pagination in Each Issue   For a journal in which each issue begins with page 1, add a period and the issue number after the volume number.

Sipes, R. G. "War, Sports, and Aggression: An Empirical Test of Two
Rival Theories." <u>American Anthropologist</u> 4.2 (1973): 65–84.

21. An Article in a Weekly Magazine (Signed/Unsigned)   In dates, the day precedes the month.

Traub, James. "The Hearts and Minds of City College." <u>New Yorker</u>
7 June 1993: 42–53.

For unsigned articles, start with the title of the article.

"Solzhenitsyn: A Candle in the Wind." <u>Time</u> 23 Mar. 1970: 70.

22. An Article in a Monthly Magazine
Roll, Lori. "Careers in Engineering." <u>Working Woman</u> Nov. 1982: 62.

23. An Article That Is Not Printed on Consecutive Pages
When, for example, an article begins on page 120 and then skips to page 186, include only the first page number and a plus sign.

Griska, Linda. "Stress and Job Performance." <u>Psychology Today</u>
Nov.-Dec. 1995: 120+.

24. An Article in a Newspaper (Signed/Unsigned)
Oates, Joyce Carol. "When Characters from the Page Are Made Flesh
on the Screen." <u>New York Times</u> 23 Mar. 1986, late ed.: C1+.

"Soviet Television." <u>Los Angeles Times</u> 13 Dec. 1990, sec. 2: 3+.

25. An Editorial
"Tough Cops, Not Brutal Cops." Editorial. <u>New York Times</u>
5 May 1994, late ed.: A26.

26. A Letter to the Editor
Bishop, Jennifer. Letter. <u>Philadelphia Inquirer</u> 10 Dec. 1995: A17.

27. A Book Review

Fox-Genovese, Elizabeth. "Big Mess on Campus." Rev. of <u>Illiberal Education: The Politics of Race and Sex on Campus</u>, by Dinesh D'Souza. <u>Washington Post</u> 15 Apr. 1991, ntnl. weekly ed.: 32.

28. An Article with a Title within Its Title If the article you are citing contains a title that is normally enclosed within quotation marks, use single quotation marks for the interior title.

Nash, Robert. "About 'The Emperor of Ice Cream.'" <u>Perspectives</u> 7 (1954): 122-24.

If the article you are citing contains a title that is normally underlined to indicate italics, underline it in your Works Cited entry.

Leicester, H. Marshall, Jr. "The Art of Impersonation: A General Prologue to <u>The Canterbury Tales</u>." <u>PMLA</u> 95 (1980): 213–24.

Sample MLA Works Cited Entries: Other Sources

29. A Lecture

Sandman, Peter. "Communicating Scientific Information." Communications Seminar, Dept. of Humanities and Communications. Drexel U, 26 Oct. 1999.

30. A Personal Interview

West, Cornel. Personal interview. 28 Dec. 1998.

Tannen, Deborah. Telephone interview. 8 June 1999.

31. A Published Interview

Stavros, George. "An Interview with Gwendolyn Brooks." <u>Contemporary Literature</u> 11.1 (Winter 1970): 1–20.

32. A Personal Letter

Tan, Amy. Letter to the author. 7 Apr. 1997.

33. A Letter Published in a Collection

Joyce, James. "Letter to Louis Gillet." 20 Aug. 1931. <u>James Joyce</u>. By Richard Ellmann. New York: Oxford UP, 1965. 631.

34. A Letter in a Library's Archives

Stieglitz, Alfred. Letter to Paul Rosenberg. 5 Sept. 1923. Stieglitz Archive. Yale Lib., New Haven.

35. A Film

<u>Citizen Kane</u>. Dir. Orson Welles. Perf. Orson Welles, Joseph Cotten, Dorothy Comingore, and Agnes Moorehead. RKO, 1941.

If you are focusing on the contribution of a particular person, begin with that person's name.

Welles, Orson, dir. <u>Citizen Kane</u>. . . .

36. A Videotape, DVD, or Laser Disk   Include the medium before the name of the distributor.

Miller, Arthur. Interview. <u>The Crucible</u>. Dir. William Schiff.
    Videocassette. The Mosaic Group, 1987.

37. A Radio or Television Program
"Prime Suspect 3." Writ. Lynda La Plante. Perf. Helen Mirren. <u>Mystery!</u>
    WNET, New York. 28 Apr. 1994.

38. A Recording
Boubill, Alain, and Claude-Michel Schönberg. <u>Miss Saigon</u>. Perf. Lea
    Salonga, Claire Moore, and Jonathan Pryce. Cond. Martin Koch.
    Geffen, 1989.

Marley, Bob. "Crisis." Lyrics. <u>Bob Marley and the Wailers</u>. Kava Island
    Records, 1978.

39. A Cartoon
Trudeau, Garry. "Doonesbury." Cartoon. <u>Philadelphia Inquirer</u> 19 July
    1999: E 13.

40. An Advertisement
Microsoft. Advertisement. <u>National Review</u> 28 June 1999: 11.

Sample MLA Works Cited Entries: Electronic Sources   The documentation style for electronic sources presented here conforms to the most recent guidelines published in the *MLA Handbook for Writers of Research Papers* (5th ed.) and found online at <http://mla.org>. (If your instructor prefers that you use Columbia Online Style for citing electronic sources, see p. 182.)

MLA style recognizes that full source information is not always available for electronic sources. Include in your citation whatever information you can reasonably obtain. MLA recommends that you include *both* the date of the electronic publication (if available) and the date you accessed the source. MLA also requires that you enclose the electronic address within angle brackets to distinguish the address from the punctuation in the rest of the citation. (If you have to carry an electronic address over to the next line, divide it after a slash or, if that is not possible, at a logical place—after a punctuation mark, for example.) Be sure to give the complete electronic address, including the **access mode identifier** (*http, ftp, gopher, telnet,* or *news*) and all appropriate path and file names.

41. A Scholarly Project or Information Database
<u>Philadelphia Writers Project</u>. Ed. Miriam Kotzen Green. May 1998.
    Drexel U. 12 June 2001 <http://www.Drexel.edu/letrs/wwp/>.

42. A Document within a Scholarly Project or Information Database
"D Day: June 7th, 1944." <u>The History Channel Online</u>. 1999. History
    Channel. 7 June 2002 <http://historychannel.com/thisday/
    today/997690.html>.

43. A Web Site or Home Page
Wilton, D. D. <u>Wilton's Etymology Page</u>. 15 June 1999
    <http://www.wilton.net/Etyma1.htm>.

Gainor, Charles. Home page. 22 July 1999 <http://
    www.chass.utoronto.ca:9094/~char/>.

44. On Online Book
Douglass, Frederick. <u>My Bondage and My Freedom</u>. Boston, 1855. 8
    June 2000 <gopher://gopher.vt.edu:10024/22/178/3>.

When you cite information from an online source that has a
print version, include the publication information for the
printed source, the number of pages or paragraphs (if available), and the date you accessed it.

45. An Article in an Online Scholarly Journal
Dekoven, Marianne. "Utopias Limited: Post-Sixties and Postmodern
    American Fiction." <u>Modern Fiction Studies</u> 41.1 (1995): 13 pp.
    17 Mar. 1999 <http://must.jhu.edu/journals/
    mfs.v041/41.1dwkovwn.html>.

46. An Article in an Online Newspaper
Lohr, Steve, "Microsoft Goes to Court." <u>New York Times on the Web</u>
    19 Oct. 1998. 29 Apr. 1999 <http://www.nytimes.com/web/
    docroot/library.ciber/week/1019business.html>.

47. An Article in an Online Newsletter
"Unprecedented Cutbacks in History of Science Funding." <u>AIP Center
    for History of Physics</u> 27.2 (Fall 1995). 26 Feb. 1996 <http://
    www.aip.org/history/fall95.html>.

48. An Article in an Online Magazine
Weister, Jay. "The Tyranny of Informality." <u>Time</u> 26 Feb. 1996. 1 Mar.
    2002 <http://www.enews.com/magazines.tnr/current/
    022696.3.html>.

49. A Review
Ebert, Roger. Rev. of <u>Star Wars: Episode 1—The Phantom Menance</u>,
    dir. George Lucas. <u>Chicago Sun-Times Online</u> 8 June 2000. 22
    June 2000 <http://www.suntimes.com/output/ebert1/
    08show.html>.

50. A Letter to the Editor

Chen-Cheng, Henry H. Letter. <u>New York Times on the Web</u> 19 July
1999. 19 July 1999 <http://www.nytimes.com/hr/mo/day/
letters/ichen-cheng.html>.

51. An Article in an Online Encyclopedia

"Hawthorne, Nathaniel." <u>Britannica Online</u>. Vers. 98.2. Apr. 1998.
Encyclopaedia Britannica. 16 May 2000 <http://www.eb.com/>.

52. Material from an Online Subscription Service

Online services can be divided into those you subscribe to,
such as America Online, and those that your college library subscribes to, such as InfoTrac, Lexis-Nexis, and ProQuest Direct.

If the service you are subscribing to provides a URL, follow
the examples in entries 41–51. If the subscription service enables you to use a keyword to access material, provide the keyword at the end of the entry.

"Kafka, Franz." <u>Compton's Encyclopedia Online</u>. Vers. 3.0. 2000.
America Online, 8 June 2001. Keyword: Compton's.

If, instead of using a keyword, you follow a series of topic labels, list them (separated by semicolons) after the word *Path.*

"Elizabeth Adams." History Resources. 11 Nov. 2001. America Online.
28 Apr. 2001. Path: Research; Biography; Women in Science;
Biographies.

To cite information from an online service to which your library subscribes, include the underlined name of the database
(if known), the name of the service, the library, the date of access, and the URL of the online service's home page.

Luckenbill, Trent. "Environmental Litigation: Down the Endless
Corridor." <u>Environment</u> 8 June 2001: 34–42. <u>ABI/INFORM
Global</u>. ProQuest Direct. Drexel U Lib., Philadelphia. 12 Oct.
2001 <http://www.umi.com/proquest/.>.

53. A Linked Site

If you get information from a linked site—that is, if you
connect from one site to another—include the title of the
document you cite (followed by its date) and the abbreviation
Lkd. (followed by the original site from which you accessed
your document). Follow this with the date of access and the
URL.

Harris, Robert. "Evaluating Information: Tests of Interpreting Quality."
17 Nov. 1997. Lkd. <u>The Holt Handbook</u>. 28 May 2002
<http://holthandbook.heinle.com/6e/student/resources/
computer/evalu8.html>.

54. A Nonperiodical Publication on DVD, CD-ROM, or Diskette

Cite a nonperiodical publication on DVD, CD-ROM, or diskette the same way you would cite a book, but also include a description of the medium of publication.

"Windhover." The Oxford English Dictionary. 2nd ed. DVD. Oxford:
   Oxford UP, 2001.

"Whitman, Walt." DiskLit: America Authors. CD-ROM. Boston: Hall,
   2000.

55. A Periodical Publication on a DVD or CD-ROM Database

Zurbach, Kate. "The Linguistic Roots of Three Terms." Linguistic
   Quarterly 37 (1994): 12–47. InfoTrac: Magazine Index Plus.
   CD-ROM. Information Access. Jan. 2001.

56. A Painting or Photograph

Lange, Dorothea. Looking at Pictures. 1936. Museum of Mod. Art,
   New York. 28 June 1999 <http://moma.org/exhibitions/
   lookingatphotographs/lang-fr.html>.

57. A Map

"Philadelphia, Pennsylvania." Map. U.S. Gazetteer. U.S. Census
   Bureau. 17 July 2000 <http://www.census.gov/cgi-
   bin/gazetteer>.

58. An E-Mail

Adkins, Camille. E-mail to the author. 28 June 2001.

59. An Online Posting

Gilford, Mary. "Dog Heroes in Children's Literature." Online posting.
   17 Mar. 1999. 12 Apr. 1999 <news: alt.animals.dogs>.

Schiller, Stephen. "Paper Cost and Publishing Costs." Online posting.
   24 Apr. 1999. 11 May 1999. Book Forum. 17 May 1999
   <www.nytimes.com/webin/webx?13A^41356.ee765e/0>.

60. A Synchronous Communication (MOO or MUD)

To cite a communication obtained on a MOO or a MUD, give the name (or names) of the writer(s), a description of the event, the date of the event, and the forum (LinguaMOO, for example), the date of access, and the URL (starting with *telnet://*).

Guitar, Gwen. Online discussion of Cathy in Emily Brontë's Wuthering
   Heights. 17 Mar. 1999. LinguaMOO. 17 Mar. 1999 <telnet://
   lingua.utdallas.edu:8888>.

COLUMBIA ONLINE STYLE

Columbia Online Style (COS) was developed to accommodate the wide variety of sources that are available in an electronic environment. For this reason, some instructors prefer their students to use COS style instead of MLA style when they document electronic sources. Remember that the MLA does not recognize COS, so be sure to check with your instructor before you use it.

Format
Author's Last Name, First Name. "Title of Document." *Title of Complete Work* [if applicable]. Version or File Number [if applicable]. Document date or date of last revision [if different from access date]. Protocol and address, access path or directories. Access date.

1. A World Wide Web Site
Sandy, Adam. "Roller Coaster History." *Coney Island History.* 2001. http://www.ultimaterollercoaster.com/coasters/history/history-coney.html (12 Nov. 2001).

2. An Online Journal Article
Dekoven, Marianne. "Utopias Unlimited: Post Sixties and Postmodern American Fiction." *Modern Fiction Studies.* 41:1(1995). http://muse.jhu.edu/journals/ mfs.v041/41.1dwkovwn.html (17 Mar. 1999).

3. An Online Magazine
Walker, Rob. "Is the Stock Market in Denial?" *Slate* 15 Nov. 2001. http://slate.msn.com/?id=2058732 (19 Nov. 2001).

4. An Online News Service or Online Newspaper
McGirk, Tim. "Deep Loyalties, Ancient Hatreds." *Time.com.* 12 Nov. 2001. http://www.time.com/time/magazine/article/0,9171, 1101011119-183964,00.html (19 Nov. 2001).

5. E-mail, Listservs, and Newsgroups
Goren, Seth. "Joke of the Week." Personal e-mail (14 Nov. 2001).

Friedlander, Sandy. "Computer Collaboration in the Writing Classroom." *Alliance for Computers and Writing Listserv.* acw-l@ unicorn.acs.ttu.edu (17 June 2000).

continued on the following page

continued from the previous page

Provizor, Norman. "Jazz in the 1990s." 2 Mar. 2000.
    alt.music.jazz. (5 Mar. 2000).

6. A Gopher Site

Douglass, Stephen. "Can Computers Think?" *Journal of
    Experimental and Artificial Intelligence* (1999).
    gopher://gopher.liv.ac.uk:80/00/phil/philos-12-
    files/searle.harnad (7 Aug. 2000).

7. An FTP Site

Johnson, Cassandra. "Cleaning Up Hypertext Links." 3 Dec.
    2000. ftp://ftp.daedalus.com/pub/ CCCC95/johnson (14
    Oct. 2001).

8. A Telnet Site

Rigg, Doreen. "Lesson Plan for Teaching about the Hubble
    Telescope." *Space News.* 11 Oct. 2000.
    telnet://spacelink.msfc.nasa.gov.guest (2 Dec. 2000).

9. A Synchronous Communication Site

Guitar, Gwen. "Update." *DaMOO.* telnet://damoo.csun.edu:
    7777 (4 Dec. 1996).

10. An Online Reference Source

Kevles, D. J. "Human Genome Project." *Columbia
    Encyclopedia.* 6th ed. NY: Columbia UP, 2001. America
    Online. Reference Desk/Encyclopedias/Columbia
    Encyclopedia (17 Nov. 2001).

11. Electronic Publications and Online Databases

Cinbac, James. "Wishing Won't Do It: Baby Boomers Save for
    Retirement." *Business Week* 1 Apr. 2000: 50. *InfoTrac
    SearchBank.* File #9606273898 (12 Aug. 2000).

12. Software Programs and Video Games

Mac Washer. Vers. 2.1. St. Louis: Webroot Software, 2000.

Abuse. Vers. 3.2. Chicago: Bungie Software Products, 1996.

(3) Content Notes

Content notes—multiple bibliographical citations or other
material that does not fit smoothly into the text—are indicated
by a **superscript** (raised numeral) in the paper. Notes can appear either as footnotes at the bottom of the page or as endnotes on a separate sheet entitled *Notes,* placed after the last
page of the paper and before the Works Cited list. Content notes
are double-spaced within and between entries.

For Multiple Citations
In the Paper

Many researchers emphasize the necessity of having dying patients share their experiences.[1]

In the Note

[1]Kübler-Ross 27; Stinnette 43; Poston 70; Cohen and Cohen 31–34; Burke 1:91–95.

For Other Material
In the Paper

The massacre during World War I is an event the survivors could not easily forget.[2]

In the Note

[2]For a firsthand account of these events, see Bedoukian 178–81.

31b MLA Manuscript Guidelines

Although MLA papers do not usually include abstracts, internal headings, tables, or graphs, this situation is changing. Be sure you know what your instructor expects.

The following guidelines are based on the latest version of the *MLA Handbook for Writers of Research Papers*.

☑ CHECKLIST: TYPING YOUR PAPER

(Use the paper on p. 188 as your model.)

✔ Type your paper with a one-inch margin at the top and bottom and on both sides. Double-space your paper throughout.

✔ Capitalize all important words in your title, but not prepositions, articles, coordinating conjunctions, or the *to* in infinitives (unless they begin or end the title or subtitle). Do not underline your title or enclose it in quotation marks. Never put a period after the title, even if it is a sentence. Double-space between the last line of your title and the first line of the paper.

✔ Indent the first line of every paragraph, as well as the first line of every item on the Works Cited list, five spaces (or one-half inch).

continued on the following page

continued from the previous page

✔ Set a long prose quotation (more than four lines) off from the text by indenting the whole quotation ten spaces (or one inch). If you quote a single paragraph or part of a paragraph, do not indent the first line. If you quote two or more paragraphs, indent the first line of each paragraph an additional quarter inch. (If the first sentence does not begin a paragraph, do not indent it. Indent the first line only in successive paragraphs.)

✔ Number all pages of your paper consecutively—including the first—in the upper right-hand corner, one-half inch from the top, flush right. Type your name before the page number on every page.

✔ If you use source material in your paper, follow **MLA documentation style**.

See 31a

✔ CHECKLIST: PREPARING THE MLA WORKS CITED LIST

✔ Begin the Works Cited list on a new page after the last page of text or **content notes**, numbered as the next page of the paper.

See 31a3

✔ Center the title *Works Cited* one inch from the top of the page. Double-space between the title and the first entry.

✔ Each entry on the Works Cited list has three divisions: author, title, and publication information. Separate divisions with a period and one space.

✔ List entries alphabetically, last name first. Use the author's full name as it appears on the title page. If a source has no listed author, alphabetize it by the first word of the title (not counting the article).

✔ Type the first line of each entry flush with the left-hand margin; indent subsequent lines five spaces (or one-half inch).

✔ Double-space within and between entries.

31c Sample MLA Research Paper

The following student paper, "The Great Digital Divide," uses MLA documentation style. It is preceded by a sentence outline and includes a Notes page and a Works Cited list.

MLA FORMAL OUTLINE

1 inch

½ inch

Romney i

Center

Outline

<u>Thesis Statement:</u> Although the Internet has changed our world for the better, it threatens to leave many people behind, creating two distinct classes—those who have access and those who do not.

I. The Internet was created in 1969 under the name ARPANET.

1 inch

A. ARPANET was designed to serve as America's communication system in case of nuclear attack.

B. It was expanded in 1972 into a system of interconnected networks.

C. In the 1980s, HTML was created to allow information on the Internet to be displayed graphically.

II. Today, many people believe the Internet has ushered in a new age.

A. Former Vice President Al Gore sees the Internet as an empowering tool.

B. Gore believes the Internet will bring knowledge and prosperity to the entire world.

III. For many people, however, the benefits of the Internet are not nearly this obvious or far-reaching.

A. The Internet is still out of reach for many Americans.

1. The elderly and the physically disabled are less likely than others to use the Internet.

2. Low-income and minority households are less likely than others to have computers.

B. People without Internet access have difficulties at school, trouble obtaining employment, and fewer opportunities to save money and time as consumers.

MLA FORMAL OUTLINE

C. Two groups that make up much of the "have-not" population are the physically disabled and the elderly.

1. For the physically disabled, the Internet could be highly beneficial, eliminating physical barriers to sources of entertainment, education, and employment.

2. Computer programmers often overlook the needs of the physically disabled when designing Web sites.

3. Although the Web offers the elderly opportunities to converse with family members and access health information, their physical and mental deficits often prevent them from using the Internet.

4. Content providers and engineers must consider the special needs of the elderly.

IV. Both government and nonprofit organizations are making efforts to bridge the gap between the "haves" and the "have-nots."

A. The federal government has launched programs like Neighborhood Networks to provide Internet access to impoverished communities.

B. Congress is making efforts to decrease the gap between the "haves" and the "have-nots."

C. Nonprofit organizations, such as PBS, are working to raise public awareness.

V. Despite these efforts, much still needs to be done.

A. We must examine the content available on the Internet, which often fails to reflect the needs of minorities, the elderly, and those with disabilities.

B. We must continue to provide training to people unfamiliar with new technology.

C. We must target the most likely "have-nots."

1 inch

$^1/_2$ inch

Romney 1

Double-space

Kimberly Larson Romney

Professor Wilson

English 102

20 April 2002

The Great Digital Divide

One of the most exciting digital technologies

1 inch

available is the information superhighway, or the Internet,

1 inch

which has dramatically changed the way we access and

see information. The Internet offers great promise, but it

has also created some serious problems. Although the

Thesis statement

Internet has changed our world for the better, it threatens

to leave many people behind, creating two distinct

classes—those who have access and those who do not.

Paragraph 2 presents background on history of the Internet, summarizing information from two sources.

The Internet was created in 1969 under the name

ARPANET (ARPA stood for Advanced Research Projects

Agency). Funded by the United States government, ARPA

was designed to serve as America's communication system

in case of a nuclear attack. The first ARPANET system

consisted of just four connected computers, but by 1972,

fifty universities and research facilities were linked (Gibbs

and Smith 5). Beginning in 1972, researchers increased

the number of computers that could be on ARPANET, and

this new system was given the name Internet. In the

1980s, a computer language called HTML (Hyper Text

Markup Language) was created to allow information on

the Internet to be displayed graphically. This advance gave

rise to the World Wide Web, which allowed users to

access text, graphics, sound, and even video while using

hyperlinks to move from one site to another (Wendall).

Today, many people believe the Internet has ushered

in a new age, one in which instant communication will

Romney 2

bring people closer together and eventually eliminate national boundaries. Former Vice President Al Gore, for example, sees the Internet as a means "to deepen and extend our oldest, and most cherished global values: rising standards of living and literacy, an ever-widening circle of democracy, freedom, and individual empowerment" (par. 4). Gore says that he can see the day when we will "extend our knowledge and our prosperity to our most isolated inner cities, to the barrios, the favelas, the colonias, and our most remote rural villages" (par. 32).

Despite the optimistic predictions of Gore and others, for many people, the benefits of the Internet are not nearly this obvious or far-reaching. In fact, the Internet remains out of reach for many Americans, creating what the NAACP and others have called a "digital divide" ("NAACP Targets Minority Gap"). Large percentages of the poor, the elderly, and the disabled, as well as members of many minority groups, are excluded from current technological advancements; thus, a gap exists between those who have access to this new technology and those who do not.

A recent survey by the Department of Commerce shows that some significant advances were made between 1998 and 2000 but that inequalities in computer ownership and Internet access continue to exist. The elderly and the physically disabled are two groups that still fall into the "have-not" category. For example, the Internet use rate for individuals 50 years of age and older is only about 30%. Further, people with a disability are half as likely to have access to the Internet as

Side annotations:

Parenthetical references cite paragraph numbers because electronic source does not include page numbers

Parenthetical documentation refers to an article accessed from the Internet.

MLA RESEARCH PAPER SAMPLE PAGE

Romney 3

those without a disability: 21.6% compared to 42.1% (<u>Falling through the Net</u>).

The Department of Commerce report reveals that although all households are more likely to have computers than they were in 1989, people with higher annual household incomes and whites remain more likely to own computers than minorities and people from low-income households. Approximately 70% of households with an income of $75,000 or above have computers, compared to 19% of households earning less than $15,000. The survey also found that only 33% of African-American and 34% of Hispanic households have computers, whereas 56% of white households have computers. This disparity exists even at household incomes lower than $15,000. According to a <u>New York Times</u> article, "at the lowest income levels, the gap is great—a child in a low-income white family is three times as likely to have Internet access as a child in a low-income black family" (Belluck).

Paragraph synthesizes information from a Department of Commerce study and a newspaper article

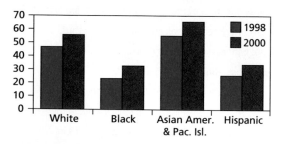

Fig. 1. Percent of U.S. Households with a Computer by Income by Race/Hispanic Origin, 1998 and 2000. United States Dept. of Commerce and Natl. Telecommunications and Information Admin., <u>Falling through the Net: Toward Digital Inclusion</u>, Dec. 2000 <http://www.ntia. doc.gov/ntiahome/ fttn00/chartI-13.htm#f13>.

Source information is typed directly below the figure.

MLA RESEARCH PAPER SAMPLE PAGE

Romney 4

Although the Commerce Department study indicates that financial circumstances, age, race, and physical disabilities contribute to the "digital divide," the gap in computer ownership across incomes suggests that other factors may also contribute to the disparity. As Henry Louis Gates, Jr., argues, bridging this gap will "require more than cheap PC's, it will involve content." African Americans are not interested in the Internet, Gates writes, because the content rarely appeals to them. He compares the lack of interest in the Internet with the history of African-Americans' relationship with the recording industry: "Blacks began to respond to this new medium only when mainstream companies like Columbia Records introduced so-called race records, blues and jazz discs aimed at a nascent African-American market." Gates believes that Web sites that address the needs of African Americans can play the same role that "race records" did for the music industry. Ignoring the problem, he warns, will lead to a form of cyber-segregation that will devastate the African-American community.[1]

Regardless of the causes of the "digital divide," it is clear that those without Internet access are at a disadvantage. They have difficulty at school, trouble obtaining employment, and fewer opportunities to save time and money as consumers. Those to whom the Internet is not available are denied access to special airline discounts, savings on long-distance carriers, and lower prices on computer software. More importantly, they lack access to educational and research materials and to jobs posted on the Web. With access to only a portion of available goods and services, people who are offline do

Summary of newspaper op-ed piece includes two quotations. Because author is mentioned in identifying tag, no parenthetical documentation is needed.

Superscript identifies content note.

MLA RESEARCH PAPER SAMPLE PAGE

Romney 5

not have the advantages that people who are online can routinely get.

1 inch ⟵⟶

> Their choices will be restricted, and they're going to pay a little bit more for things and they'll have fewer options [...] and it's not going to be one of these things where you see the digital homeless on the street, or sleeping on the steps of City Hall. It's going to be an invisible problem. The people who are digitally dispossessed may not even appreciate that they are dispossessed. (Belluck)

Clearly, the Internet is widening the economic and social divide that already separates people in this country.

Two groups that make up much of the "have-not" population are the physically disabled and the elderly. Both are less likely than others to have access to the Internet and therefore suffer some of the greatest consequences. For the physically disabled, the Internet could be highly beneficial, actually eliminating physical barriers to sources of entertainment, education, and employment. Ironically, however, attitudinal barriers may lead educators, employers, and even family members to dismiss a physically disabled person's ability to use a computer and the Internet. Furthermore, computer programmers often forget to consider the needs of the physically disabled when designing Web sites (Lester). Sadly, those who might gain the most from this technology are overlooked by those who control access.

Similarly, the elderly, who might also benefit greatly from services that the Internet can provide, are often overlooked as potential users of new technology. According to Jennifer O'Neill, speakers at the "Older

Romney 6

Adults, Health Information, and the World Wide Web" conference at the National Institutes of Health noted that even if they want to use the Internet, many elderly Americans have difficulty doing so. Although the Web offers the elderly opportunities to converse with family members and access health information, their physical and mental deficits may prevent them from using the Internet: "Seniors often have difficulty navigating the Web, finding information, and sometimes even remembering the object of their search" (O'Neill). Unless content providers and engineers consider their special needs, the elderly will continue be "have-nots."

Both public and private sectors recognize the potential danger of the "digital divide" and are taking steps to narrow the gap. For example, the federal government is sponsoring several programs aimed at those groups who are in danger of becoming "have-nots." One such effort is Neighborhood Networks, a program sponsored by the U.S. Department of Housing and Urban Development (HUD) that works to provide computer-training centers to people living in homes that are assisted or insured by HUD ("About Neighborhood Networks").

Congress, too, is targeting the gap between the "haves" and the "have-nots." In the Telecommunications Act of 1996, the Federal Communications Commission was directed to "set rules requiring telephone and cable television companies to provide universal access to new services like the Internet" (Lohr). Legislators hope this language will encourage regulators to "mandate access and cut-rate service for schools and public libraries" (Lohr).[2]

Exact wording of a piece of key legislation is used to eliminate any possibility of misinterpretation. Each quotation requires its own parenthetical documentation, even though both cite the same source.

193

MLA RESEARCH PAPER SAMPLE PAGE

Romney 7

Nonprofit organizations are also entering the war to close the "digital divide." In an effort to raise public awareness, the Public Broadcasting Corporation (PBS) created a series called <u>Digital Divide</u> to examine race and gender gaps in technology in the classroom and at work. According to "Virtual Diversity," one program in this series, both the dynamic of a co-ed classroom and the lack of appealing content make technology seem inaccessible to women and minorities. Only by changing the way classes are conducted and by including content that is interesting to women and minorities can technology and the Internet be made accessible to these populations.

Conclusion recommends solutions for problem of "digital divide." Because no new material is introduced (the paragraph presents the student's original conclusions), no documentation is needed.

Despite the efforts of government and nonprofit organizations, as well as many businesses, much still needs to be done to ensure that everyone has access to the Internet. First, we must examine the content available on the Internet, which often fails to reflect the needs of minorities, the elderly, and those with disabilities. We must also continue to provide training to people unfamiliar with new technology, and we must ensure that the instructors who are teaching these new technology skills understand the equipment and software they are explaining. Finally, we must target the most likely "have-nots": the poor, minorities, the elderly, the disabled, and girls and young women. Unless we take steps to make the Internet available to all, we will quickly become two separate and unequal societies, one "plugged-in" and privileged and one "unplugged" and marginalized.

MLA CONTENT NOTES PAGE

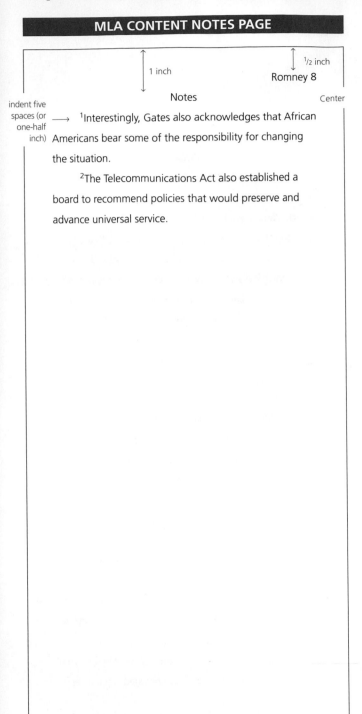

1 inch

½ inch

Romney 8

Center

Notes

indent five
spaces (or
one-half
inch)

⟶ ¹Interestingly, Gates also acknowledges that African
Americans bear some of the responsibility for changing
the situation.

²The Telecommunications Act also established a
board to recommend policies that would preserve and
advance universal service.

MLA WORKS CITED LIST

Works Cited

center

indent five spaces (or ¹/₂ inch) →

"About Neighborhood Networks." Neighborhood

Networks. 3 May 2000. 26 June 2000

<http://www.digitaldividenetwork.org/frameset.adp

?url=http%3a%2f%2fwww%2ehud%2egov%2fn

nw%2fnwindex%2ehtml>.

Belluck, Pam. "What Price Will Be Paid by Those Not on

the Net?" <u>New York Times on the Web</u> 22 Sept.

1999. 26 July 2000 <http://search3.nytimes.com/

search/daily/binfastweb?getdoc+site+site+124947+

32+wAA+What%7Eprice%Ewukk%7Ebe%7ePaid

%7Eby%7Ethose%7Enot%7Eon%7Ethe%7Enet>.

Long URLs should be broken after a slash. If this is not possible, break at a logical point—for example after a punctuation mark.

Gates, Henry Louis, Jr. "One Internet, Two Nations." <u>New</u>

<u>York Times</u> 31 Oct. 1999, late ed.: A25.

Gibbs, Mark, and Richard Smith. <u>Navigating the Internet</u>.

Indianapolis: SAMS, 1993.

Gore, Al. "Building a Global Community." Remarks

Prepared for the 15th International ITU Conference.

12 Oct. 1998. 69 pars. 5 July 2000 <http://

www.itu.int/Newsarchive/press/PP98/

Documents/Statement_Gore.html>.

Lester, Mary. "The Internet and People with Disabilities."

<u>Digital Divide Network</u>. 2002. 5 Mar. 2002.

<http://www.digitaldividenetwork.org/content/

sections/index.cfm>.

Lohr, Steve. "The Great Unplugged Masses Confront the

Future." *New York Times on the Web* 21 Apr. 1996.

26 July 2000 <http://search3.nytimes.com/

search/daily/bin/fastweb?getdoc+site+site+29519+0

+wAA+The%7Egreat%7Eunplugged%7Emasses.>

MLA 31c

MLA WORKS CITED LIST

"NAACP Targets Minority Gap in Internet Use, TV Roles."
    <u>CNN.Com</u> 13 July 1999. 3 July 2000 <http://
    www.cnn.com/US/9907/13/naacp.gap/>.

O'Neill, Jennifer. "Limited Mobility Doesn't Stop Senior
    Surfers." <u>CNN.Com</u> 5 Mar. 2001. 17 Dec. 2001
    <http://www.cnn.com/2001/TECH/internet/03/05/
    senior.surfers.idg/index.html>.

United States. Dept. of Commerce and Natl.
    Telecommunications and Information Admin.
    <u>Falling through the Net: Toward Digital Inclusion</u>.
    Dec. 2000 <http://www.ntia.doc.gov/ntiahome>.

"Virtual Diversity." <u>Digital Divide</u>. 1 Apr. 2000. 24 June
    2000 <http://www.pbs.org/digitaldivide/
    about.about.htm#series>.

Wendall, Kyla. "Internet History." University of Regina
    Student Connection Program. 18 Aug. 1997. 27
    June 2000 <http://tdi.uregina.ca/~ursc/internet/
    history.html>.

Entries for Electronic Sources

CHAPTER 32

APA DOCUMENTATION STYLE

32a Using APA Style

APA* style is used extensively in the social sciences. APA documentation has three parts: *parenthetical references in the body of the paper*, a *reference list*, and optional *content footnotes*.

(1) Parenthetical References

APA documentation uses short parenthetical references in the body of the paper keyed to an alphabetical list of references that follows the paper. A typical parenthetical reference consists of the author's last name (followed by a comma) and the year of publication.

Many people exhibit symptoms of depression after the death of a pet (Russo, 2000).

If the author's name appears in the introductory phrase, include the year of publication there as well.

According to Russo (2000), many people exhibit symptoms of depression after the death of a pet.

When you are using material from a source, the author's name and the date may appear either in the introductory phrase or in parentheses at the end of the paraphrase or summary.

According to Zinn (1995), this program has had success in training teenage fathers to take financial and emotional responsibility for their offspring.

This program has had success in training teenage fathers to take financial and emotional responsibility for their offspring (Zinn, 1995).

When quoting directly, include the page number in parentheses after the quotation.

According to Weston (1996), children from one-parent homes read at "a significantly lower level than those from two-parent homes" (p. 58).

---

*APA documentation format follows the guidelines set in the *Publication Manual of the American Psychological Association*, 5th ed. Washington, DC: APA, 2001.

Long quotations (forty words or more) are double-spaced and indented five spaces from the left margin. Parenthetical documentation is placed after the final punctuation.

Sample APA Parenthetical References

1. A Work by a Single Author
Many college students suffer from sleep deprivation (Anton, 1999).

2. A Work by Two Authors
There is growing concern over the use of psychological testing in elementary schools (Albright & Glennon, 1982).

3. A Work by Three to Five Authors   If a work has more than two but fewer than six authors, mention all names in the first reference; in subsequent references in that same paragraph, cite the first author followed by *et al.* Add the year when the reference appears in later paragraphs.
   First Reference
(Sparks, Wilson, & Hewitt, 2001).
   Subsequent Reference in Same Paragraph
(Sparks et al.).
   First Reference in Later Paragraphs
(Sparks et al., 2001).

4. A Work by Six or More Authors   When a work has six or more authors, cite the name of the first author followed by *et al.* and the year in all references.
(Miller et al., 1995).

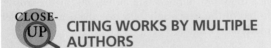

CLOSE-UP CITING WORKS BY MULTIPLE AUTHORS

When referring to multiple authors in the text of your paper, join the last two names with *and.*

According to Rosen, Wolfe, and Ziff (1988). . . .

In parenthetical documentation, however, use an ampersand.

(Rosen, Wolfe, & Ziff, 1988).

5. A Work by a Corporate Author   If the name of a corporate author is long, abbreviate it after the first citation.
   First Reference
(National Institute of Mental Health [NIMH], 2001)
   Subsequent Reference
(NIMH, 2001)

6. A Work with No Listed Author If a work has no listed author, cite the first two or three words of the title (capitalized) and the year.

("New Immigration," 2000).

NOTE: Use quotation marks around titles of articles or chapters; use italics for titles of periodicals, books, brochures, and reports.

7. A Personal Communication
(R. Takaki, personal communication, October 17, 2001).

NOTE: Cite letters, memos, telephone conversations, personal interviews, e-mail, messages from electronic bulletin boards, and the like only in the text—*not* in the reference list.

8. An Indirect Source
Cogan and Howe offer very different interpretations of the problem (as cited in Swenson, 1999).

9. A Specific Part of a Source Use abbreviations for the words *page* (p.), *chapter* (chap.), and *section* (sec.).

These theories have an interesting history (Lee, 1966, chap. 2).

10. An Electronic Source For an electronic source that does not show page numbers, use the paragraph number preceded by a ¶ symbol or by the abbreviation *para.*

Conversation at the dinner table is an example of a family ritual (Kulp, 2001, ¶ 3).

For an electronic source that does not show either page numbers or paragraph numbers, cite a heading in the source and the number of the paragraph following the heading under which the material is located.

Healthy growing is a never-ending series of free choices (Shapiro, 2001, Introduction section, para. 1).

11. Two or More Works within the Same Parenthetical Reference List works by different authors—separated by semicolons—in alphabetical order.

This theory is supported by several studies (Barson & Roth, 1985; Rose, 1987; Tedesco, 1982).

List works by the same author or authors in order of date of publication, with the earliest date first.

This theory is supported by several studies (Weiss & Elliot, 1982, 1984, 1985).

For works by the same author published in the same year, designate the work whose title comes first alphabetically *a*, the one whose title comes next *b*, and so on; repeat the year in each citation.

This theory is supported by several studies (Hossack, 1995a, 1995b).

12. A Table If you use a table from a source, give credit to the author in a note at the bottom of the table. This information is not included in the reference list.

Note. From "Predictors of Employment and Earnings Among JOBS Participants," by P. A. Neenan and D. K. Orthner, 1996, *Social Work Research, 20*(4), p. 233.

(2) Reference List

The **reference list** gives the publication information for all the sources you cite. It should appear at the end of your paper on a new numbered page entitled *References* (or *Bibliography* if you are listing all the works you consulted, whether or not you cited them in your paper).

Sample APA Reference List Entries: Books Book citations include the author's name; the year of publication (in parentheses); the book title (italicized); and publication information. Capitalize only the first word of the title and subtitle and any proper nouns. Include additional information necessary for retrieval—edition, report number, or volume number, for example—in parentheses after the title.

1. A Book with One Author Use a short form of the publisher's name. Write out the names of associations, corporations, and university presses. Include the words *Book* and *Press*, but do not include terms such as *Publishers, Co.,* and *Inc.*

Maslow, A. H. (1974). *Toward a psychology of being.* Princeton: Van Nostrand.

2. A Book with More Than One Author List all the authors—by last name and initials—regardless of how many there are.

Wolfinger, D., Knable, P., Richards, H. L., & Silberger, R. (1990). *The chronically unemployed.* New York: Berman Press.

3. An Edited Book
Lewin, K., Lippitt, R., & White, R. K. (Eds.). (1985). *Social learning and imitation.* New York: Basic Books.

4. A Book with No Listed Author or Editor
Writing with a computer (4th ed.). (2000). Philadelphia: Drexel Publications.

5. A Work in Several Volumes
Jones, P. R., & Williams, T. C. (Eds.). (1990–1993). *Handbook of therapy* (Vols. 1–2). Princeton: Princeton University Press.

6. A Work with a Corporate Author
League of Women Voters of the United States. (2001). *Local league handbook.* Washington, DC: Author.

NOTE: When the author and publisher are the same, list *Author* at the end of the citation instead of repeating the publisher's name.

7. A Government Report

National Institute of Mental Health. (1987). *Motion pictures and violence: A summary report of research* (DHHS Publication No. ADM 91-22187). Washington, DC: U.S. Government Printing Office.

8. One Selection from an Anthology

A title of a selection in an anthology is not underlined or enclosed in quotation marks. Give inclusive page numbers preceded by *pp.* (in parentheses) after the title of the anthology.

Lorde, A. (1984). Age, race, and class. In P. S. Rothenberg (Ed.), *Racism and sexism: An integrated study* (*pp.* 352–360). New York: St. Martin's.

NOTE: If you cite two or more selections from the same anthology, give the full citation for the anthology in each entry.

9. An Article in a Reference Book

Edwards, P. (1987). Determinism. In *The encyclopedia of philosophy* (Vol. 2, pp. 359–373). New York: Macmillan.

10. The Foreword, Preface, or Afterword of a Book

Taylor, T. (1979). Preface. In B. B. Ferencz, *Less than slaves* (pp. ii–ix). Cambridge: Harvard University Press.

Sample APA Reference List Entries: Articles Article citations include the author's name; the date of publication (in parentheses); the title of the article; the title of the periodical (italicized); the volume number (italicized); the issue number (if any), in parentheses; and the inclusive page numbers. Capitalize only the first word of the article's title and subtitle. Do not underline or italicize the title of the article or enclose it in quotation marks. Give the periodical title in full, and capitalize all major words. Use *p.* or *pp.* when referring to page numbers in newspapers, but omit this abbreviation when referring to page numbers in journals and popular magazines.

11. An Article in a Scholarly Journal with Continuous Pagination through an Annual Volume

Miller, W. (1969). Violent crimes in city gangs. *Journal of Social Issues 27,* 581–593.

12. An Article in a Scholarly Journal with Separate Pagination in Each Issue

Williams, S., & Cohen, L. R. (1984). Child stress in early learning situations. *American Psychologist, 21*(10), 1–28.

13. A Magazine Article

McCurdy, H. G. (1983, June). Brain mechanisms and intelligence. *Psychology Today, 46,* 61–63.

14. A Newspaper Article

James, W. R. (1993, November 16). The uninsured and health care.
     Wall Street Journal, pp. A1, A14.

NOTE: If an article appears on two non-consecutive pages, give all the page numbers separated by commas—for example, A1, A17.

15. A Personal Letter References to personal letters, like other references to personal communications, should be included only in the text of the paper, not in the reference list.

16. A Letter to the Editor

Williams, P. (2000, July 19). Self-fulfilling stereotypes [Letter to the
     editor]. *Los Angeles Times,* p. A22.

17. A Published Letter

Joyce, J. (1931). Letter to Louis Gillet. In Richard Ellmann, *James Joyce*
     (p. 631). New York: Oxford University Press.

Sample APA Reference List Entries: Electronic Sources APA guidelines for documenting electronic sources focus on Web sources, which often do not contain all the bibliographic information that print sources do. For example, Web sources may not contain page numbers or a place of publication. At a minimum, a Web citation should have a title, a date (the date of publication, update, or retrieval), and an electronic address (URL). If possible, also include the author(s) of a source. When you need to break the URL at the end of a line, break it after a slash or a period (do not add a hyphen). Do not add a period at the end of the URL.

18. An Internet Article Based on a Print Source

Winston, E. L. (2000). The role of art therapy in treating chronically
     depressed patients [Electronic version]. *Journal of Bibliographic
     Research, 5,* 54–72. Retrieved September 15, 2001, from
     http://jbr.org/articles.html

NOTE: If you have seen the article only in electronic form, include the phrase *Electronic version* in brackets after the title.

19. An Article in an Internet-Only Journal

Hornaday, J. A., & Bunker, C. S. (2001). The nature of the entrepreneur.
     Personal Psychology, 23, Article 2353b. Retrieved November 21,
     2001, from http://jjournals.apa.org/personal/ volume23/
     pre002353b.html

20. An Abstract

Guinot, A., & Peterson, B. R. (1995). *Forgetfulness and partial
     cognition* (Drexel University Cognitive Research Report No. 21).
     Abstract retrieved December 4, 2001, from http://www.Drexel.
     edu/~guinot/deltarule-abstract.html

21. An E-Mail As with all personal communication, references to e-mail sent from one person to another should be included only in the text, not in the reference list.

22. A Message Posted to a Newsgroup List the author's full name or, if that is not available, the screen name. Provide, in brackets after the title, information that will help readers access the message.

Shapiro, R. (2001, April 4). Chat rooms and interpersonal communication [Msg 7]. Message posted to news://sci.psychology. communication

23. A Daily Newspaper

Farrell, P. D. (1997, March 23). New high-tech stresses hit traders and investors on the information superhighway. *Wall Street Journal.* Retrieved April 4, 1999, from http://wall-street-news.com/ forecasts/stress/stress.html

24. A Searchable Database

Nowroozi, C. (1992). What you lose when you miss sleep. *Nation's Business, 80*(9), 73–77. Retrieved April 22, 2001, from Expanded Academic ASAP database.

25. Computer Software

Sharp, S. (1995). Career Selection Tests (Version 5.0) [Computer software]. Chico, CA: Avocation Software.

(3) Content Notes

APA format permits content notes, indicated by **superscripts** (raised numerals) in the text. The notes are listed on a separate numbered page, entitled *Footnotes,* following the last page of text. Double-space all notes, indenting the first line of each note five to seven spaces and beginning subsequent lines flush left. Number the notes so they correspond to the numbers in your text.

32b APA Manuscript Guidelines

Social science papers include internal headings (for example, *Introduction, Methods, Results, Background of Problem, Description of Problem, Solutions,* and *Conclusions*). Each section of a social science paper is a complete unit with a beginning and an end so that it can be read separately, out of context, and still make sense. The body of the paper may include and discuss charts, graphs, maps, photographs, flowcharts, or tables.

The following guidelines are based on the latest version of the *Publication Manual of the American Psychological Association.*

✔ CHECKLIST: TYPING YOUR PAPER

✔ Leave a one-inch margin at the top and bottom and on both sides.

✔ Double-space your paper throughout.

✔ Indent the first line of every paragraph, and the first line of every footnote, five to seven spaces (or 1/2 inch) from the left-hand margin. Set off a long quotation of more than forty words in a block format by indenting the entire quotation five to seven spaces (or 1/2 inch) from the left-hand margin.

✔ Number all pages consecutively. Each page should include a **page header** (an abbreviated title) and a page number 1/2 inch from the top and one inch from the right-hand edge of the page. Leave a 1/2 inch space between the page header and the page number.

✔ Center and type major **headings** with upper-case and lower-case letters. Place minor headings flush left, typed with upper-case and lower-case letters and italicized.
See 34a

✔ Format items in a series as a numbered **list**.
See 34a

✔ Arrange the pages of the paper in the following order:
  - Title page (page 1) that includes a page header, running head, title, and byline (your name)
  - Abstract (page 2)
  - Text of paper (beginning on page 3)
  - Reference List (new page)
  - Appendixes (start each on a new page)
  - Footnotes (new page)
  - Tables (start each on a new page)
  - List of captions for figures (new page)
  - Figures (start each on a new page)

✔ Number all tables consecutively, and refer to them by numbers in the text (for example, See Table 4). Tables should be placed on separate pages at the end of the paper. Each table should have a brief explanatory title. Type the word *Table* along with an Arabic numeral flush left above the table (for example, Table 7).

continued on the following page

continued from the previous page

✔ Double-space and type the title of each table (in italics) flush left. Capitalize the first letters of principal words of the title (for example, *Frequency of Negative Responses of Dorm Students to Questions Concerning Alcohol Consumption*).

✔ Number all figures consecutively, and refer to them by numbers in the text (for example, See Figure 1). Figures should be placed on separate pages at the end of the paper. In addition to a number, each figure should have a caption that explains the figure and that serves as a title. Do not include the captions with the figures themselves. Instead, list captions for all the figures together on a separate page.

✔ Type the word *Figure* followed by the number (in italics). Then, type the caption (not italicized). (For example, *Figure 1*. Duration of responses measured in seconds).

See 32a

✔ If you use source material in your paper, citations should be consistent with **APA documentation style**.

✔ CHECKLIST: PREPARING THE APA REFERENCE LIST

✔ Begin the reference list on a new page after the last page of text or content notes, numbered as the next page of the paper.

✔ Center the title *References* at the top of the page.

✔ List the items on the reference list alphabetically (with author's last name first).

✔ Type the first line of each entry at the left-hand margin. Indent subsequent lines five to seven spaces (or 1/2 inch).

✔ Separate the major divisions of each entry with a period and one space.

✔ Double-space the reference list within and between entries.

☑ CHECKLIST: ARRANGING WORKS IN THE APA REFERENCE LIST

✔ Single-author entries precede multiple-author entries that begin with the same name.

Field, S. (1987).

Field, S., & Levitt, M. P. (1984).

✔ Entries by the same author or authors are arranged according to date of publication, starting with the earliest date.

Ruthenberg, H., & Rubin, R. (1985).

Ruthenberg, H., & Rubin, R. (1987).

✔ Entries with the same author or authors and date of publication are arranged alphabetically according to the title. Lower-case letters (*a, b, c,* and so on) are placed within parentheses.

Wolk, E. M. (1996a). Analysis. . . .

Wolk, E. M. (1996b). Hormonal. . . .

32c Sample APA Research Paper

The following student paper, "Sleep Deprivation in College Students," uses APA documentation style. It includes a title page, an abstract, a list of references, and two tables.

APA TITLE PAGE

Sleep Deprivation 1

Page header, page number

Type running head flush with left-hand margin.

Running head: SLEEP DEPRIVATION

Sleep Deprivation in

College Students

Andrew J. Neale

Dr. Reiss

May 6, 2002

Title

Byline

APA ABSTRACT

Center   Abstract

Page header and number on every page

The present study examined the extent to which sleep deprivation affects college students' scholastic performance. A survey of 50 first-year college students in an Introduction to Biology class was conducted. The survey consisted of five questions regarding the causes and results of sleep deprivation and specifically addressed the students' study methods and the grades they received on the fall midterm. The study's hypothesis was that although students believe that forgoing sleep to study will yield better grades, sleep deprivation actually causes a decrease in scholastic performance. In support of this hypothesis, 70% of the students who received either an A or a B on the fall midterm did not deprive themselves of sleep in order to cram for the test.

Abstract typed as a single paragraph in block format

APA RESEARCH PAPER SAMPLE PAGE

Sleep Deprivation 3

Sleep Deprivation and
College Students

Full title (centered) ⟶

For many college students, sleep is a luxury that they

feel they cannot afford. Bombarded with tests and   *Introduction*

assignments and limited by a 24-hour day, students often

attempt to make up time by forgoing sleep. Ironically,

students may actually impair their scholastic performance

by failing to get adequate sleep. According to several

psychological and medical studies, sleep deprivation can

lead to memory loss and health problems, both of which

are more likely to harm a student's academic performance

than to help it.

Internal heading ⟶   Background

*Literature
review
(para-
graphs
2-6)*

Sleep is often overlooked as an essential component

of a healthy lifestyle. More than 75% of Americans

"wake up regularly to alarms, and almost as many sleep

more than an hour or two longer on weekends than on

weekdays" (Nowroozi, 1992, p. 74). Both of these

behaviors are results of sleep deprivation, indicating that

*Author's
name and
year of
publi-
cation are
placed in a
paren-
thetical
reference
when not
mentioned
in the text.
Note that
the
quotation
requires
separate
document
ation and
a page
number.*

for most people, sleep is viewed as a luxury rather than a

necessity (Nowroozi, 1992). This is particularly true for

college students, many of whom are required to

memorize a great deal of material before their exams.

Students believe that if they read and review immediately

before the test—even though this invariably means losing

sleep—they will remember more information and thus

get better grades. However, this is not true.

In fact, according to Dr. Charles Pollak, head of the

sleep-disorder center at Cornell University's New York

Hospital in Westchester County, "people who don't get

enough sleep can't think, they can't make appropriate

APA RESEARCH PAPER SAMPLE PAGE

judgments, and they can't maintain long attention spans"
(as cited in Toufexis, 1990, p. 80). Thus, students who
choose studying over sleep might actually be limiting their
ability to perform well.

Clearly, sleep deprivation harms, rather than
improves, academic performance. A study conducted by
professors Mary Carskadon at Brown University in
Providence, Rhode Island, and Amy Wolfson at the
College of the Holy Cross in Worcester, Massachusetts,
showed that high school students who get adequate
sleep were more likely to do well in their classes
(Carpenter, 2001). According to their study of the
correlation between grades and sleep, students who went
to bed earlier on both weeknights and weekends earned
mainly A's and B's. The students who received D's and F's
averaged about 35 minutes less sleep per day than the
high achievers (as cited in Carpenter, 2001). Apparently,
then, sleep is essential to high academic achievement.

Once students reach college, however, sleep
becomes expendable. For example, students believe that
if they use the time they would normally sleep to study,
they will do better on exams. A recent survey of 144
undergraduate students in introductory psychology
classes contradicted this assumption. According to this
study, long sleepers, or those individuals who slept 9 or
more hours out of a 24-hour day, had significantly higher
grade point averages (GPAs) than short sleepers, or
individuals who slept less than 7 hours out of a 24-hour
day. Thus, contrary to the belief of many college students,
more sleep is often required to achieve a high GPA (Kelly,
Kelly, & Clanton, 2001).

> Student uses past tense when discussing other researchers' work.

APA RESEARCH PAPER SAMPLE PAGE

Many students believe that they will be able to remember more material if they do not sleep at all before an exam. They fear that sleeping will interfere with their ability to retain information. A study of the cognitive abilities of 44 college students, however, showed that sleep deprivation actually impaired learning skills (Pilcher & Walters, 1997). College students were either deprived of 24 hours of sleep or allowed to sleep 8 hours before taking the Watson-Glaser Critical Thinking Appraisal, a test that measures critical thinking skills. The participants were then asked to complete two questionnaires about the test, one assessing their effort, concentration, and estimated performance, the other assessing their off-task cognitions. According to the researchers, "sleep-deprived participants performed significantly worse than the nondeprived participants on the cognitive task" (Pilcher & Walters,1997, p.123). Surprisingly, "the sleep-deprived participants rated their concentration and effort higher than the nondeprived participants did" (Pilcher & Walters, 1997, p. 124). Thus, this study confirms that sleep deprivation actually harms cognitive performance, while simultaneously explaining that students nevertheless continue to believe that the less sleep they get, the better they will do.

A survey of students in an Introduction to Biology class at the University of Texas demonstrated the effects of sleep deprivation on scholastic performance and supported the hypothesis that despite students' beliefs, forgoing sleep does not lead to better test scores.

Student uses past tense when discussing the results of his own survey.

Methods

To ascertain the causes and results of sleep deprivation, a study of the relationship between sleep and

APA RESEARCH PAPER SAMPLE PAGE

Sleep Deprivation 6

test performance was conducted. A survey of 50 first-year college students in an Introduction to Biology class and their performance on the fall midterm was competed and analyzed.

Each student was asked to complete a survey composed of the following five questions about their sleep patterns and their performance on the fall midterm.

1. Did you deprive yourself of sleep when studying for the fall midterm?
2. Do you regularly deprive yourself of sleep when studying for an exam?
3. What was your grade on the exam?
4. Do you feel that your performance was improved or harmed by the amount of sleep you had?
5. Will you deprive yourself of sleep when you study for the final exam?

Lists are indented 1/2 inch from left margin.

To encourage honest responses, the students were not asked to put their names on the survey. Also, to determine whether the students answered question 3 accurately, their responses were compared to the grades the professor gave for the class. The grade distribution on the surveys corresponded to the numbers of A's, B's, C's, and D's given on the test.

Results

Analysis of the results of the survey indicates a significant difference between the grades of students who were sleep-deprived and the grades of those who were not. The results of the survey are presented in Table 1. The results of the survey are shown as percentages of the class in Table 2.

Tables discussed here are placed at end of the paper.

Sleep Deprivation 7

The grades in the class were curved so that out of 50 students, 10 received A's, 20 received B's, 10 received C's, and 10 received D's. For the purposes of this survey, an A or B on the exam indicates that the student performed well. A grade of C or D on the exam is considered a poor grade.

Statistical findings reported

Of the 50 students in the class, 31 (or 62%) said that they deprived themselves of sleep when studying for the fall midterm. Of these students, 17 (or 34%) of the class answered yes to the second question, admitting that they regularly deprive themselves of sleep before an exam.

Of the 31 students who said they deprived themselves of sleep when studying for the fall midterm, only 4 earned A's, and the majority of the A's in the class were received by those students who were not sleep-deprived. Even more significant was the fact that of the 4 students who were sleep-deprived and got A's, only one student claimed usually to be sleep-deprived on the day of an exam. Thus assuming that the students who earn A's in a class do well in general, it is possible that sleep deprivation did not help or harm these students' grades. Not surprisingly, of the 4 students who received A's and were sleep-deprived, all said they would continue to use sleep deprivation to enable them to study for longer hours.

The majority of those who used sleep deprivation in an effort to obtain a higher grade received B's and C's on the exam. A total of 20 students earned a grade of B on the exam. Of those students, only 9, or 18% of the class, said that they were deprived of sleep when they took the test.

APA RESEARCH PAPER SAMPLE PAGE

Students who said that they were sleep-deprived when they took the exam received the majority of the poor grades. Ten students got C's on the midterm, and of these 10 students, 100% said that they were sleep-deprived when they took their test. Of the 10 students (20% of the class) who got D's, 8 said they were sleep-deprived. Thus, a significant correlation between poor grades on the exam and sleep deprivation was found.

Conclusions

For many students, sleep is viewed as a luxury rather than a necessity. Particularly during the exam period, students use the hours in which they would normally sleep to study. However, this method does not seem to be effective. The survey discussed above reveals a clear correlation between sleep deprivation and lower exam scores. In fact, the majority of students who performed well on the exam, earning either an A or a B, were not deprived of sleep. Therefore, students who choose studying over sleep should rethink their approach and consider that sleep deprivation may actually impair academic performance.

Sleep Deprivation 9

References

Carpenter, S. (2001). Sleep deprivation may be undermining teen health. *Monitor on Psychology, 32* (9). Retrieved November 9, 2001, from http://www.apa.org/ monitor/oct01/sleepteen.html

Kelly, W. E., Kelly, K. E., & Clanton, R. C. (2001). The relationship between sleep length and grade-point average among college students. *College Student Journal, 35*(1), 84–90.

Nowroozi, C. (1992). What you lose when you miss sleep. *Nation's Business, 80*(9), 73–77. Retrieved April 22, 2001, from Expanded Academic ASAP database.

Pilcher, J. J., & Walters, A. S. (1997). How sleep deprivation affects psychological variables related to college students' cognitive performance. *Journal of American College Health, 46*(3), 121–131.

Toufexis, A. (1990, May 8). Drowsy America: For millions of people caught in the nation's 24-hour whirl, sleep is the last thing on their mind. *Time, 136*, 78–85.

APA 32c

APA TABLES

Table 1
Results of Survey of Students in University of Texas Introduction to Biology Class
Examining the Relationship between Sleep Deprivation and Academic Performance

Grade Totals	Sleep-Deprived	Not Sleep-Deprived	Usually Sleep-Deprived	Improved	Harmed	Continue Sleep Deprivation?
A=10	4	6	1	4	0	4
B=20	9	11	8	8	1	8
C=10	10	0	6	5	4	7
D=10	8	2	2	1	3	2
Total	31	19	17	18	8	21

Table 2
Results of Survey of Students in University of Texas Introduction to Biology Class
Examining the Relationship between Sleep Deprivation and Academic Performance:
Results Shown as Percentages of Total Class

Grade Totals	Sleep-Deprived	Not Sleep-Deprived	Usually Sleep-Deprived	Improved	Harmed	Continue Sleep Deprivation?
A=20%	8%	12%	2%	8%	0	8%
B=40%	18%	22%	16%	16%	2%	16%
C=20%	20%	0%	12%	10%	8%	14%
D=20%	16%	4%	4%	2%	6%	4%
Total	62%	38%	34%	36%	16%	42%

DIRECTORY OF CHICAGO STYLE ENDNOTE AND BIBLIOGRAPHY ENTRIES

CHAPTER 33

CHICAGO AND OTHER DOCUMENTATION STYLES

33a Using Chicago Style

The Chicago Manual of Style is used in history and some social science and humanities disciplines. **Chicago Style*** has two parts: notes at the end of the paper (endnotes) and a list of bibliographic citations. (Although Chicago style encourages the use of endnotes, it also allows the use of footnotes at the bottom of the page.)

(1) Endnotes and Footnotes

The notes format calls for a **superscript** (raised numeral) in the text after source material you have either quoted or referred to. This numeral, which is placed after all punctuation marks except dashes, corresponds to the numeral that accompanies the note.

Endnote and Footnote Format: Chicago Style
In the Text
By November of 1942, the Allies had proof that the Nazis were engaged in the systemic killing of Jews.[1]
In the Note
1. David S. Wyman, *The Abandonment of the Jews: America and the Holocaust 1941–1945* (New York: Pantheon Books, 1984), 65.

(2) Bibliography

In addition to the heading *Bibliography*, Chicago style allows *Selected Bibliography, Works Cited, Literature Cited, References,* and *Sources Consulted.*

Sample Chicago Style Entries: Books Capitalize the first, last, and all major words of titles and subtitles. Although underlining to indicate italics is acceptable, Chicago style recommends the use of italics for titles.

1. A Book by One Author
Endnote
1. Herbert J. Gans, *The Urban Villagers,* 2d ed. (New York: Free Press, 1982), 100.

*Chicago style follows the guidelines set in *The Chicago Manual of Style,* 14th ed. Chicago: University of Chicago Press, 1993.

Bibliography

Gans, Herbert J. *The Urban Villagers,* 2d ed. New York: Free Press, 1982.

2. A Book by Two or Three Authors
Endnote

2. Jack Watson and Grant McKernie, *A Cultural History of the Theatre* (New York: Longman, 1993), 72.

Bibliography

Watson, Jack and Grant McKernie. *A Cultural History of the Theatre.* New York: Longman, 1993.

3. A Book by More than Three Authors
Endnote

3. Robert E. Spiller et al., eds., *Literary History of the United States* (New York: Macmillan, 1974), 24.

Bibliography

Spiller, Robert E., et al., eds. *Literary History of the United States.* New York: Macmillan, 1974.

4. An Edited Book
Endnote

4. William Bartram, *The Travels of William Bartram,* ed. Mark Van Doren (New York: Dover Press, 1955), 85.

Bibliography

Bartam, William. *The Travels of William Bartram.* Edited by Mark Van Doren. New York: Dover Press, 1955.

5. A Chapter in a Book or an Essay in an Anthology
Endnote

5. Peter Kidson, "Architecture and City Planning," in *The Legacy of Greece,* edited M. I. Finley (New York: Oxford University Press, 1981), 379.

Bibliography

Kidson, Peter. "Architecture and City Planning." In *The Legacy of Greece,* ed. M. I. Finley, 376–400. New York: Oxford University Press, 1981.

6. A Multivolume Work
Endnote

6. Kathleen Raine, *Blake and Tradition* (Princeton: Princeton University Press, 1968), 1: 143.

Bibliography

Raine, Kathleen. *Blake and Tradition.* Vol. 1. Princeton: Princeton University Press, 1968.

Sample Chicago Style Entries: Articles

7. An Article in a Scholarly Journal with Continuous Pagination through an Annual Volume
Endnote

7. John Huntington, "Science Fiction and the Future," *College English* 37 (fall 1975): 341.

Bibliography

Huntington, John. "Science Fiction and the Future." *College English* 37 (fall 1975): 340–58.

8. An Article in a Scholarly Journal with Separate Pagination in Each Issue

Endnote

8. R. G. Sipes, "War, Sports, and Aggression: An Empirical Test of Two Rival Theories," *American Anthropologist* 4, no. 2 (1973): 80.

Bibliography

Sipes, R. G. "War, Sports, and Aggression: An Empirical Test of Two Rival Theories." *American Anthropologist* 4, no. 2 (1973): 65–84.

9. An Article in a Weekly Magazine

Endnote

9. James Traub, "The Hearts and Minds of City College," *New Yorker,* 7 June 1993, 45.

Bibliography

Traub, James. "The Hearts and Minds of City College." *New Yorker,* 7 June 1993, 42–53.

10. An Article in a Monthly Magazine

Endnote

10. Lori Roll, "Careers in Engineering," *Working Woman,* November 1982, 62.

Bibliography

Roll, Lori. "Careers in Engineering." *Working Woman,* November 1982, 62.

11. An Article in a Newspaper

Endnote

11. Raymond Bonner, "A Guatemalan General's Rise to Power," *New York Times,* 21 July 1982, sec. 3A.

Bibliography

Bonner, Raymond. "A Guatemalan General's Rise to Power." *New York Times,* 21 July 1982, sec. 3A.

Sample Chicago Style Entries: Other Sources

12. A Personal Interview

Endnote

12. Cornel West, interview by author, tape recording, St. Louis, Mo., 8 June 1994.

Bibliography

West, Cornel. Interview by author. Tape recording. St. Louis, Mo., 8 June 1994.

13. A Published Interview

Endnote

13. Gwendolyn Brooks, interview by George Stravos, *Contemporary Literature* 11, no. 1 (winter 1970): 12.

Bibliography

Brooks, Gwendolyn. Interview by George Stravos. *Contemporary Literature* 11, no. 1 (winter 1970): 1–20.

14. A Letter
Endnote

14. Amy Tan, letter to author, 7 April 1990.

Bibliography

Tan, Amy. Letter to author. 7 April 1990.

15. A Film or Videotape
Endnote

15. *Interview with Arthur Miller,* dir. William Schiff, 17 min., The Mosaic Group, 1987, videocassette.

Bibliography

Miller, Arthur. *Interview with Arthur Miller.* Directed by William Schiff. 17 min. The Mosaic Group, 1987. Videocassette.

16. A Recording
Endnote

16. Bob Marley, "Crisis," on *Bob Marley and the Wailers,* Kava Island Records compact disk 423 095-3.

Bibliography

Marley, Bob. "Crisis." On *Bob Marley and the Wailers.* Kava Island Records compact disk 423 095-3.

Sample Chicago Style Entries: Electronic Sources

17. Computer Software
Endnote

17. *Reunion: The Family Tree Software,* vers. 2.0 for Macintosh, Lester Productions, Cambridge, Mass.

Bibliography

Reunion: The Family Tree Software. Vers. 2.0 for Macintosh. Lester Productions, Cambridge, Mass.

18. An Electronic Document *The Chicago Manual of Style* recommends following the guidelines developed by the International Standards Organization (ISO). List the authors, the title, the electronic medium (*electronic bulletin board,* for example), information about a print version, access dates, and electronic address (URL) or location information.

Endnote

18. Arthur Sklar, "Survey of Legal Opinions Regarding the Death Penalty in New Jersey," in NL-KR (Digest vol. 3, no. 2) [electronic bulletin board] (Newark, N.J., 1995 [cited 17 March 1997]); available from nl-kr@cs.newark.edu; INTERNET.

Bibliography

Sklar, Arthur. "Survey of Legal Opinions Regarding the Death Penalty in New Jersey," in NL-KR (Digest vol. 3, no. 2) [electronic bulletin board]. (Newark, N.J., 1995 [cited 17 March 1997]). Available from nl-kr@cs.newark.edu; INTERNET.

33b Chicago Style Manuscript Guidelines

✓ CHECKLIST: TYPING YOUR PAPER

✔ On the title page include the full title of your paper as well as your name. You may also be asked to include the course title, the instructor's name, and the date.

✔ Type your paper with a one-inch margin at the top, at the bottom, and on both sides.

✔ Double-space your paper throughout.

✔ Indent the first line of each paragraph five spaces. Set off a long prose quotation (ten or more typed lines or more than one paragraph) from the text by indenting one-half inch from the left-hand margin. If the quotation is a full paragraph, include the paragraph indentation.

✔ Number all pages consecutively in the upper right-hand corner, one-half inch from the top, flush right. Although it is not required, you may include your name before the page number. Although the title page is counted as page 1, it is not numbered. The first full page of the paper will be numbered page 2.

✔ Use superscript numbers to indicate in-text citations. Type superscript numbers at the end of cited material (quotations, paraphrases, or summaries). Leave no space between the superscript number and the preceding letter or punctuation mark.

✔ if you use source material in your paper, use **Chicago documentation style**.

See 33a

✓ CHECKLIST: PREPARING CHICAGO STYLE ENDNOTES

✔ Begin the endnotes on a new page after the last page of the paper.
✔ Center the title *Notes* one inch from the top of the page.

continued on the following page

continued from the previous page

✔ Number the page on which the endnotes appear as the next page of the paper.

✔ Type and number notes in the order in which they appear in the paper, beginning with number 1.

✔ Type the note number on (not above) the line, followed by a period and one space.

✔ Indent the first line of each note three spaces; type subsequent lines flush with the left-hand margin.

✔ Double-space within and between entries.

SUBSEQUENT REFERENCES TO THE SAME WORK

In the first reference to a work, use the full citation; in subsequent references to the same work, list only the author's last name, followed by a comma and a page number.

First Note on Espinoza

   1. J. M. Espinoza, *The First Expedition of Vargas in New Mexico, 1692* (Albuquerque: University of New Mexico Press, 1949), 10–12.

Subsequent Note

   5. Epinoza, 29.

NOTE: *The Chicago Manual of Style* allows the use of the abbreviation *ibid.* ("in the same place") for subsequent references to the same work as long as there are no intervening references. *Ibid.* takes the place of the author's name and the work's title—but not the page number.

First Note on Espinoza

   1. J. M. Espinoza, *The First Expedition of Vargas in New Mexico, 1692* (Albuquerque: University of New Mexico Press, 1949), 10–12.

Subsequent Note

   2. Ibid., 23.

Keep in mind, however, that the use of *ibid.* is giving way to the use of the author's last name and the page number for subsequent references to the same work.

☑ CHECKLIST: PREPARING THE CHICAGO STYLE BIBLIOGRAPHY

- ✔ Type entries on a separate page after the endnotes.
- ✔ List entries alphabetically according to the author's last name.
- ✔ Type the first line of each entry flush with the left-hand margin; indent subsequent lines three spaces.
- ✔ Double-space the bibliography within and between entries.

33c Sample Chicago Style Research Paper

The following excerpts from a paper that uses Chicago Style documentation include a title page, endnotes, and a bibliography.

Native Americans and the Reservation System

By

Angela M. Womack

Title centered and capitalized, followed by name

American History 301

Dr. Adkins

December 3, 2000

*Course title
Instructor
Date*

Indent → 5 spaces

It is July 7, and ten thousand Navajo Indians prepare to leave land in Arizona that they have called home for generations. This land has been assigned to the Hopi tribe by the U. S. government to settle a boundary dispute between the two tribes.[1] Ella Bedonie, a member of the Navajo tribe, says, "The Navajo and the Hopi people have no dispute. It's the government that's doing this to us. I think the Hopis may have the land for a while, but then the government . . . will step in."[2] The Hopis are receiving 25,000 acres to compensate them for the 900,000 acres they will lose in this land deal; however, the groundwater on this land is suspect because of possible contamination by a uranium mine upstream. To mitigate this situation, the government has sweetened this deal with incentives of livestock.[3]

Superscript numbers

This was the fate many native Americans faced as western expansion swept across the North American continent. However, the incident mentioned above occurred not on July 7, 1886, but on July 7, 1986. Indian relations with the U. S. government remain as problematic as they once were, for the federal government's administration of the reservation system both promotes and restricts the development of Native American culture.

2

A reservation is an area of land reserved for Indian use. At present, there are approximately 260 reservations in the United States.[4] The term *reservation* can be traced back to the time when land was "reserved" for Indian use in treaties between whites and Native Americans. Figures from 1986 . . .

10

Notes

1. Trebbe Johnson, "Indian Land, White Greed," *Nation,* 4 July 1987, 15.

2. Johnson, 17.

3. Johnson, 16.

4. Ted Williams, "On the Reservation: America's Apartheid," *National Review,* 8 May 1987, 28.

Sources listed in order in which they appear in paper. Second and subsequent references to sources include only author's last name and page number.

11

Entries are listed alpha-
betically according to
author's last name

11

Bibliography   ←— Center
         ←— Double-
          space

"Adrift in Their Own Land." *Time,* 6 July 1987, 89.

Arrandale, Tom. "American Indian Economic
    Development." *Editorial Research Reports,* 17 Feb.
    1984, 127–142.

Battise, Carol. Personal interview, 25 Sept. 1987.

Cook, J. "Help Wanted—Work, Not Handouts." *Forbes,*
    4 May 1987, 68–71.

Horswell, Cindy. "Alabama-Coushattas See Hope in U.S.
    Guardianship." *Houston Chronicle,* 26 May 1987, 11.

Johnson, Trebbe. "Indian Land, White Greed." *Nation,*
    4 July 1987, 15–18.

Martin, Howard N. "Alabama-Coushatta Indians of Texas:
    Alabama-Coushatta Historical Highlights." Brochure,
    Alabama-Coushatta Indian Reservation: Livingston,
    Tex., n.d.

"A New Brand of Tribal Tycoons." *Time,* 16
    March 1987, 56.

Philip, K. R. "Dillon S. Myer and the Advent of
    Termination: 1950–1953." *Western Historical*
    Quarterly 3 (January 1988): 37–59.

U.S. Bureau of Indian Affairs. "Information About . . . The
    Indian People." Washington, D.C.: GPO, 1981.
    Mimeographed.

Williams, Ted. "On the Reservation: America's
    Apartheid." *National Review,* 8 May 1987, 28–30.

Young, J., and T. Williams. *American Realities: Historical*
    Realities from the First Settlements to the Civil War.
    Boston: Little, Brown, 1981.

Article
has no
listed
author;
alpha-
betized
accord-
ing to
first
signifi-
cant
word
of title

First line of
each entry
is flush
with left-
hand
margin;
subsequent
lines
indented 3
spaces

33d Using CBE Style

CBE style, recommended by the Council of Biology Editors (CBE) and used in biology, zoology, physiology, anatomy, and genetics, has two parts: documentation in the text and a reference list.

(1) Documentation in the Text

CBE Style* recommends two documentation formats: citation-sequence format and name-year format.

Citation-Sequence Format   The citation-sequence format calls for either raised numbers in the text of the paper (the preferred form) or numbers inserted parenthetically in the text of the paper.

One study[1] has demonstrated the effect of low dissolved oxygen.

These numbers correspond to a list of references at the end of the paper. When the writer refers to more than one source in a single note, the numbers are separated by a dash if they are in sequence[2-3] and by a comma if they are not[3,6].

Name-Year Format   This system calls for the author's name and the year of publication to be inserted parenthetically in the text. If the author's name is used to introduce the source material, only the date of publication is needed.

A great deal of heat is often generated during this process (McGinness 1999).

According to McGinness, a great deal of heat is often generated during this process (1999).

*CBE style follows the guidelines set in the style manual of the Council of Biology Editors: *Scientific Style and Format: The CBE Manual for Authors, Editors, and Publishers*, 6th ed. New York: Cambridge UP, 1994.

When two or more works are cited in the same parentheses, the sources are arranged chronologically (from earliest to latest) and separated by a semicolon.

Epidemics can be avoided by taking tissue cultures (Domb 1998) and by intervention with antibiotics (Baldwin and Rigby 1984; Martin and others 1992; Cording 1998).

NOTE: The first citation, *Baldwin and Rigby,* 1984, refers to a work by two authors; the second citation, *Martin and others,* refers to a work by three or more authors.

(2) Reference List

The format of the reference list depends on the documentation format you use. If you use the name-year documentation format, your reference list will resemble the reference list for an **APA** paper. If you use the citation-sequence documentation style, your sources will be listed by number, in the order in which they appear in your text, on a *References* page. This section presents guidelines for assembling the citation-sequence reference list.

See 32a2

Sample CBE Reference List Entries: Books   List the author or authors (last name first), the title (not underlined, and with only the first word capitalized), the place of publication (followed by a colon), the full name of the publisher (followed by a semicolon), the year (followed by a period), and the total number of pages (followed by a period).

1. A Book with One Author

1. Key K. Plant biology. Fort Worth: Harcourt Brace; 1995. 437 p.

2. A Book with More Than One Author

2. Krause KF, Paterson MK. Tissue culture: methods and application. New York: Academic Press; 1993. 217 p.

3. An Edited Book

3. Marzacco MP, editor. A survey of biochemistry. New York: Bowker; 1985. 523 p.

4. A Specific Section of a Book

4. Baldwin LD, Rigby CV. A study of animal virology. New York: Wiley; 1984: p 121-33.

5. A Chapter in a Book or an Essay in an Anthology

5. Brydon RB, Ellis J, Scott CD. Cell division and cancer treatment. In Gotlieb, JM, editor. Current research in cancer treatment. New York: Springer-Verlag; 1996: p 34-47.

Sample CBE Reference List Entries: Articles List the author or authors (last name first), the title of the article (with only the first word capitalized), the abbreviated name of the journal (with all major words capitalized, but not underlined), the year (followed by a semicolon), the volume number (followed by a colon), and inclusive page numbers. No spaces separate the year, the volume, and the page numbers.

6. An Article in a Journal with Continuous Pagination through an Annual Volume

> 6. Bensley KR. Profiling women physicians. Medica 1985;1:140-145.

7. An Article in a Journal with Separate Pagination in Each Issue

> 7. Paul DR, Wang AR, Richards L. The human genome project. Sci Am 1995 Sept; 285(2):43-52.

8. An Article with No Listed Author

> 8. [Anonymous]. Developments in microbiology. Int. J. Microbiol 1987; 6:234-48.

9. An Electronic Source
List the author or authors, the title (followed by the journal title, along with the date and volume number, in the case of journal articles), the electronic medium (*serial online* for periodicals and *monograph online* for books), the date of publication, the words *Available from* followed by a colon and the electronic address, and the date of access.

> 9. Bensley KR. Profiling women physicians. Medica [serial online] 1985; 1. Available from: ftp.lib.nscu.edu via the INTERNET. Accessed 1997 Feb 18.

33e CBE Manuscript Guidelines

Because writing in the sciences focuses on the experiment, not on those conducting the experiment, writers often use the passive voice ("The mixture *was heated* . . ." not "I *heated* the mixture....") Another stylistic convention concerns verb tense: a conclusion or a statement of generally accepted fact should be in the present tense ("Objects in motion *tend* to stay in motion"); a summary of a study, however, should be in the past tense ("Watson and Crick *discovered* the structure of DNA"). Finally, note that direct quotations are seldom used in scientific papers.

Because you are writing to inform or persuade other scientists, you should write clearly and concisely. Remember to use technical terms only when they are necessary to convey your meaning. Too many terms can make your paper difficult to understand—even for scientists familiar with your discipline.

Tables and illustrations are an important part of scientific papers. Be sure to place tables as close to your discussion of them as possible and to number and label any illustration or diagram so that you can refer to it in your text.

✔ CHECKLIST: TYPING YOUR PAPER

✔ Type your name, the course, and the date flush left one inch from the top of the first page.

✔ If required, include an abstract (a 250-word summary of the paper) on a separate page following the title page.

✔ Indent the first line of each paragraph five spaces.

✔ Insert tables and figures in the body of the paper. Number tables and figures in separate sequences (Table 1, Table 2; Figure 1, Figure 2; and so on).

✔ Number pagers consecutively in the upper right-hand corner.

✔ If you use source material in your paper, follow **CBE documentation style**.

See
33d

✔ CHECKLIST: PREPARING THE CBE REFERENCE LIST

✔ Begin the reference list on a new page after the last page of the paper, numbered as the next page of the paper.

✔ Center the title *References, Literature Cited,* or *References Cited* about one inch from the top of the page.

✔ List the items in the order in which they appear in the paper, not alphabetically.

✔ Number the entries consecutively; type the note numbers on (not above) the line, followed by a period.

✔ Type the first line of each entry flush with the left-hand margin; align subsequent lines directly beneath the first letter of the author's last name.

✔ Double-space within and between entries.

33f Sample CBE Research Paper

The following excerpts are from a biology research paper that illustrates the citation-sequence format recommended by the *CBE Style Manual*.

June M. Fahrman

Biology 306

April 17, 2000

Maternal Smoking: Deleterious
Effects on the Fetus

Introduction

The placenta, lifeline between fetus and
mother, has been the subject of various studies
aimed at determining the mechanisms by which
substances in the mother's bloodstream affect the
fetus. For example, cigarette smoking is clearly
associated with an increased risk in the incidence of
low-birthweight infants,[1] due both to prematurity
and to intrauterine growth retardation.[2]

Development of the Placenta

At the morula stage of development, less
than one week after fertilization, two types of
cells can be distinguished. . . .

Conclusion

In summary, abundant evidence exists as to the harmful effects maternal smoking may have on the fetus. These effects include low birthweight, low IQ scores, minimal brain dysfunction, shorter stature, prenatal mortality, and premature birth. . . .

References

1. Rakel RE. Conn's current therapy 1988. Philadelphia: W. B. Saunders; 1988. 360 p.

2. Meberg A, Sande H, Foss, OP, Stenwig JT. Smoking during pregnancy—effects on the fetus and on thiocyanate levels in mother and baby. Acta. Paediatr Scand 1979; 68:547-552.

3. Lehtovirta P, Forss, M. The acute effect of smoking on intervillous blood flow of the placenta. Brit Obs Gyn 1978; 85:729-731.

4. Phelan JP. Diminished fetal reactivity with smoking. Amer Obs Gyn 1980;136:230-233.

5. VanDerVelde WJ. Structural changes in the placenta of smoking mothers: a quantitative study. Placenta 1983; 4:231-240.

33g Using Other Documentation Styles

The following style manuals describe documentation formats used in various fields.

Chemistry
Dodd, Janet S. American Chemical Society. *The ACS Guide: A Manual for Authors and Editors.* 2nd ed. Washington: Amer. Chemical Soc., 1997.

Government Documents
Garner, Diane L. *The Complete Guide to Citing Government Information Resources: A Manual for Writers and Librarians.* Rev. Ed. Bethesda: Congressional Information Service, 1993.

Geology
United States Geological Survey. *Suggestions to Authors of the Reports of the United States Geological Survey.* 7th ed. Washington: GPO, 1991.

Journalism
Associated Press Staff. *Associated Press Stylebook and Libel Manual.* New York: Associated Press, 1998.

Law
The Bluebook: A Uniform System of Citation. Comp. Editors of *Columbia Law Review* et al. 16th ed. Cambridge: Harvard Law Rev. Assn., 1996.

Mathematics
American Mathematical Society. *AMS Author Handbook.* Providence: Amer. Mathematical Soc., 1997.

Medicine
Iverson, Cheryl. *Manual of Style: A Guide for Authors and Editors.* 9th ed. Chicago: Amer. Medical Assn., 1997.

Music
Holman, D. Kirn, ed. *Writing about Music: A Style Sheet from the Editors of 19th-Century Music.* Berkeley: U California P, 1988.

Physics
American Institute of Physics. *AIP Style Manual.* 5th ed. New York: Am. Inst. of Physics, 1995.

Scientific and Technical Writing
Rubens, Philip, ed. *Science and Technical Writing: A Manual of Style.* Fort Worth: Harcourt, 1992.

PART 8

PRACTICAL
WRITING

CHAPTER 34

DESIGNING DOCUMENTS
AND WEB PAGES

This chapter presents general guidelines for designing documents (papers, letters, reports, and so on) and Web pages, as well as specific advice for making all your papers easier to read.

34a Understanding Document Design

Document design refers to the conventions that determine the way a document—a research paper, memo, report, business letter, or résumé, for example—looks on a page. In general, well-designed documents have the following characteristics:

- An effective format
- Clear headings
- Useful lists
- Attractive visuals

(1) Creating an Effective Format

Margins Your document should have at least a one-inch margin on all sides. Keep in mind that specific assignments often have specific requirements for margins. Before you prepare an academic document, consult the appropriate style sheet.

Line Spacing Line spacing refers to the amount of space between the lines of a document. The type of writing you do often determines line spacing. For example, the paragraphs of business letters are usually single-spaced and separated by a double-space, and the paragraphs of academic papers are usually double-spaced and indented.

Font Size To create a readable document, use a 10- or 12-point font. Avoid fonts that will distract readers (script or cursive fonts, for example).

White Space You can use white space around a block of text—a paragraph or a section, for example—to focus readers' attention on the material you are isolating.

(2) Using Headings

Headings tell readers what to expect in a section before they actually read it. In addition, because they break up a text, headings make a document inviting and easy to read.

Number of Headings   The number of headings depends on the document. A long, complicated document will need more headings than a shorter, less complex one. Keep in mind that too few headings may not be of much use, but too many headings will make your document look like an outline.

Phrasing   Headings should be brief, descriptive, and to the point. They can be single words—*Summary* or *Introduction*, for example. Headings can also be phrases (always stated in **parallel** terms): *Choosing a dog, Caring for the dog, Housebreaking the dog.* They can also be questions (*How do you choose a dog?*) or statements (*Choose the right dog.*).

See
12a

Placement   Headings and subheadings may be centered, placed flush left, or indented. The most important thing to remember is that headings at the same level should be in the same format. For example, if one first-level heading is boldfaced and centered, all other first-level headings must be boldfaced and centered.

Typographical Emphasis   You can emphasize headings by using **boldface,** *italics,* or ALL CAPITAL LETTERS. Used in moderation, these distinctive typefaces make a text more readable. Used excessively, however, they slow readers down.

(3) Constructing Lists

A list makes material easier to understand by breaking complicated statements into a series of key ideas. Lists are easiest to read when all the elements are parallel and about the same length. When rank is important, number the items on the list; when it isn't, use **bullets** (as in the list below). Make sure you introduce the list with a complete sentence followed by a colon.

We must take several steps to reduce spending:
- We must cut our workforce by 10 percent.
- We must utilize less expensive vendors.
- We must decrease overtime payments.

Because the items on the list above are complete sentences, each ends with a period. Do not use periods if the items are not sentences.

(4) Creating Effective Visuals

Visuals, such as tables, graphs, diagrams, and photographs, can enhance your documents. You can create your own tables and graphs by using a computer program such as *Excel*, *Lotus*, or *Microsoft Word*. In addition, you can get diagrams and photographs by photocopying or scanning them from a print source, or by downloading them from the Internet or from CD-ROMs or DVDs. Remember, however, that if you use a visual from a source, you must supply appropriate **documentation.**

See
Pt. 7

Tables Tables present data in a condensed visual format—arranged in rows and columns. Tables most often present numerical data, although occasionally they include words as well as numbers. Keep in mind that tables may distract readers, so include only those that are necessary to support your discussion. The following table reports the writer's original research and therefore needs no documentation.

McVay 3

As the following table shows, the Madison location now employs more workers in every site than the St. Paul location.

Table 1 — Heading

Number of Employees at Each Location — Descriptive caption

Employees	Madison	St. Paul
Plant	461	254
Warehouse	45	23
Outlet Stores	15	9

Data

Because the Madison location has grown so quickly, steps must be taken to. . . .

Graphs Whereas tables present specific numerical data, graphs convey the general pattern or trend that the data suggest. Because graphs tend to be more general (and therefore less accurate) than tables, they are frequently accompanied by tables. The following is an example of a bar graph reproduced from a source.

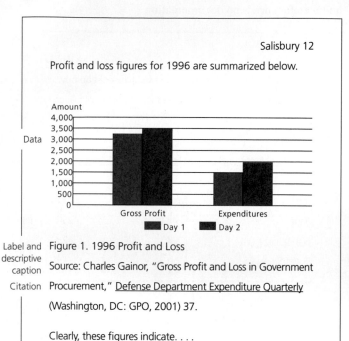

Salisbury 12

Profit and loss figures for 1996 are summarized below.

Data

Label and descriptive caption — Figure 1. 1996 Profit and Loss

Source: Charles Gainor, "Gross Profit and Loss in Government

Citation — Procurement," <u>Defense Department Expenditure Quarterly</u>

(Washington, DC: GPO, 2001) 37.

Clearly, these figures indicate. . . .

Diagrams A diagram enables you to focus on specific details of a mechanism or object. Diagrams are often used in scientific and technical writing to clarify concepts while eliminating the need for paragraphs of detailed and confusing description. The diagram below, which illustrates the ancient Greek theater, serves a similar purpose in a literature paper.

Dixon 10

The design of the ancient Greek theater is similar to that of a present-day sports stadium, as Figure 2 illustrates.

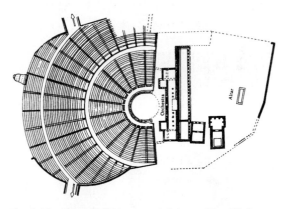

Fig. 2. The Theater of Dionysus at Athens, from W. B. Worthen, <u>The Harcourt Brace Anthology of Drama,</u> 3rd Edition (Fort Worth: Harcourt, 2000) 16.

Citation

Label and descriptive caption

This design, with its tiered seats, enabled the audience to view the actors onstage as well as. . . .

Photographs Photographs enable you to show exactly what something or someone looks like—an animal in its natural habitat, a work of fine art, or an actor in costume, for example. Although computer technology that enables you to paste photographs directly into a text is widely available, you should use it with restraint. Not every photograph will support or enhance your written text; in fact, an irrelevant photograph will distract readers.

Robes 3

In the later years of his life, Twain was seen more as a personality than as a writer. Figure 3 shows him in a characteristic pose.

Fig. 3. Mark Twain, <u>On Porch with Kitten, Mark Twain and His Times,</u> 17 April 1999, U of Virginia, 18 June 2000 <http://etext.virginia.edu/railton/index2html>

Citation

Label and descriptive caption

The white suit he wears in this photograph. . . .

> ☑ **CHECKLIST: INCLUDING VISUALS IN THE TEXT**
>
> ✔ Use a visual only when it contributes something important to the discussion, not for embellishment.
> ✔ Include the visual in the text only if you plan to discuss it in your paper (place the visual in an appendix if you do not).
> ✔ Introduce each visual with a complete sentence.
> ✔ Follow each visual with a discussion of its significance.
> ✔ Leave wide margins around each visual.
> ✔ Place each visual as close as possible to the section of your document in which it is discussed.
> ✔ Label each visual appropriately.
> ✔ Determine whether a borrowed visual falls under the **fair use doctrine**. See 34b1
> ✔ Document each visual that is borrowed from a source.

34b Designing Web Pages

Because many colleges and universities provide students with a full range of Internet services, you may have the opportunity to create a Web page—or even a full Web site. Like other documents, Web pages are subject to specific conventions of document design.

The easiest way to create a Web page is to use one of the many Web creation software packages that are commercially available. These programs automatically convert text and graphics into HTML (the programming language by which standard documents are converted into World Wide Web hypertext documents) so that they can be posted on the Web.

(1) Building a Web Site

A personal **home page** usually contains information about how to contact the author, a brief biography, and links to other Web sites. A home page can be expanded into a full **Web site** (a group of related Web pages). Basic Web pages contain only text, but more advanced Web pages include photographs, animation, and even film clips. You can get ideas for your Web page by examining other Web pages and determining what appeals to you. Keep in mind, however, that although you may borrow formatting ideas from a Web site, it is never acceptable to appropriate a site's content.

WEB SITES AND COPYRIGHT

As a rule, you should assume that any material on the Web is copyrighted unless the author makes an explicit statement to the contrary. This means that you must receive written permission if you are going to reproduce this material on your Web site. The only exception to this rule is the **fair use doctrine,** which allows the use of copyrighted material for the purpose of commentary, parody, or research and education. How much of the work you use is also of consideration, and so is the purpose of your use—whether or not you are using it commercially. Thus you can quote a sentence of an article from the *New York Times* for the purpose of commenting on it, but you must get permission from the *New York Times* to reproduce the article in its entirety on your Web site. As of now, you do not, however, have to get permission to provide a link to the article on the *New York Times's* Web site. (Material you quote in a research paper for one of your classes falls under the fair use doctrine and does not require permission.)

(2) Organizing Information

Before creating a Web site, sketch a basic plan on a piece of paper. Consider how your Web pages will be connected and what links you will provide to other Web sites. Your home page should provide an overview of your site and give readers a clear sense of what material the site will contain. Beginning with the home page, users will navigate from one piece of information to another.

As you plan your Web site, consider how your pages will be organized. If your site is relatively uncomplicated, you can arrange pages so that one page leads sequentially to the next. If your site is relatively complicated, however, you will have to group pages in order of their importance or of their relevance to a particular category. The home page of the *Pocket Handbook's* Web site, for example, indicates that information is grouped under various headings—Learning Resources, Review, and Online Writing Centers, for example (see Figure 1).

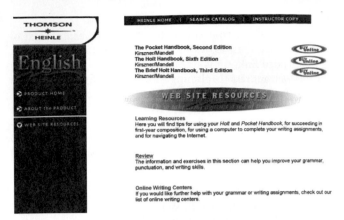

Figure 1 Home page of The Pocket Handbook's *Web site*

(3) Designing a Web Site

When you design your Web site, lay out text and graphics so that they present your ideas clearly and logically. Because your home page is the first thing readers will encounter, it should be clear and easy to follow. Present related items next to each other, and use text sparingly. Make sure you identify items on the same topic by highlighting them in the same color or by using the same font or graphic. Remember, however, that using too many graphics or fancy type styles will confuse readers.

(4) Providing Links

Your home page will probably include buttons and links. **Buttons**—graphic icons, such as arrows or pictures—enable readers to move from one page of a Web site to another. **Links** (short for hyperlinks)—words or URLs (electronic addresses) highlighted and underlined in blue—enable readers to navigate from one site to another. When you provide a link, you are directing people to the Web site to which the link refers. For this reason, be certain that the site is up and running and that the information that appears there is reliable.

(5) Proofreading Your Text

Before you post your site on the Web, proofread the text of your Web pages just as you would any other document. If you have included links on your Web site, be sure you have entered the full Web address (beginning with http://). If you have used a colored background or text, be sure you have avoided color combinations that make your pages difficult to read (purple on black, for example). Finally, make certain you have received permission to use all material—graphics as well as text—that you have borrowed from a source and that you have documented this material.

(6) Posting Your Web Site

Once you have designed a Web site, you will need to upload, or **post,** it so you can view it on the Web. Most commonly, Web pages are posted with **FTP** (File Transfer Protocol) software.

See 29b4

To get your site up on the Web, you transfer your files to an **Internet server,** a computer that is connected at all times to the Internet. Your Internet service provider will instruct you on how to use FTP to transfer your files. Once your site is up and running, you will instantly be able to see if you have made any mistakes. These errors will be apparent as soon as you view your pages on the Web.

Your next step is to publicize your new Web site. Even though many search engines automatically search for new Web sites, you should give formal notification to them that you have launched a new site. Most search engines have links to pages where you can register new sites. In addition, you can access Web sites that automatically send your information to a number of different search engines. (By doing this, you avoid having to repeat the same information each time you register. You can find these sites by doing a keyword search of the phrase "site registration.")

✔ CHECKLIST: CREATING A WEB SITE

- ✔ Decide what content and design appeal to you.
- ✔ Make sure you do not plagiarize another site's content.
- ✔ Consider how you want your site to be organized.
- ✔ Draw a basic plan of your site.
- ✔ Lay out text and graphics so that they present your ideas clearly and logically.
- ✔ Keep both text and graphics simple.
- ✔ Provide clear and informative links.

continued on the following page

continued from the previous page

✔ Proofread your text.
✔ Make sure your site looks the way you want it to.
✔ Make sure all your links are active.
✔ Makes sure you have acknowledged all material that you have borrowed from a source.
✔ Post your site to an Internet server.
✔ Notify search engines that your site is up and running.

CHAPTER 35

WRITING FOR
THE WORKPLACE

Whether you are writing letters of application, résumés, memos, or e-mail, you should always be concise, avoid digressions, and try to sound as natural as possible.

35a Writing Letters of Application

A letter of application summarizes your qualifications for a particular job. Begin by identifying the job and telling where you heard about it. In the body of your letter, provide the information that will convince readers you are qualified for the position. Conclude by reinforcing your desire for the job and by stating that you have enclosed your résumé.

Single-space within paragraphs and double-space between paragraphs. Proofread carefully to make sure there are no errors in spelling or punctuation. Most business letters use **block** format, with all parts of the letter aligned on the left-hand margin.

SAMPLE LETTER OF APPLICATION: BLOCK FORMAT

246 Hillside Drive
Urbana, IL 61801
October 20, 2002
kr237@metropolis.105.com

Mr. Maurice Snyder, Personnel Director
Guilford, Fox, and Morris
22 Hamilton Street
Urbana, IL 61822

Dear Mr. Snyder:

My college advisor, Dr. Raymond Walsh, has told me that you are interested in hiring a part-time accounting assistant. I believe that my academic background and my work experience qualify me for this position.

I am presently a junior accounting major at the University of Illinois. During the past year, I have taken courses in taxation, trusts, and business law. I am also proficient in *Lotus* and *ClarisWorks*. Last spring, I gained practical accounting experience by working in our department's tax clinic.

After I graduate, I hope to get a master's degree in taxation and then return to the Urbana area. I believe that my experience in taxation as well as my familiarity with the local business community will enable me to make a contribution to your firm.

I have enclosed a résumé for your examination. I will be available for an interview any time after midterm examinations, which end October 25. I look forward to hearing from you.

Sincerely yours,

Sandra Kraft

Sandra Kraft
Enc.: Résumé

Heading

Inside address

Salutation

Body

← Double-space

← Single-space

Complimentary close

Typed signature

Additional data

35b Preparing Résumés

A résumé lists relevant information about your education, job experience, goals, and personal interests. The most common way to arrange the information in your résumé is in chronological order, listing your education and work experience in sequence, moving from earliest to latest. Your résumé should be brief (one page, if possible), clear, and logically organized. Emphasize important information with italics, bullets, boldface, or different fonts. Print your résumé on high-quality paper, and proofread carefully for errors.

SCANNABLE RÉSUMÉS

Although the majority of résumés are submitted on paper, an increasing number of résumés are designed to be scanned into a database. If you submit such a résumé, format it accordingly. Because scanners will not pick up columns, bullets, or italics, you should not use them in a scannable résumé. Whereas in print résumés you use strong action verbs to describe your accomplishments (*performed computer troubleshooting,* for example), in a scannable résumé you use key nouns or adjectives (*computer troubleshooter,* for example) to attract employers who carry out a keyword search for applicants with certain skills. (To facilitate such a search, you should include a Keyword section at the bottom of your scannable résumé.)

SAMPLE PRINT RÉSUMÉ: EMPHATIC ORDER

MICHAEL D. FULLER

SCHOOL
27 College Avenue
University of Maryland
College Park, MD 20742
(301) 357-0732

HOME
1203 Hampton Road
Joppa, MD 21085
(301) 877-1437
mful532@aol.com

RESTAURANT EXPERIENCE

McDonald's Restaurant, Pikesville, MD. Cook.
Prepared hamburgers. Acted as assistant manager for two weeks while manager was on vacation. Supervised employees, helped prepare payroll and work schedules. Was named employee of the month. Summer 1999.

University of Maryland, College Park, MD. Cafeteria busboy. Cleaned tables, set up cafeteria, and prepared hot trays. September 1998–May 1999.

OTHER WORK EXPERIENCE

University of Maryland Library, College Park, MD. Reference assistant. Filed, sorted, typed, shelved, and cataloged. Earnings offset college expenses. September 1997–May 1998.

EDUCATION

University of Maryland, College Park, MD (sophomore). Biology major. Expected date of graduation: June 2001.
Forest Park High School, Baltimore, MD.

INTERESTS

Member of University Debating Society.
Tutor in University's Academic Enrichment Program.

REFERENCES

Mr. Arthur Sanducci, Manager
McDonald's Restaurant
5712 Avery Road
Pikesville, MD 22513

Mr. William Czernick, Manager
Cafeteria
University of Maryland
College Park, MD 20742

Ms. Stephanie Young, Librarian
Library
University of Maryland
College Park, MD 20742

SAMPLE RÉSUMÉ: SCANNABLE

CONSTANTINE G. DOUKAKIS

2000 Clover Lane   Phone: (817) 735-9120
Fort Worth, TX 76107   E-Mail: Douk@aol.com

Employment Objective: Entry-level position in an organization that will enable me to use my academic knowledge and the skills that I learned in my work experience.

EDUCATION:

University of Texas at Arlington, Bachelor of Science in Civil Engineering. June 2001. Major: Structural Engineering. Graduated Magna Cum Laude. Overall GPA: 3.754 on a 4.0 base.

SCHOLASTIC HONORS AND AWARDS:

Member of Phi Eta Sigma First-Year Academic Honor Society, Chi Epsilon Civil Engineering Academic Society, Tau Beta Pi Engineering Academic Society, Golden Key National Honor Society

Jack Woolf Memorial Scholarship for Outstanding Academic Performance

COOPERATIVE EMPLOYMENT EXPERIENCE:

Dallas-Fort Worth International Airport, Tarrant County, TX, Dec. 1999 to June 2000. Assistant Engineer. Supervised and inspected airfield paving, drainage, and utility projects as well as terminal building renovations. Performed on-site and laboratory soil tests. Prepared concrete samples for load testing.

Dallas-Fort Worth International Airport, Tarrant County, TX, Jan. 2000 to June 2000. Draftsman in Design Office. Prepared contract drawings and updated base plans as well as designed and estimated costs for small construction projects.

Johnson County Electric Cooperative, Cleburne, TX, Jan. 1999 to June 1999. Junior Engineer in Plant Dept. of Maintenance and Construction Division. Inspected and supervised in-plant construction. Devised solutions to construction problems. Estimated costs of materials for small construction projects. Presented historical data relating to the function of the department.

KEY WORDS:

Organizational and leadership skills. Written and oral communication skills. IBM microcomputer hardware. DOS, Windows 2000, and Mac OS. Word, Excel, FileMaker Pro, PowerPoint, WordPerfect, and various Internet client software. Computer model development.

35c Writing Memos

Memos communicate information within an organization. A memo can be short or long, depending on its purpose. Begin your memo with a purpose statement that presents your reason for writing the memo. Follow this statement with a summary section that tells readers what to expect in the rest of the memo. Then, in the body of your memo, present your support: the detailed information that supports the main point of your memo. If your memo is short, use numbered or bulleted lists to emphasize information. If it is long, use headings to designate the various parts of the memo (*Summary, Background, Benefits,* and so on). End your memo with a statement of your conclusions and recommendations.

SAMPLE MEMO

TO: Ina Ellen, Senior Counselor
FROM: Kim Williams, Student Tutor Supervisor   Opening
SUBJECT: Construction of a Tutoring Center   component
DATE: November 10, 2001

This memo proposes the establishment of a tutoring center in the Office of Student Affairs.   Purpose
                                                    statement

BACKGROUND

Under the present system, tutors must work with students
at a number of facilities scattered across the university
campus. As a result, tutors waste a lot of time running
from one facility to another and are often late for
appointments.

NEW FACILITY

I propose that we establish a tutoring facility adjacent to
the Office of Student Affairs. The two empty classrooms Body
next to the office, presently used for storage of office fur-
niture, would be ideal for this use. We could furnish these
offices with the desks and file cabinets already stored in
these rooms.

BENEFITS

The benefits of this facility would be the centralizing of
the tutoring services and the proximity of the facility to the
Office of Student Affairs. The tutoring facility could also
use the secretarial services of the Office of Student Affairs.

RECOMMENDATIONS   Conclusion

To implement this project, we would need to do the
following:

1. Clean up and paint rooms 331 and 333
2. Use folding partitions to divide each room into five
   single-desk offices
3. Use stored office equipment to furnish the center

I am certain these changes would do much to improve the
tutoring service. I look forward to discussing this matter
with you in more detail.

35d Writing E-Mails

In many workplaces, virtually all internal (and some external) communications are transmitted as e-mail. Although personal e-mail tends to be quite informal, business e-mail observes the conventions of standard written communication. The following rules can help you communicate effectively in an electronic environment.

- Write in complete sentences. Avoid the slang, imprecise diction, and abbreviations that are commonplace in personal e-mail.
- Use an appropriate tone. Address readers with respect, just as you would in a standard business letter.
- Include a subject line that clearly identifies your content. If your subject line is vague, your e-mail may be deleted without being read.
- Make your message as short as possible. Because most e-mails are read on the screen, long discussions are difficult to follow.
- Use short paragraphs, leaving an extra space between paragraphs.
- Use lists and internal headings to focus your discussion and to break it into parts. This strategy will make your message easier to understand.
- Take the time to edit your e-mail after you have written it. Delete excess words and phrases.
- Proofread carefully before sending your e-mail. Look for errors in grammar, spelling, and punctuation.
- Make sure that your list of recipients is accurate and that you do not send your e-mail to unintended recipients.
- Do not send your e-mail until you are absolutely certain that your message says exactly what you want it to say.
- Do not forward an e-mail unless you have the permission of the sender.
- Watch what you write. Keep in mind that e-mail written at work is the property of the employer, who has the legal right to access it—even without your permission.

CHAPTER 36

MAKING ORAL PRESENTATIONS

At school and on the job, you may sometimes be called upon to make an oral presentation. In a college course, you might be asked to explain your ideas, to defend your position, or to present your research. At work, you might be asked to discuss a process, propose a project, or solve a problem. Although many people are uncomfortable about making oral presentations, the guidelines that follow can make the process easier and less stressful.

Getting Started

Just as with writing an essay, the preparation phase of an oral presentation is as important as the speech itself. The time you spend here will make your job easier later on.

Identify your Topic The first thing you should do is to identify the topic of your speech. Sometimes you are assigned a topic; at other times you are given the option of choosing your own. Once you have a topic, you should decide how much information, as well as what kind of information, you will need.

Consider Your Audience The easiest way to determine what kind of information you will need is to consider the nature of your audience. Is your audience made up of experts or of people who know very little about your topic? How much background information will you have to provide? Can you use technical terms, or should you avoid them? Do you think your audience will be interested in your topic, or will you have to create interest? What opinions or ideas about your topic will the members of your audience bring with them?

 AUDIENCE

An **expert audience** is made up of people who have intimate knowledge of your particular field or subject.

continued on the following page

continued from the previous page

A **collegial audience** is made up of people who share the same frame of reference as you do.

A **general audience** is made up of people who have no specific knowledge of your topic or field.

A **mixed audience** is made up of people who have varying degrees of knowledge about your topic or field.

Consider Your Purpose   Your speech should have a specific purpose that you can sum up concisely—for example, *to suggest ways to make registration easier for students.* To help you zero in on your purpose, ask yourself what you are trying to accomplish with your presentation. Are you trying to inform? To instruct? To stimulate an exchange of ideas? To get support for a project? To solicit feedback? To persuade? It is good a idea to keep this purpose statement in front you on an index card so that it will help keep you focused as you plan your speech.

Consider Your Constraints   How much time do you have for your presentation? (Obviously a ten-minute presentation requires more information and preparation than a three-minute presentation.) Do you already know enough about your topic, or will you have to do research? Where will you go to find information? The library? The Internet? Somewhere else?

36b Planning Your Speech

In the planning phase, you focus your ideas about your topic and develop a thesis; then, you decide what specific points you will discuss and divide your speech into a few manageable sections.

Develop a Thesis Statement   Before you can actually begin to plan your speech, you should develop a thesis statement that clearly and concisely presents your main idea—the key idea you want to present to your audience. For example, the student who wrote the purpose statement above came up with this thesis statement for her speech: *The university needs to implement a three-step plan to make registration easier for students.* If you know a lot about your topic, you can develop a thesis on your own. If you do not, you will have to gather information and review it before you can decide on a thesis. As you plan your speech, remember to refer to your thesis to make sure that you stay on track.

Decide on Your Points Once you have developed a thesis, you can decide what points you will discuss. Unlike readers, who can reread a passage until they understand it, listeners must understand information the first time they hear it. For this reason, speeches usually focus on points that are clear and easy to follow. Frequently, your thesis statement states or strongly implies these points: *There are three steps that the university should take to make registration easier for students.*

Outline the Individual Parts of Your Speech Every speech has a beginning, a middle, and an end. Your **introduction** should introduce your subject, engage your audience's interest, and state your thesis—but it should not present an in-depth discussion or a summary of your topic. The **body,** or middle section, of your speech should present the points that support your thesis. It should also include the facts, examples, and other information that will clarify your points and help convince listeners that your thesis is reasonable. As you present your points, use strong topic sentences to lead listeners from one point to another: *The first step, The second step,* and so on. Your **conclusion** should bring your speech to a definite end and reinforce your thesis. Because an audience remembers best what it hears last, this section is extremely important. In your conclusion, you should restate your thesis and reaffirm how your speech supports it.

36c Preparing Your Notes

Most people use notes of some form when they give a speech. Each system of notes has advantages and disadvantages.

Full Text Some people like to write out the full text of their speech and refer to it during their presentation. If the type is large enough, and if you triple-space, such notes can be useful. One disadvantage of using of a full text of your speech is that it is easy to lose your place and become disoriented; another is that you may find yourself simply reading your speech. In either case, you not only stop relating to your audience but also lose their interest.

3 × 5 Cards Some people write parts of their speech—for example, a list of key points or definitions—on 3 × 5 notecards, which can be rearranged easily. They are also small, so they can be placed inconspicuously on a podium or a table. With some practice, you can use notecards effectively. You have to be careful, however, not to become so dependent on the cards that you lose eye contact with your audience or begin fidgeting with the cards as you give your speech.

Outlines   Some people like to refer to an outline when they give their speech. As they speak, they can glance down at the outline to get their bearings or to remind themselves of a point they may have forgotten. Because an outline does not contain the full text of a speech, the temptation to read is eliminated. However, if for some reason you draw a blank, an outline gives you very little to fall back on.

Computer Presentation Software   Finally, some people like to use a computer presentation program like Microsoft's *Power-Point* to keep them on track.

36d   Preparing Visuals

As you plan your speech, you should decide whether you want to use some type of visual aid. Visual aids—such as overhead transparencies, posters, or computer presentation software—can reinforce important information and make your speech easier to understand. They can also break the monotony of a speech and help focus an audience's attention.

For a simple speech, a visual aid may be no more than a definition or a few key terms, names, or dates written on the board. For a more complicated presentation, you might need charts, graphs, diagrams, or photographs—or even objects. The major consideration for including a visual aid is whether it actually adds something to your speech. If a poster will help your listeners understand some key concepts, then by all means use one. However, if it will do little to highlight the information in your speech, then don't use it. Finally, if you are using equipment such as a slide projector or a laptop, make sure you know how to operate it—and have a contingency plan just in case the equipment doesn't work the way it should. For example, it is a good idea to back up a PowerPoint presentation with overhead transparencies just in case the computer at school or at work will not open your files.

If possible, visit the room in which you will be giving your speech, and see whether it has the equipment you need. Some college classrooms are equipped with overhead projectors, VCRs, or computer interfaces. At other schools, you have to make arrangements in advance for equipment.

Finally, make sure that whatever visual aid you use is large enough for everyone in your audience to see. Printing or typing should be neat and free of errors. Graphics should be clearly labeled and easy to see.

☑ CHECKLIST: DESIGNING VISUALS

✔ Do not put more than three or four points on a single visual.

✔ Use single words or short phrases, not sentences or paragraphs.

✔ Limit the number of visuals. For a three-to five-minute presentation, five or six visuals are enough.

✔ Use the same-size font and the same color consistently on each visual.

✔ Use type that is large enough for your audience to see (36-point type for major headings and18-point type for text).

✔ Do not use elaborate graphics or special effects just because your computer software enables you to do so (this is especially relevant for users of Microsoft's *PowerPoint*).

✔ Check your visuals for correctness. Make sure your graphics do not contain typos, mislabelings, or other kinds of errors.

36e Rehearsing Your Speech

There is a direct relationship between how thoroughly you prepared and how effective your speech is. For this reason, you should practice your speech often—at least five times. Do not try to memorize your entire speech, but be sure you know it well enough so that you can move from point to point without constantly looking at your notes. If possible, rehearse your speech in the actual room you will be using, and try standing in the back of the room to make sure that your visuals can be seen clearly. You should also practice in front of some friends and get some constructive criticism about both the content and the delivery of your speech. Another strategy is to use a tape recorder to help you rehearse. When you play back the tape, you can hear whether you are pronouncing your words clearly and whether you are saying "uh" or "you know" throughout your presentation. Finally, time yourself. Make certain that your three-minute speech actually takes three minutes to deliver.

36f Delivering Your Speech

The most important part of your speech is your delivery. Keep in mind that a certain amount of nervousness is normal, so try not to focus on your nervousness too much. While you are waiting to begin, take some deep breaths and calm down. Once you get to the front of the room, do not start right away. Take the time to make sure that everything you will need is there and that all your equipment is positioned properly.

Before you speak, make sure that both feet are flat on the floor and that you face the audience. When you begin speaking, pace yourself. Speak slowly and clearly, and look at the entire audience, one person at a time. Make sure that you speak *to* your audience, not *at* them. Even though your speech is planned, it should sound natural and conversational. Speak loudly enough for everyone in the room to hear you, and remember to vary your pitch and your volume so that you do not speak in a monotone. Try using pauses to emphasize important points and to give listeners time to consider what you have said. Finally, sound enthusiastic about your subject. If you appear to be bored or distracted, your audience will be too.

Your movements should be purposeful and natural. Do not pace or lean against something. Move around only when the need arises—for example, to change a visual, to point to a chart, or to distribute something. Never turn your back to your audience; if you have to write on the board, make sure that you are angled toward the audience. Try to use hand movements to emphasize points, but do not play with pens or notecards as you speak, and do not put your hands in your pockets. Also, resist the temptation to deliver your speech from behind a podium or a table: come around to the front and address the audience directly.

Finally, dress appropriately for the occasion. How you look will be the first thing that listeners notice about you. (Although shorts and a T-shirt may be appropriate for an afternoon in the park, they are not suitable for a classroom presentation.) Dressing appropriately not only demonstrates your respect for your audience but also shows that you are someone who deserves to be taken seriously.

PART 9

GRAMMAR, USAGE, AND ESL REVIEW

APPENDIX A
GRAMMAR REVIEW
PAGE 269

APPENDIX B
USAGE REVIEW
PAGE 278

APPENDIX C
ESL REVIEW
PAGE 288

GRAMMAR REVIEW

A1 Parts of Speech

The **part of speech** to which a word belongs depends on its function in a sentence.

(1) Nouns

Nouns name people, animals, places, things, ideas, actions, or qualities.

A **common noun** names any of a class of people, places, or things: *artist, judge, building, event, city.*

A **proper noun,** always **capitalized**, refers to a particular person, place, or thing: *Mary Cassatt, World Trade Center, Crimean War.*

See 22a

A **collective noun** designates a group thought of as a unit: *committee, class, family.*

An **abstract noun** refers to an intangible idea or quality: *love, hate, justice, anger, fear, prejudice.*

(2) Pronouns

Pronouns are words used in place of nouns. The noun for which a pronoun stands is its **antecedent.**

Although different types of pronouns may have the same form, they are distinguished from one another by their function in a sentence.

A **personal pronoun** stands for a person or thing: *I, me, we, us, my, mine, our, ours, you, your, yours, he, she, it, its, him, his, her, hers, they, them, their, theirs.*

<u>They</u> made <u>her</u> an offer <u>she</u> couldn't refuse.

An **indefinite pronoun** does not refer to any particular person or thing, so it does not require an antecedent. Indefinite pronouns include *another, any, each, few, many, some, nothing, one, anyone, everyone, everybody, everything, someone, something, either,* and *neither.*

See 5a4, 5b3

<u>Many</u> are called, but <u>few</u> are chosen.

A **reflexive pronoun** ends with *-self* and refers to a recipient of the action that is the same as the actor: *myself, yourself, himself, herself, itself, oneself, themselves, ourselves, yourselves.*

They found <u>themselves</u> in downtown Pittsburgh.

Intensive pronouns have the same form as reflexive pronouns; an intensive pronoun emphasizes a preceding noun or pronoun.

Darrow <u>himself</u> was sure his client was innocent.

A **relative pronoun** introduces an adjective or noun clause in a sentence. Relative pronouns include *which, who, whom, that, what, whose, whatever, whoever, whomever,* and *whichever.*

Gandhi was the man <u>who</u> led India to independence. (introduces adjective clause)

<u>Whatever</u> happens will be a surprise. (introduces noun clause)

An **interrogative pronoun** introduces a question. Interrogative pronouns include *who, which, what, whom, whose, whoever, whatever,* and *whichever.*

<u>Who</u> was that masked man?

A **demonstrative pronoun** points to a particular thing or group of things. *This, that, these,* and *those* are demonstrative pronouns.

<u>This</u> is one of Shakespeare's early plays.

A **reciprocal pronoun** denotes a mutual relationship. The reciprocal pronouns are *each other* and *one another. Each other* indicates a relationship between two individuals; *one another* denotes a relationship among more than two.

Cathy and I respect <u>each other</u> for our differences.

Many of our friends do not respect <u>one another</u>.

(3) Verbs

Verbs can be classified into two groups: *main verbs* and *auxiliary verbs.*

Main Verbs **Main verbs** carry most of the meaning in a sentence or clause. Some main verbs are action verbs.

He <u>ran</u> for the train. (physical action)

He <u>thought</u> about taking the bus. (emotional action)

Other main verbs are linking verbs. A **linking verb** does not show any physical or emotional action. Its function is to link the subject to a **subject complement,** a word or phrase that renames or describes the subject. Linking verbs include *be, become,* and *seem* and verbs that describe sensations—*look, appear, feel, taste, smell,* and so on.

Parts of Speech

Carbon disulfide <u>smells</u> bad.

Auxiliary Verbs **Auxiliary verbs** (also called **helping verbs**), such as *be* and *have,* combine with main verbs to form **verb phrases.** Auxiliary verbs indicate tense, voice, or mood.

[auxiliary] [main verb]   [auxiliary]   [main verb]

The train <u>has started</u>. We <u>are leaving</u> soon.

[verb phrase] [verb phrase]

Certain auxiliary verbs, known as **modal auxiliaries,** indicate necessity, possibility, willingness, obligation, or ability. These include *must, shall, might, will, should, can, would, may, could, need* [to], and *ought* [to].

Verbals **Verbals,** such as *known* or *running* or *to go,* are verb forms that act as adjectives, adverbs, or nouns. A verbal can never serve as a sentence's main verb unless it is used with one or more auxiliary verbs (*He is running*). Verbals include *participles, infinitives,* and *gerunds.*

Participles Virtually every verb has a **present participle,** which ends in *-ing* (*loving, learning*) and a **past participle,** which usually ends in *-d* or *-ed* (*agreed, learned*). Some verbs have **irregular** past participles (*gone, begun, written*). Participles may function in a sentence as adjectives or as nouns. _{See 6a}

Twenty brands of <u>running</u> shoes were on display. (participle serves as adjective)

The <u>wounded</u> were given emergency first aid. (participle serves as noun)

Infinitives An **infinitive**—the *to* form of the verb—may function as an adjective, an adverb, or a noun.

Ann Arbor was clearly the place <u>to be</u>. (infinitive serves as adjective)

Carla went outside <u>to think</u>. (infinitive serves as adverb)

<u>To win</u> was everything. (infinitive serves as subject)

Gerunds **Gerunds,** which like present participles end in *-ing*, always function as nouns.

<u>Seeing</u> is <u>believing</u>.

Andrew loves <u>skiing</u>.

(4) Adjectives

Adjectives describe, limit, qualify, or in some other way modify nouns or pronouns.

Descriptive adjectives name a quality of the noun or pronoun they modify.

After the game, they were <u>exhausted</u>.

They ordered a <u>chocolate</u> soda and a <u>butterscotch</u> sundae.

When articles, pronouns, numbers, and the like function as adjectives, limiting or qualifying nouns or pronouns, they are referred to as **<u>determiners</u>**.

See C1.3

(5) Adverbs

Adverbs describe the action of verbs or modify adjectives or other adverbs (or complete phrases, clauses, or sentences). They answer the questions "How?" "Why?" "When?" "Under what conditions?" and "To what extent?"

He walked <u>rather hesitantly</u> toward the front of the room.

Let's meet <u>tomorrow</u> for coffee.

Adverbs that modify other adverbs or adjectives limit or qualify the words they modify.

He pitched an <u>almost perfect</u> game yesterday.

Interrogative Adverbs The **interrogative adverbs** (*how, when, why,* and *where*) introduce questions.

See 2b

Conjunctive Adverbs **Conjunctive adverbs** act as **<u>transitional words</u>**, joining and relating independent clauses.

FREQUENTLY USED CONJUNCTIVE ADVERBS

accordingly	furthermore	meanwhile	similarly
also	hence	moreover	still
anyway	however	nevertheless	then
besides	incidentally	next	thereafter
certainly	indeed	nonetheless	therefore
consequently	instead	now	thus
finally	likewise	otherwise	undoubtedly

---

(6) Prepositions

A **preposition** introduces a noun or pronoun (or a phrase or clause functioning in the sentence as a noun), linking it to other words in the sentence. The word or word group that the preposition introduces is its **object.**

    prep obj   prep obj

They received a postcard <u>from</u> Bobby telling <u>about</u> his trip.

FREQUENTLY USED PREPOSITIONS

about	beneath	inside	since
above	beside	into	through
across	between	like	throughout
after	beyond	near	to
against	by	of	toward
along	concerning	off	under
among	despite	on	underneath
around	down	onto	until
as	during	out	up
at	except	outside	upon
before	for	over	with
behind	from	past	within
below	in	regarding	without

---

(7) Conjunctions

Conjunctions connect words, phrases, clauses, or sentences.

Coordinating Conjunctions **Coordinating conjunctions** (*and, or, but, nor, for, so, yet*) connect words, phrases, or clauses of equal weight.

Should I order chicken <u>or</u> fish?

Thoreau wrote *Walden* in 1854, <u>and</u> he died in 1862.

Correlative Conjunctions Always used in pairs, **correlative conjunctions** also link items of equal weight.

<u>Both</u> Hancock <u>and</u> Jefferson signed the Declaration of Independence.

<u>Either</u> I will renew my lease, <u>or</u> I will move.

FREQUENTLY USED CORRELATIVE CONJUNCTIONS

both . . . and	neither . . . nor
either . . . or	not only . . . but also
just as . . . so	whether . . . or

Subordinating Conjunctions Words such as *since, because,* and *although* are **subordinating conjunctions.** They introduce adverb clauses and thus connect the sentence's independent (main) clause to a dependent (subordinate) clause to form a <u>complex sentence</u>.

See 9a2

Although people may feel healthy, they can still have medical problems.

It is best to diagram your garden before you start to plant.

(8) Interjections

Interjections **Interjections** are words used as exclamations to express emotion: *Oh! Ouch! Wow! Alas! Hey!*

A2 Sentences

(1) Basic Sentence Elements

A **sentence** is an independent grammatical unit that contains a subject and a predicate and expresses a complete thought.

The quick brown fox jumped over the lazy dog.

It came from outer space.

(2) Basic Sentence Patterns

A **simple sentence** consists of at least one subject and one predicate. Simple sentences conform to one of five patterns.

Subject + Intransitive Verb (s + v)

Stock prices may fall.
$\;\;\;\;$s$\;\;\;\;\;\;$v

Subject + Transitive Verb + Direct Object (s + v + do)

Van Gogh created *The Starry Night.*
$\;\;$s$\;\;\;\;\;\;$v$\;\;\;\;\;\;$do

Caroline saved Jake.
$\;\;$s$\;\;\;\;\;$v$\;\;\;$do

Subject + Transitive Verb + Direct Object + Object Complement (s + v + do + oc)

I found the exam easy.
s$\;$v$\;\;\;\;\;\;$do$\;$oc

The class elected Bridget treasurer.
$\;\;\;$s$\;\;\;\;\;\;\;$v$\;\;\;\;\;$do$\;\;\;\;\;$oc

Subject + Linking Verb + Subject Complement (s + v + sc)

The injection was painless.
$\;\;\;\;$s$\;\;\;\;\;\;$v$\;\;\;$sc

Tony Blair became prime minister.
$\;\;$s$\;\;\;\;\;\;\;$v$\;\;\;\;\;\;$sc

Subject + Transitive Verb + Indirect Object + Direct Object
(s + v + io + do)

    s   v   io   do
<u>Cyrano</u> <u>wrote</u> Roxanne a poem. (Cyrano wrote a poem *for* Roxanne.)

    s   v   io   do
<u>Hester</u> <u>gave</u> Pearl a kiss. (Hester gave a kiss *to* Pearl.)

(3) Phrases and Clauses

A **phrase** is a group of related words that lacks a subject or predicate or both and functions as a single part of speech. It cannot stand alone as a sentence.

A **verb phrase** consists of a **main verb** and all its auxiliary verbs. (Time *is flying*.) A **noun phrase** includes a noun or pronoun plus all related modifiers. (I'll climb *the highest mountain*.)

A **prepositional phrase** consists of a <u>**preposition**</u>, its object, and any modifiers of that object (They considered the ethical implications *of the animal studies*).

See
A1.6

A **verbal phrase** consists of a <u>**verbal**</u> and its related objects, modifiers, or complements. A verbal phrase may be a **participial phrase** (*encouraged by the voter turnout*), a **gerund phrase** (*taking it easy*), or an **infinitive phrase** (*to evaluate the evidence*).

See
A1.3

An **absolute phrase** usually consists of a noun and a participle, accompanied by modifiers. It modifies an entire independent clause rather than a particular word or phrase.

<u>Their toes tapping</u>, they watched the auditions.

A **clause** is a group of related words that includes a subject and a predicate. An **independent** (main) **clause** may stand alone as a sentence, but a **dependent** (subordinate) **clause** cannot. It must always be combined with an independent clause to form a <u>**complex sentence**</u>.

See
9a2

[Lucretia Mott was an abolitionist.] [She was also a pioneer for women's rights.] (two independent clauses)

[Lucretia Mott was an abolitionist] [who was also a pioneer for women's rights.] (independent clause, dependent clause)

Dependent clauses may be adjective, adverb, or noun clauses.

Adjective clauses, sometimes called **relative clauses,** modify nouns or pronouns and always follow the nouns or pronouns they modify. They are introduced by relative pronouns—*that, what, which, who,* and so forth—or by the adverbs *where* and *when.*

Celeste's grandparents, <u>who were born in Romania</u>, speak little English.

Adverb clauses modify verbs, adjectives, adverbs, entire phrases, or independent clauses. They are always introduced by subordinating conjunctions.

Mark will go <u>wherever there's a party</u>.

Noun clauses function as subjects, objects, or complements. A noun clause may be introduced by a relative pronoun or by *whether, when, where, why,* or *how.*

<u>What you see</u> is <u>what you get</u>.

(4) Types of Sentences

A **simple sentence** is a single independent clause. A simple sentence can consist of just a subject and a predicate.

<u>Jessica</u> <u>fell</u>.

Or, a simple sentence can be expanded with modifying words and phrases.

Jessica fell in love with the mysterious Henry Goodyear on Halloween.

See
9a1
A **<u>compound sentence</u>** consists of two or more simple sentences linked by a coordinating conjunction (preceded by a comma), by a semicolon (alone or with a transitional word or phrase), by correlative conjunctions, or by a colon.

[The moon rose in the sky], <u>and</u> [the stars shone brightly].

[José wanted to spend a quiet afternoon]; <u>however</u>, [his aunt surprised him with a new set of plans.]

See
9a2
A **<u>complex sentence</u>** consists of an independent clause along with one or more dependent clauses.

   Independent clause   Dependent clause
[It was hard for us to believe] [that anyone could be so cruel].

A **compound-complex sentence** is a compound sentence—made up of at least two independent clauses—that also includes at least one dependent clause.

[My mother always worried] [when my father had to work late], and [she could rarely sleep more than a few minutes at a time].

Sentences can also be classified according to their function. **Declarative sentences** make statements; they are the most common. **Interrogative sentences** pose questions, usually by inverting standard subject-verb order (often with an interrogative word) or by adding a form of *do* (*Is Maggie at home? Where is Maggie? Does Maggie live here?*). **Imperative sentences** express commands or requests, using the second-person singular of the verb and generally omitting the pronoun subject *you* (*Go to your room. Please believe me.*). **Exclamatory sentences** express strong emotion and end with an exclamation point (*The killing must stop now!*).

APPENDIX B

USAGE REVIEW

This usage review lists words and phrases that are often troublesome for writers.

a, an   Use *a* before words that begin with consonants and words that have initial vowels that sound like consonants: *a* person, *a* one-horse carriage, *a* uniform. Use *an* before words that begin with vowels and words that begin with a silent *h: an* artist, *an* honest person.

accept, except   *Accept* is a verb that means "to receive"; *except* as a preposition or conjunction means "other than" and as a verb means "to leave out": The auditors will *accept* all your claims *except* the last two. Some businesses are *excepted* from the regulation.

advice, advise   *Advice* is a noun meaning "opinion or information offered"; *advise* is a verb that means "to offer advice to": The broker *advised* her client to take his attorney's *advice.*

affect, effect   *Affect* is a verb meaning "to influence"; *effect* can be a verb or a noun. As a verb it means "to bring about," and as a noun it means "result": We know how the drug *affects* patients immediately, but little is known of its long-term *effects.* The arbitrator tried to *effect* a settlement between the parties.

all ready, already   *All ready* means "completely prepared"; *Already* means "by or before this or that time": I was *all ready* to help, but it was *already* too late.

all right, alright   Although the use of *alright* is increasing, current usage calls for *all right.*

allusion, illusion   An *allusion* is a reference or hint; an *illusion* is something that is not what it seems: The poem makes an *allusion* to the Pandora myth. The shadows created an optical *illusion.*

a lot   *A lot* is always two words.

among, between   *Among* refers to groups of more than two things; *between* refers to just two things: The three parties agreed *among* themselves to settle the case. There will be a brief intermission *between* the two acts.

amount, number   *Amount* refers to a quantity that cannot be counted; *number* refers to things that can be counted: Even a small *amount* of caffeine can be harmful. Seeing their commander fall, a large *number* of troops ran to his aid.

an, a   See **a, an.**

and/or   In business or technical writing, use *and/or* when either or both of the items it connects can apply. In college writing, however, the use of *and/or* should generally be avoided.

as . . . as . . .   In such constructions, *as* signals a comparison; therefore, you must always use the second *as: East of Eden* is *as* long *as The Grapes of Wrath.*

as, like   *As* can be used as a conjunction (to introduce a complete clause) or as a preposition; *like* should be used as a preposition only: In *The Scarlet Letter* Hawthorne uses imagery *as* (not *like*) he does in his other works. After classes he works *as* a manager of a fast-food restaurant. Writers *like* Carl Sandburg appear once in a generation.

at, to   Many people use the prepositions *at* and *to* after *where* in conversation: *Where* are you working *at? Where* are you going *to?* This usage is redundant and should not appear in college writing.

awhile, a while   *Awhile* is an adverb; *a while,* which consists of an article and a noun, is used as the object of a preposition: Before we continue we will rest *awhile.* (modifies the verb *rest*); Before we continue we will rest for *a while.* (object of the preposition *for*)

bad, badly   *Bad* is an adjective, and *badly* is an adverb: The school board decided that *Huckleberry Finn* was a *bad* book. American automobile makers did not do *badly* this year. After verbs that refer to any of the senses or after any other linking verb, use the adjective form: He looked *bad.* He felt *bad.* It seemed *bad.*

being as, being that   These awkward phrases add unnecessary words and weaken your writing. Use *because* instead.

beside, besides   *Beside* is a preposition meaning "next to"; *besides* can be either a preposition meaning "except" or "other than," or an adverb meaning "as well": *Beside* the tower was a wall that ran the length of the city. *Besides* its industrial uses, laser technology has many other applications. Edison invented not only the lightbulb but the phonograph *besides.*

between, among   See **among, between.**

bring, take   *Bring* means to transport from a farther place to a nearer place; *take* means to carry or convey from a nearer place to a farther one: *Bring* me a souvenir from your trip. *Take* this message to the general, and wait for a reply.

can, may   *Can* denotes ability, and *may* indicates permission: If you *can* play, you *may* use my piano.

capital, capitol   *Capital* refers to a city that is an official seat of government; *capitol* refers to a building in which a legislature meets: Washington, DC, is the *capital* of the United States. When we were there, we visited the *Capitol* building.

center around   This imprecise phrase is acceptable in speech and informal writing but not in college writing. Use *center on* instead.

cite, site   *Cite* is a verb meaning "to quote as an authority or example"; *site* is a noun meaning "a place or setting": Jeff *cited* five sources in his research paper. The builder cleared the *site* for the new bank.

climactic, climatic   *Climactic* means "of or related to a climax"; *climatic* means "of or related to climate": The *climactic* moment of the movie occurs unexpectedly. If scientists are correct, the *climatic* conditions of Earth are changing.

coarse, course   *Coarse* is an adjective meaning "inferior" or "having a rough, uneven texture"; *course* is a noun meaning "a route or path," "an area on which a sport is played," or "a unit of study": *Coarse* sandpaper is used to smooth the surface. The *course* of true love never runs smoothly. Last semester I had to drop a *course*.

complement, compliment   *Complement* means "to complete or add to"; *compliment* means "to give praise": A double-blind study would *complement* their preliminary research. My instructor *complimented* me on my improvement.

conscious, conscience   *Conscious* is an adjective meaning "having one's mental faculties awake"; *conscience* is a noun that means the moral sense of right and wrong: The patient will remain *conscious* during the procedure. His *conscience* wouldn't allow him to lie.

continual, continuous   *Continual* means "recurring at intervals"; *continuous* refers to an action that occurs without interruption: A pulsar is a star that emits a *continual* stream of electromagnetic radiation. (It emits radiation at regular intervals.) A small battery allows the watch to run *continuously* for five years. (It runs without stopping.)

could of, should of, would of   The contractions *could've, should've,* and *would've* are often misspelled as the nonstandard constructions *could of, should of,* and *would of.* Use *could have, should have,* and *would have* in college writing.

council, counsel   A *council* is "a body of people who serve in a legislative or advisory capacity"; *counsel* means "to offer advice or guidance": The city *council* argued about the proposed ban on smoking. The judge *counseled* the couple to settle their differences.

couple of   *Couple* means "a pair," but *couple of* is used colloquially to mean "several" or "a few." In your college writing, specify "four points" or "two examples" rather than using "a couple of."

criterion, criteria   *Criteria,* from the Greek, is the plural of *criterion,* meaning "standard for judgment": Of all the *criteria* for hiring graduating seniors, class rank is the most important *criterion.*

data   *Data* is the plural of the Latin *datum,* meaning "fact." In everyday speech and writing, *data* is used for both singular and plural. In college writing, you should use *data* only for the plural: The *data* discussed in this section *are* summarized in Appendix A.

different from, different than   *Different than* is widely used in American speech. In college writing, use *different from.*

discreet, discrete   *Discreet* means "careful or prudent"; *discrete* means "separate or individually distinct": Because Madame Bovary was not *discreet,* her reputation suffered. Atoms can be broken into hundreds of *discrete* particles.

disinterested, uninterested   *Disinterested* means "objective" or "capable of making an impartial judgment"; *uninterested* means "indifferent or unconcerned": The American judicial system depends on *disinterested* jurors. Finding no treasure, Hernando de Soto was *uninterested* in going farther.

don't, doesn't   *Don't* is the contraction of *do not; doesn't* is the contraction of *does not.* Do not confuse the two: My dog *doesn't* (not *don't*) like to walk in the rain.

effect, affect   See **affect, effect.**

e.g.   *E.g.* is an abbreviation for the Latin *exempli gratia,* meaning "for example" or "for instance." In college writing, do not use *e.g.* Instead, use its English equivalent.

emigrate from, immigrate to   To *emigrate* is "to leave one's country and settle in another"; to *immigrate* is "to come to another country and reside there." The noun forms of these words are *emigrant* and *immigrant*: My great-grandfather *emigrated from* Warsaw along with many other *emigrants* from Poland. Many people *immigrate* to the United States for economic reasons, but such *immigrants* still face great challenges.

eminent, imminent   *Eminent* is an adjective meaning "standing above others" or "prominent"; *imminent* means "about to occur": Oliver Wendell Holmes, Jr., was an *eminent* jurist. In ancient times, a comet signaled *imminent* disaster.

enthused   *Enthused,* a colloquial form of *enthusiastic,* should not be used in college writing.

etc.   *Etc.,* the abbreviation of *et cetera,* means "and the rest." Do not use it in your college writing. Instead, say "and so on" or, better, specify exactly what *etc.* stands for.

everyday, every day   *Everyday* is an adjective that means "ordinary" or "commonplace"; *every day* means "occurring daily": In the Gettysburg Address, Lincoln used *everyday* language. She exercises almost *every day.*

everyone, every one   *Everyone* is an indefinite pronoun meaning "every person"; *every one* means "every individual or thing in a particular group": *Everyone* seems happier in the spring. *Every one* of the packages had been opened.

except, accept   See **accept, except.**

explicit, implicit   *Explicit* means "expressed or stated directly"; *implicit* means "implied" or "expressed or stated indirectly": The director *explicitly* warned the actors to be on time for rehearsals. Her *implicit* message was that lateness would not be tolerated.

farther, further   *Farther* designates distance; *further* desig-nates degree: I have traveled *farther* from home than any of my relatives. Critics charge that welfare subsidies encourage *further* dependence.

fewer, less   Use *fewer* with nouns that can be counted: *fewer* books, *fewer* people, *fewer* dollars. Use *less* with quantities that cannot be counted: *less* pain, *less* power, *less* enthusiasm.

firstly (secondly, thirdly, . . .)   Archaic forms meaning "in the first . . . second . . . third place." Use *first, second, third.*

further, farther   See **farther, further.**

good, well   *Good* is an adjective, never an adverb: She is a *good* swimmer. *Well* can function as an adverb or as an adjec-tive. As an adverb it means "in a good manner": She swam *well* (not *good*) in the meet. *Well* is used as an adjective with verbs that denote a state of being or feeling. Here *well* can mean "in good health": I feel *well.*

got to   *Got to* is not acceptable in college writing. To indicate obligation, use *have to, has to,* or *must.*

hanged, hung   Both *hanged* and *hung* are past participles of *hang. Hanged* is used to refer to executions; *hung* is used to mean "suspended": Billy Budd was *hanged* for killing the master-at-arms. The stockings were *hung* by the chimney with care.

he, she   Traditionally *he* has been used in the generic sense to refer to both males and females. To acknowledge the equality of the sexes, however, avoid the generic *he.* Use plural pronouns whenever possible. See **14d.2.**

hopefully   The adverb *hopefully,* meaning "in a hopeful man-ner," should modify a verb, an adjective, or another adverb. Do not use *hopefully* as a sentence modifier meaning "it is hoped." Rather than "*Hopefully,* scientists will soon discover a cure for AIDS," write "Scientists *hope* they will soon discover a cure for AIDS."

i.e.   *I.e.* is an abbreviation for the Latin *id est,* meaning "that is." In college writing, do not use *i.e.* Instead, use its English equivalent.

if, whether   When asking indirect questions or expressing doubt, use *whether:* He asked *whether* (not *if*) the flight would be delayed. The flight attendant was not sure *whether* (not *if*) it would be delayed.

illusion, allusion   See **allusion, illusion.**

immigrate to, emigrate from   See **emigrate from, immigrate to.**

implicit, explicit   See **explicit, implicit.**

imply, infer   *Imply* means "to hint" or "to suggest"; *infer* means "to conclude from": Mark Antony *implied* that the conspirators had murdered Caesar. The crowd *inferred* his meaning and called for justice.

infer, imply   See **imply, infer.**

inside of, outside of   *Of* is unnecessary when *inside* and *outside* are used as prepositions. *Inside of* is colloquial in references to time: He waited *inside* (not *inside of*) the coffee shop. He could run a mile in *under* (not *inside of*) eight minutes.

irregardless, regardless   *Irregardless* is a nonstandard version of *regardless*. Use *regardless* instead.

is when, is where   These constructions are faulty when they appear in definitions: A playoff *is* an additional game played to establish the winner of a tie. (not "A playoff *is when* an additional game is played. . . . ")

its, it's   *Its* is a possessive pronoun; *it's* is a contraction of *it is*: *It's* no secret that the bank is out to protect *its* assets.

kind of, sort of   *Kind of* and *sort of* to mean "rather" or "somewhat" are colloquial and should not appear in college writing: It is well known that Napoleon was *rather* (not *kind of*) short.

lay, lie   See **lie, lay.**

leave, let   *Leave* means "to go away from" or "to let remain"; *let* means "to allow" or "to permit": *Let* (not *leave*) me give you a hand.

less, fewer   See **fewer, less.**

let, leave   See **leave, let.**

lie, lay   *Lie* is an intransitive verb (one that does not take an object) that means "to recline." Its principal forms are *lie, lay, lain, lying*: Each afternoon she would *lie* in the sun and listen to the surf. *As I Lay Dying* is a novel by William Faulkner. By 1871, Troy had *lain* undisturbed for two thousand years. The painting shows a nude *lying* on a couch. *Lay* is a transitive verb (one that takes an object) meaning "to put" or "to place." Its principal forms are *lay, laid, laid, laying*: The Federalist Papers *lay* the foundation for American conservatism. In October of 1781, the British *laid* down their arms and surrendered. He had *laid* his money on the counter before leaving. We watched the stonemasons *laying* a wall.

like, as   See **as, like.**

loose, lose   *Loose* is an adjective meaning "not rigidly fastened or securely attached"; *lose* is a verb meaning "to misplace": The marble facing of the building became *loose* and fell to the sidewalk. After only two drinks, most people *lose* their ability to judge distance.

lots, lots of, a lot of   These words are colloquial substitutes for *many, much,* or *a great deal of.* Avoid their use in college writing: The students had many (not *lots of* or *a lot of*) options for essay topics.

man   Like the generic pronoun *he, man* has been used in English to denote members of both sexes. This usage is being replaced by *human beings, people,* or similar terms that do not specify gender. See **14d.2.**

may, can   See **can, may.**

may be, maybe   *May be* is a verb phrase; *maybe* is an adverb meaning "perhaps": She *may be* the smartest student in the class. *Maybe* her experience has given her an advantage.

media, medium   *Medium*, meaning a "means of conveying or broadcasting something," is singular; *media* is the plural form and requires a plural verb: The *media* have distorted the issue.

might have, might of   *Might of* is a nonstandard spelling of the contraction of *might have* (*might've*).

number, amount   See **amount, number.**

OK, O.K., okay   All three spellings are acceptable, but this term should be avoided in college writing. Replace it with a more specific word or words: The lecture was *adequate* (not *okay*), if uninspiring.

outside of, inside of   See **inside of, outside of.**

passed, past   *Passed* is the past tense of the verb *pass; past* means "belonging to a former time" or "no longer current": The car must have been going eighty miles per hour when it *passed* us. In the envelope was a bill marked *past* due.

percent, percentage   *Percent* indicates a part of a hundred when a specific number is referred to: "*10 percent* of his salary." *Percentage* is used when no specific number is referred to: "a *percentage* of next year's receipts." In technical and business writing, it is permissible to use the % sign after percentages you are comparing. Write out *percent* in college writing.

phenomenon, phenomena   A *phenomenon* is a single observable fact or event. It can also refer to a rare or significant occurrence. *Phenomena* is the plural form and requires a plural verb: Many supposedly paranormal *phenomena* are easily explained.

plus   As a preposition, *plus* means "in addition to." Avoid using *plus* as a substitute for *moreover* or *and:* Include the principal, *plus* the interest, in your calculations. Your quote was too high; moreover (not *plus*), it was inaccurate.

precede, proceed   *Precede* means "to go or come before"; *proceed* means "to go forward in an orderly way": Robert Frost's *North of Boston* was *preceded* by an earlier volume. In 1532, Francisco Pizarro landed at Tumbes and *proceeded* south.

principal, principle   As a noun, *principal* means "a sum of money (minus interest) invested or lent" or "a person in the leading position"; as an adjective it means "most important." A *principle* is a rule of conduct or a basic truth: He wanted to reduce the *principal* of the loan. The *principal* of the high school is a talented administrator. Women are the *principal* wage earners in many American households. The Constitution embodies certain fundamental *principles.*

quote, quotation   *Quote* is a verb. *Quotation* is a noun. In college writing, do not use *quote* as a shortened form of *quotation:* Scholars attribute those *quotations* (not *quotes*) to Shakespeare.

raise, rise   *Raise* is a transitive verb, and *rise* is an intransitive verb—that is, *raise* takes an object, and *rise* does not: My grandparents *raised* a large family. The sun will *rise* at 6:12 this morning.

real, really   *Real* means "genuine" or "authentic"; *really* means "actually." In your college writing, do not use *real* as an adjective meaning "very."

reason is that, reason is because   *Reason* should be used with *that* and not with *because,* which is redundant: The *reason* he left *is that* (not *is because*) you insulted him.

regardless, irregardless   See **irregardless, regardless.**

respectably, respectfully, respectively   *Respectably* means "worthy of respect"; *respectfully* means "giving honor or deference"; *respectively* means "in the order given": He skated quite *respectably* at his first Olympics. The seminar taught us to treat others *respectfully.* The first- and second-place winners were Tai and Kim, *respectively.*

rise, raise   See **raise, rise.**

set, sit   *Set* means "to put down" or "to lay." Its principal forms are *set* and *setting:* After rocking the baby to sleep, he *set* her down carefully in her crib. *Sit* means "to assume a sitting position." Its principal forms are *sit, sat, sat,* and *sitting:* Many children *sit* in front of the television five to six hours a day.

shall, will   *Will* has all but replaced *shall* to express all future action.

should of   See **could of, should of, would of.**

since   Do not use *since* for *because* if there is any chance of confusion. In the sentence "*Since* President Nixon traveled to China, trade between China and the United States has increased," *since* could mean either "from the time that" or "because."

sit, set   See **set, sit.**

so   Avoid using *so* alone as a vague intensifier meaning "very" or "extremely." Follow *so* with *that* and a clause that describes the result: She was *so* pleased with their work *that* she took them out to lunch.

sometime, sometimes, some time   *Sometime* means "at some time in the future"; *sometimes* means "now and then"; *some time* means "a period of time": The president will address Congress *sometime* next week. All automobiles, no matter how reliable, *sometimes* need repairs. It has been *some time* since I read that book.

sort of, kind of   See **kind of, sort of.**

stationary, stationery   *Stationary* means "staying in one place"; *stationery* means "materials for writing" or "letter paper": The communications satellite appears to be *stationary* in the sky. The secretaries supply departmental offices with *stationery.*

supposed to, used to   *Supposed to* and *used to* are often misspelled. Both verbs require the final *d* to indicate past tense.

take, bring   See **bring, take.**

than, then   *Than* is a conjunction used to indicate a comparison; *then* is an adverb indicating time: The new shopping center is bigger *than* the old one. He did his research; *then* he wrote a report.

that, which, who   Use *that* or *which* when referring to a thing; use *who* when referring to a person: It was a speech *that* inspired many. The movie, *which* was a huge success, failed to impress her. Anyone *who* (not *that*) takes the course will benefit.

their, there, they're   *Their* is a possessive pronoun; *there* indicates place and is also used in the expressions *there is* and *there are*; *they're* is a contraction of *they are*: Watson and Crick did *their* DNA work at Cambridge University. I love Los Angeles, but I wouldn't want to live *there*. *There* is nothing we can do to resurrect an extinct species. When *they're* well treated, rabbits make excellent pets.

themselves; theirselves, theirself   *Theirselves* and *theirself* are nonstandard variants of *themselves*.

then, than   See **than, then.**

till, until, 'til   *Till* and *until* have the same meaning, and both are acceptable. *Until* is preferred in college writing. *'Til*, a contraction of *until*, should be avoided.

to, at   See **at, to.**

to, too, two   *To* is a preposition that indicates direction; *too* is an adverb that means "also" or "more than is needed"; *two* expresses the number 2: Last year we flew from New York *to* California. "Tippecanoe and Tyler, *too*" was Harrison's campaign slogan. The plot was *too* complicated for the average reader. Just north of *Two* Rivers, Wisconsin, is a petrified forest.

try to, try and   *Try and* is the colloquial equivalent of *try to*: He decided to *try to* (not *try and*) do better.

-type   Deleting this empty suffix eliminates clutter and clarifies meaning: Found in the wreckage was an *incendiary* (not *incendiary-type*) device.

uninterested, disinterested   See **disinterested, uninterested.**

unique   Because *unique* means "the only one," not "remarkable" or "unusual," you should never use constructions like "the most unique" or "very unique."

until   See **till, until, 'til.**

used to   See **supposed to, used to.**

utilize   In most cases, it is best to replace *utilize* with *use* (*utilize* often sounds pretentious).

wait for, wait on   To *wait for* means "to defer action until something occurs." To *wait on* means "to act as a waiter": I am *waiting for* (not *on*) dinner.

weather, whether   *Weather* is a noun meaning "the state of the atmosphere"; *whether* is a conjunction used to introduce an alternative: The *weather* outside is frightful, but the fire inside is delightful. It is doubtful *whether* we will be able to ski tomorrow.

well, good   See **good, well.**

were, we're   *Were* is a verb; *we're* is the contraction of *we are:* The Trojans *were* asleep when the Greeks attacked. We must act now if *we're* going to succeed.

whether, if   See **if, whether.**

which, who, that   See **that, which, who.**

who, whom   When a pronoun serves as the subject of its clause, use *who* or *whoever;* when it functions in a clause as an object, use *whom* or *whomever:* Sarah, *who* is studying ancient civilizations, would like to visit Greece. Sarah, *whom* I met in France, wants me to travel to Greece with her. To determine which to use at the beginning of a question, use a personal pronoun to answer the question: *Who* tried to call me? *He* called. (subject); *Whom* do you want for the job? I want *her.* (object)

who's, whose   *Who's* means "who is"; *whose* indicates possession: *Who's* going to take calculus? The writer *whose* book was in the window was autographing copies.

will, shall   See **shall, will.**

would of   See **could of, should of, would of.**

your, you're   *Your* indicates possession, and *you're* is the contraction of *you are:* You can improve *your* stamina by jogging two miles a day. *You're* certain to be the winner.

APPENDIX C

ENGLISH FOR SPEAKERS OF OTHER LANGUAGES

✔ CHECKLIST: ENGLISH LANGUAGE BASICS

✔ **In English, words may change their form according to their function.** For example, verbs change form to communicate whether an action is taking place in the past, present, or future.

✔ **In English, context is extremely important to understanding function.** In the following sentences, for instance, the very same words can perform different functions according to their relationships to other words.

Juan and I are taking a <u>walk</u>. (*Walk* is a noun, a direct object of the verb *taking*, with an article, *a*, attached to it.)

If you <u>walk</u> instead of driving, you will help conserve the Earth's resources. (*Walk* is a verb, the predicate of the subject *you*.)

See
Ch. 21

✔ **Spelling in English is not always phonetic and sometimes may seem illogical.** <u>Spelling</u> in English may be related more to the history of the word and to its origins in other languages than to the way the word is pronounced. Therefore, learning to spell correctly is often a matter of memorization, not sounding out the word phonetically. For example, "ough" is pronounced differently in *tough, though,* and *thought*.

See
C6

✔ <u>Word order</u> **is extremely important in English sentences.** In English sentences, word order may indicate which word is the subject of the sentence and which is the object, whether the sentence is a question or a statement, and so on.

C1 Nouns

A **noun** names things: people, animals, objects, places, feel-
ings, ideas. If a noun names one thing, it is <u>**singular**</u>; if a noun
names many things, it is <u>**plural**</u>.

See
21b7

(1) Noncount Nouns

Some English nouns do not have a plural form. These are
called **noncount nouns** because what they name cannot be
counted.

 NONCOUNT NOUNS

The following commonly used nouns are noncount
nouns. These words have no plural forms. Therefore, you
should never add *s* to them.

advice	homework
clothing	information
education	knowledge
equipment	luggage
evidence	merchandise
furniture	revenge

(2) Articles with Nouns

English has two **articles:** *a* and *the. A* is called the **indefinite**
article; *the* is the **definite article.** *A* is replaced by *an* if the word
that follows begins with a *vowel* (*a, e, i, o,* or *u*) or with a vowel
sound: a book, *an* apple, *an* honor. If the vowel is pronounced
like a consonant, use *a: a one-time offer.*

Use an **indefinite article** (*a* or *an*) with a noun when the
reader has no reason to be familiar with the noun you are naming—when you are introducing the noun for the first time, for
example. To say, "Jatin entered *a* building," signals to the audience that you are introducing the idea of the building for the
first time. The building is indefinite, or not specific, until it has
been identified.

Use the **definite article** (*the*) when the noun you are naming
has already been introduced. To say, "Jatin walked through *the*
building," signals to readers that you are referring to the same
building you mentioned earlier.

USING ARTICLES WITH NOUNS

There are two exceptions to the rules governing the use of articles with nouns.

- **Plural nouns** do not require **indefinite articles:** "I love horses," not "I love <u>a</u> horses." (Plural nouns do, however, require definite articles: "I love <u>the</u> horses in the national park near my house.")
- **Noncount nouns** may not require articles: "Love conquers all," not "<u>A</u> love conquers all" or "<u>The</u> love conquers all."

(3) Using Other Determiners with Nouns

See C4

Determiners are words that function as <u>adjectives</u> to limit or qualify the meaning of nouns. In addition to articles, **demonstrative pronouns, possessive nouns and pronouns, numbers** (both **cardinal** and **ordinal**), and other words indicating *number* and *order* can function in this way.

1. **Demonstrative pronouns** (*this, that, these, those*) communicate

   - the relative nearness or fairness of the noun from the speaker's position (*this* and *these* for things that are *near*, *that* and *those* for things that are *far*): *this* book on my desk, *that* book on your desk; *these* shoes on my feet, *those* shoes in my closet.
   - the *number* of things indicated (*this* and *that* for *singular* nouns, *these* and *those* for *plural* nouns): *this* (or *that*) flower in the vase, *these* (or *those*) flowers in the garden.

2. **Possessive nouns** and **possessive pronouns** (*Ashraf's, his, their*) show who or what the noun belongs to: *Maria's* courage, *everybody's* fears, the *country's* natural resources, *my* personality, *our* groceries.

3. **Cardinal** numbers (*three, fifty, a thousand*) indicate how many of the noun you mean: *seven* continents. **Ordinal** numbers (*first, tenth, thirtieth*) indicate in what order the noun appears among other items: *third* planet.

4. Words other than numbers may indicate **amount** (*many, few*) and **order** (*next, last*) and function in the same ways as cardinal and ordinal numbers: *few* opportunities, *last* chance.

C2 Pronouns

Any English noun may be replaced by a **pronoun**. Pronouns enable you to avoid repeating a noun over and over. For example, *doctor* may be replaced by *he* or *she, books* by *them,* and *computer* by *it.*

See A1.2

C3 Verbs

(1) Person and Number

Person refers to *who* or *what* is performing the action of the verb (for example, *myself, you,* or someone else), and **number** refers to *how many* people or things are performing the action (one or more than one). Unless you use the correct person and number in the verbs in your sentences, you will confuse your English-speaking audience by communicating meanings you do not intend.

See 11a4

(2) Tense

Tense refers to *when* the action of the verb takes place. One problem that many nonnative speakers of English have with English verb tenses results from the large number of **irregular verbs** in English. For example, the first-person singular present tense of *be* is not "I be" but "I am," and the past tense is not "I beed" but "I was."

See 6b

See 6a

Another problem occurs for some nonnative speakers of English when they use tenses that are more complicated than they need to be. Such speakers may do this because their native language uses more complicated tenses where English does not or because they are nervous about using simple tenses and "overcorrect" their verbs into complicated tenses.

Specifically, nonnative speakers tend to use **progressive** and **perfect** verb forms instead of **simple** verb forms. To communicate your ideas clearly to an English-speaking audience, choose the simplest possible verb tense.

(3) Auxiliary Verbs

Meaning is also communicated in English through the use of **auxiliary verbs** (also known as **helping verbs**), such as forms of the verbs *be* and *have* ("Julio *is taking* a vacation," "I *have been* tired lately.") and **modal auxiliaries** such as *would, should,* and *can* ("We *should conserve* more of our resources," "You *can succeed* if you try").

See A1.3

See A1.3

AUXILIARY VERBS

Only auxiliary verbs, not the verbs they "help," change form to indicate person, number, and tense.

We ~~have~~ had to ~~went~~ go downtown yesterday. (Only the auxiliary verb *had* should be in the past tense.)

Modal auxiliaries do not change form to indicate tense, person, or number.

(4) Negative Verbs

The meaning of a verb may be made negative in English in a variety of ways, chiefly by adding the words *not* or *does not* to the verb (is, *is not;* can ski, *can't* ski; drives a car, *does not* drive a car).

CORRECTING DOUBLE NEGATIVES

A **double negative** occurs when the meaning of a verb is negated not just once but twice in a single sentence.

Henry doesn't have ~~no~~ any friends. (*or* Henry ~~doesn't~~ has no friends.)

I looked for articles in the library, but there weren't none. (*or* I looked for articles in the library, but there weren't ~~none~~ any.)

 C4 **Adjectives and Adverbs**

Adjectives and adverbs are words that modify (describe, limit, or qualify) other words.

(1) Position of Adjectives and Adverbs

Adjectives in English usually appear *before* the nouns they modify. A native speaker of English would not say, "*Cars red and black* are involved in more accidents than *cars blue or green*" but would say instead, "*Red and black cars* are involved in more accidents than *blue or green cars.*"

However, adjectives may appear *after* linking verbs ("The name seemed *familiar*"), direct objects ("The coach found them *tired* but *happy*."), and indefinite pronouns ("Anything *sad* makes me cry.")

Adverbs may appear *before or after* the verbs they describe, but they should be placed as close to the verb as possible: not "I *told* John that I couldn't meet him for lunch *politely*," but "I *politely* told John that I couldn't meet him for lunch" or "I *told* John *politely* that I couldn't meet him for lunch." When an adverb modifies an adjective or another adverb, it usually comes *before* the adjective or the adverb: "The essay has *basically sound* logic." However, adverbs may appear in a greater variety of positions than adjectives can.

(2) Order of Adjectives

A single noun may be modified by more than one adjective, perhaps even by a whole list of adjectives in a row. Given a list of three or four adjectives, most native speakers would arrange them in a sentence in the same order. If shoes are to be described as *green* and *big*, numbering *two*, and of the type worn for playing *tennis*, a native speaker would say "two big green tennis shoes." Generally, the adjectives that are most important in completing the meaning of the noun are placed closest to the noun.

ORDER OF ADJECTIVES

1. Articles (*a, the*), demonstratives (*this, those*), and possessives (*his, our, Maria's, everybody's*)
2. Amounts (*one, five, many, few*), order (*first, next, last*)
3. Personal opinions (*nice, ugly, crowded, pitiful*)
4. Sizes and shapes (*small, tall, straight, crooked*)
5. Age (*young, old, modern, ancient*)
6. Colors (*black, white, red, blue, dark, light*)
7. Nouns functioning as adjectives to form a unit with the noun (*soccer* ball, *cardboard* box, *history* class)

C5 Prepositions

In English, **prepositions** (such as *to, from, at, with, among, between*) give meaning to nouns by linking them with other words and other parts of the sentence. Prepositions convey several different kinds of information. See A1.6

- Relations to **time** (*at* nine o'clock, *in* five minutes, *for* a month)
- Relations of **place** (*in* the classroom, *at* the library, *beside* the chair) and **direction** (*to* the market, *onto* the stage, *toward* the freeway)

- Relations of **association** (go *with* someone, the tip *of* the iceberg)
- Relations of **purpose** (working *for* money, dieting *to* lose weight)

In some languages, prepositions may be used in quite different ways, may exist in forms quite different from English, or may not exist at all—and any of these situations may cause problems. However, speakers of languages with prepositions very similar to those in English—especially Romance languages such as Spanish, French, and Italian—may also have trouble with English prepositions because they may be tempted to translate prepositional phrases directly from their own language into English.

 PREPOSITIONS IN IDIOMATIC EXPRESSIONS

Common Nonnative Speaker Usage	*Native Speaker Usage*
according *with*	according *to*
apologize *at*	apologize *to*
appeal *at*	appeal *to*
believe *at*	believe *in*
different *to*	different *from*
for least, *for* most	*at* least, *at* most
refer *at*	refer *to*
relevant *with*	relevant *to*
similar *with*	similar *to*
subscribe *with*	subscribe *to*

 Word Order

In English, word order is extremely important, contributing a good deal to the meaning of a sentence.

(1) Standard Word Order
Like Chinese, English is an "SVO" language, or one in which the most typical sentence pattern is "subject-verb-object." (Arabic, by contrast, is an example of a "VSO" language.) Deviation from the SVO pattern tends to confuse English speakers.

(2) Word Order in Questions
Word order in questions can be particularly troublesome for speakers of languages other than English, partly because there are so many different ways to form questions in English.

WORD ORDER IN QUESTIONS

1. To create a yes/no question from a statement using the verb *be*, simply invert the order of the subject and the verb:

   <u>Rasheem is</u> researching the depletion of the ozone layer.

   <u>Is Rasheem</u> researching the depletion of the ozone layer?

2. To create a yes/no question from a statement using a verb other than *be*, use a form of the auxiliary verb *do* before the sentence without inverting the subject and verb:

   <u>Does</u> Rasheem want to research the depletion of the ozone layer?

   <u>Do</u> Rasheem's friends want to help him with his research?

   <u>Did</u> Rasheem's professors approve his research proposal?

3. You can also form a question by adding a **tag question**—such as *won't he?* or *didn't I?*—to the end of a statement. If the verb of the main statement is *positive*, then the verb of the tag question is *negative*; if the verb of the main statement is *negative*, then the verb of the tag question is *positive*:

   Rasheem <u>is</u> researching the depletion of the ozone layer, <u>isn't he</u>?

   Rasheem <u>doesn't</u> intend to write his dissertation about the depletion of the ozone layer, <u>does</u> he?

4. To create a question asking for information, use **interrogative** words (*who, what, where, when, why, how*), and invert the order of the subject and verb (note that *who* functions as the subject of the question in which it appears):

   <u>Who is</u> researching the depletion of the ozone layer?

   <u>What is Rasheem</u> researching?

   <u>Where is Rasheem</u> researching the depletion of the ozone layer?

INDEX

Index

Index

Index

Index

Index

Index

Index